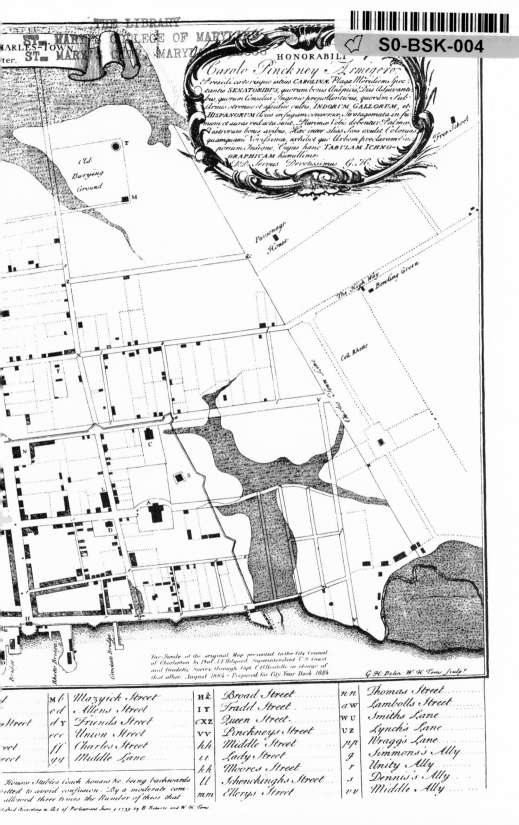

The Letterbook of
Eliza Lucas Pinckney
1739-1762

*Publication of this volume is sponsored
and supported in part by
The South Carolina Historical Society,
Charleston, South Carolina.*

The Letterbook of
Eliza Lucas Pinckney

1739-1762

·

Edited by

Elise Pinckney

with the editorial assistance of

Marvin R. Zahniser

and an Introduction by

Walter Muir Whitehill

·

The University of North Carolina Press
Chapel Hill

Manufactured in the United States of America.
Printed by Heritage Printers, Inc., Charlotte, N. C.
ISBN 0–8078–1182–3.
Library of Congress Catalog Card Number 76–174783.

Contents

ㄥ፧ㄨ

Illustrations

ᘛᘚ

Introduction

No one could claim that Eliza Lucas Pinckney of Charleston is a little-known or unappreciated figure. As a person "identified with the development of indigo as a staple of colonial South Carolina" she merited a life in the *Dictionary of American Biography* on an equal footing with her sons, Charles Cotesworth Pinckney and Thomas Pinckney. As long ago as 1850 selections of her writings were included by George Wymberley Jones De Renne in the series of historical quartos privately printed at Wormsloe Plantation near Savannah. In 1896 her biography was written by her great-granddaughter, Mrs. St. Julien Ravenel, who drew extensively upon her letters. While quotations from her lively letters appear in an extraordinary number of places, no text of them is currently available. The Wormsloe Quarto was printed in the ultralimited edition of nineteen copies, while Mrs. Ravenel's biography, although published commercially, is now long out of print. This documentary publication of Eliza Lucas Pinckney's letterbook by its present owner, the South Carolina Historical Society, adds a new and vivid dimension to our knowledge of this remarkable woman. It also makes available to present-day readers a group of letters so delightful that they will, I feel sure, appeal not only to historians but to a far wider audience.

Although many chronological series of documents, like biographies, offer heavy sledding in the earlier pages, there are conspicuous exceptions. The *Papers of Benjamin Franklin* get off to a lively start with ballads and the Silence Dogood letters. The nineteen-year-old Thomas Jefferson makes a mock-heroic event out of rats demolishing his pocketbook, garters, and half a dozen new minuets. Similarly, at the beginning of her letterbook, the eighteen-year-old Eliza Lucas firmly but politely tells her absent father that she will not marry the elderly suitor he proposes, begging father "to pay my thanks to the old Gentleman for his Generosity and favourable sentiments of me and let him know my thoughts on the affair in such civil terms as you know much better than any I can dictate; and beg leave to say to you that the riches of Peru and Chili if he had them put together could not purchase a sufficient Esteem for him to make him my husband." She flicks aside another gentleman suggested as a candidate for her hand with the assurance "that a single life is my only Choice and if it were not as I am yet but Eighteen, hope you will [put] aside the thoughts of my marrying yet these two or three years at least." Here is a dramatic situation, with a girl who clearly knows her own mind. It is also, in family terms, one that requires a certain elucidation. Father, Lieutenant Colonel George Lucas of the British Army, based in Antigua, had in 1738 moved his ailing wife and two daughters, the fifteen-year-old Eliza and a younger sister, Polly, to Wappoo plantation near Charleston, a South Carolina property that his father, John Lucas, also of Antigua, had owned for at least a quarter of a century. Colonel Lucas returned the next year to Antigua, where he was a councilor and later lieutenant governor. Mrs. Lucas is a shadowy figure. Young Eliza seems to have run the plantation, with advice by letter rather than the personal presence of her father, whom, nevertheless, she greatly admired and respected. This, then, is the curious domestic setting depicted in the years 1739 to 1743, when Eliza, from seventeen to twenty-one, is running Wappoo plantation and carrying out the experiments in the growing of indigo that eventually provided a staple for South Carolina.

The choice of setting was Eliza's. In 1740 she wrote to Mrs. Boddicott, with whom she earlier lived while at school in England:

My Papa and Mama's great indulgence to me leaves it to me to chose our place of residence either in town or Country, but I think it more prudent as well as most agreeable to my Mama and self to be in the Country during my Father's absence. We are 17 mile by land and 6 by water from Charles Town—where we have about 6 agreeable families around us with whom we live in great harmony.

I have a little library well furnished (for my papa left me most of his books) in which I spend part of my time. My Musick and the Garden, which I am very fond of, take up the rest of my time that is not imployed in business, of which my father has left me a pretty good share—and indeed, 'twas inavoidable as my Mama's bad state of health prevents her going through any fatigue.

I have the business of 3 plantations to transact, which requires much writing and more business and fatigue of other sorts than you can imagine. But least you should imagine it too burthensom to a girl at my early time of life, give me leave to answer you: I think myself happy that I can be useful to so good a father, and by rising very early I find I can go through much business. But least you should think I shall be quite moaped with this way of life I am to inform you there is two worthy Ladies in Charles Town, Mrs. Pinckney and Mrs. Cleland, who are partial enough to me to be always pleased to have me with them, and insist on my making their houses my home when in town and press me to relax a little oftener than 'tis in my honor to accept of their obliging intreaties. But I some times am with one or the other for 3 weeks or a month at a time, and then enjoy all the pleasures Charles Town affords.

To her brothers, who were living with the Boddicotts in England, Eliza sent a deal of good advice, sprinkled with exhortations to virtue. To her father in Antigua, she communicated news of the plantation, the military moves of Spaniards, the loss of negroes, sale of cows, planting of indigo, the prophesying of a crazy man. And to Mrs. Charles Pinckney in Charleston, to her lawyer husband, and to their niece Mary Bartlett, there are affectionate letters of friendly thanks for numerous kindnesses. Charles Pinckney set Eliza to reading John Locke. He lent her Virgil, from whom she derived agricultural counsel as well as literary pleasure. Virgil inspired her to plant a cedar grove. She further set out a plantation of oaks, with an eye to the day when their timber would be useful for shipbuilding.

Eliza's days were long. She rose at five, read until seven, and then walked in the garden or field to "see that the Servants are at their respective business, then to breakfast." An hour of music, an hour of French and shorthand, and teaching her sister Polly and two Negro girls to read occupied the time from breakfast to dinner. After dinner came another hour of music, followed by needlework, "till candle light, and from that time to bed time read or write." Fortunately this bluestocking schedule was now and then interrupted by visits to the Pinckneys in Charleston. On returning from one such period of "giddy gayety and want of reflection," Eliza confessed by letter to Mrs. Pinckney that she had been forced to read John Locke "over and over to see wherein personal identity consisted and if I was the very same self."

One wishes that Eliza Lucas had persevered with her letterbook consistently through life. Alas, she did not, and we thus miss any account of the most important event of her life. In January, 1744, her good friend Mrs. Pinckney died. On the following May 27 Eliza married the widower. When the entries resume in 1753 Eliza and Charles Pinckney are in England where he is serving as colonial agent for South Carolina. In the interval they have had four children: Charles Cotesworth and Thomas, another son who died, and a daughter Harriott. After five years they returned to South Carolina, taking Harriott with them, but leaving the boys at school. Hardly had they returned when Charles Pinckney died of malaria. The later pages of the letterbook contain the record of Eliza's grief. Although less than half the age of her husband at the time of her marriage, Eliza described herself as "for more than 14 years the happiest mortal upon Earth!" In letters conveying the news of his death to England, he is "the beloved of my soul! all that was valuable and aimiable in man! my dear, dear Mr. Pinckney," "the most aimable, tender, and affectionate of husbands," "the best of men, of husbands, and of fathers, and equally good in every relation and connection in life." Yet even in her grief, Eliza Pinckney was meticulous in attention to business, as when she attempts to ship live turtles and ducks to her late husband's friends in England.

Eliza Lucas Pinckney's letterbook records only part of a remarkable life, but for the periods that it covers it is more vivid than any consecutive biography. I am happy that the South Carolina Historical Society is making it available to a wider audience than those who are able to come to the society's quarters in the Robert Mills Greek Revival Fireproof Building in Charleston. Since my first visit there in the autumn of 1959 I have had respect and admiration for what the South Carolina Historical Society and its director, Mrs. Granville T. Prior, accomplish with very limited resources. I am happy that *The South Carolina Historical Magazine*, which has appeared every quarter throughout the present century, is now supplemented by this ably edited volume, which I hope will be followed

by others that will contain similar texts of other manuscripts owned
by the society. It would be hard to find a more attractive eighteenth-
century document for the launching of such a series than this letterbook of Eliza Lucas Pinckney.

WALTER MUIR WHITEHILL

Boston Athenaeum

Eliza Lucas Pinckney

Biographical Sketch

꙳

When British Army officer George Lucas moved his family to the province of South Carolina in 1738, his fifteen-year-old daughter Eliza was already a well-traveled and rather cosmopolitan young lady. Born in the West Indies, she had spent several years at school in England and had lived briefly in Antigua before going to the nearby mainland colony.[1]

Her father's decision to move to Carolina was probably motivated by several reasons: his wife's health, his desire to better himself economically, and, because of the threat of war with Spain, his anxiety to give his family physical security. The plantation on which the Lucas family settled overlooked Wappoo Creek, seventeen miles

1. It is difficult to establish the year of Eliza's birth, but 1722 is indicated by most references; her birthday was December 28. *City Gazette*, Charleston, S. C., July 17, 1793, obituary reprinted in *South Carolina Historical Magazine* (hereafter *SCHM*) 21 (1920): 158–59; Prayers, Book E, Ravenel Papers, South Carolina Historical Society, Charleston; Harriott Pinckney Holbrook, ed., *Journal and Letters of Eliza Lucas* (Wormsloe, Ga., 1850), p. 3; Eliza Lucas to Lady Carew, September, 1743, quoted in C. C. Pinckney, *Life of General Thomas Pinckney* (Boston and New York, 1895), p. 14. The name is recorded "Elizabeth" in her marriage record, husband's will, and death notice, but the signature is "Eliza." in the letterbook. Although her father addresses her as "Betsey," tradition indicates that she was called "Eliza." Mabel L. Webber, ed., "South Carolina Gleanings in England" (the will of Charles Pinckney), *SCHM* 8 (1907): 218–19; Mabel L. Webber, ed., "Register of St. Andrew's Parish, Berkeley County, South Carolina," *SCHM* 14 (1913): 29; George Lucas to Charles Pinckney, July 12, 1745, Middleton Collection, Pinckney Papers, South Carolina Historical Society, Charleston (hereafter PP/SCHS); George Lucas to Charles Pinckney, September 17, 1745, Pinckney Family Papers, Manuscripts Division, Library of Congress (hereafter PP/LC).

by land and six by water from Charleston. Wappoo was one of three Carolina plantations which Major Lucas's father, John Lucas of Antigua, had owned as early as 1713. From his home on Wappoo, Major Lucas directed his other plantations: fifteen-hundred-acre Garden Hill, on the Combahee River, which supplied pitch, tar, salt pork, and other products; and some three thousand acres in three parcels of rice-growing lands along the Waccamaw River. In 1739 the responsibilities of six-hundred-acre Wappoo with its "20 able-bodied slaves" fell to young Eliza, as did supervision of the overseers at Combahee and Waccamaw.[2]

Mrs. Lucas remains an enigma partly because of her reluctance to write letters. About the "Dear Papa" of Eliza's letters, however, we know more. The son of an assemblyman of Antigua, George Lucas was captain of a company by 1724, "heir to one of the best estates," and a councilor of that island colony in 1733. His political importance and military connection acted to terminate his later move to Carolina. The political conflict between England and Spain that was soon to erupt in the War of Jenkins' Ear forced Lucas to return in 1739 to his military post in Antigua. Three years later he was appointed lieutenant governor of that island. England's involvement in the War of the Austrian Succession prevented him from ever reaching Carolina again. With the rank of lieutenant colonel, he participated in several campaigns in the Caribbean area; taken prisoner by the French, he died at Brest January 11, 1747. Eliza's letters to him indicate that he provided the chief source of parental advice for the children and that she viewed him with deep affection and respect. His few remaining letters and Eliza's entries in her letterbook reveal Lucas as enterprising and resourceful, and it was at his instigation that Eliza undertook the indigo experiments with which her name was ever after linked.[3]

2. Letterbook, p. 7; Henry A. M. Smith, "Old Charles Town and Its Vicinity," *SCHM* 16 (1915): 63–64 and map; Beatrice St. J. Ravenel, "Notes on John and George Lucas," *SCHM* 46 (1945): 185–89; Records of Mesne Conveyance, Charleston, S.C., Charleston County Courthouse, 200: 175; Wills, Inventories and Miscellaneous Records, Probate Court, Charleston County, 75A: 95–106. The Lucas house was probably located near the end of the present Betsey Road, just south of U.S. Highway 17. A description of Wappoo is given in an advertisement for sale, *South-Carolina Gazette* (hereafter *SCG*), Charleston, S.C., June 11, 1744.

3. Vere Langford Oliver, *The History of the Island of Antigua*, 3 vols. (London, 1894–99), 2: 199–202; Ravenel, "Notes on John and George Lucas," pp. 185–89; *Gentleman's Magazine* (London) (December, 1742), p. 659, and (January, 1747), p. 47; Frances Leigh Williams, *Plantation Patriot* (New York, 1967), pp. 132–38;

The choice *Indigofera Tinctoria* of the Caribbean islands had showed promise briefly in the early years of Carolina, but it was soon abandoned because of the problems it posed in cultivation and because rice, though expensive to ship, proved sufficiently remunerative to discourage commercial planting of other commodities. But when the War of Jenkins' Ear severed Carolina from its established markets, the province desperately needed a substitute export.[4] Of this need George Lucas must have been well aware. Partly for this reason, perhaps, Lucas began to send his daughter various seeds from the West Indies to plant on his Carolina lands.

By 1740 Eliza was experimenting with indigo, for which she entertained "greater hopes" than for the other seeds her father sent. Indefatigable in purpose and energy, she overcame one obstacle after another during the next few years to bring these hopes to fruition. Frost ruined her first crop before it could dry, and from the seed she saved for the next year's planting only one hundred bushes grew. Meanwhile her father had sent from Montserrat an experienced dye-maker, Nicholas Cromwell, to make the vats and assist her in the process.[5] Despite the small size of the 1741 crop and the handicap that "the works were new and not dry enough in time" Wappoo plantation succeeded in producing "20 weight" of indigo. The 1741 output was marked also by difficulties with Cromwell. "He made a great mistery of the process," recalled Eliza many years later; "said he repented coming as he should ruin his own Country by it . . . and threw in so large a quantity of Lime water as to spoil the colour."[6]

George Lucas to Charles Pinckney, September 17, 1745, December 24, 1744, and June 14, 1744/5, PP/LC; *SCG*, March 5, 1737, and March 28, 1743; Robert Pringle to Andrew Lessley, August 29, 1739, Robert Pringle Letterbook, 1737–1745, SCHS.

4. "The Shaftesbury Papers," South Carolina Historical Society *Collections*, 5 vols. (Charleston, S.C., 1857–97), 5: 125, 127, 297, 334, 347, 349, 350, 388; David D. Wallace, *History of South Carolina*, 4 vols. (New York, 1934), 1: 132, 185–86. See also Thomas Ashe, "Carolina," in A. S. Salley, ed., *Narratives of Early Carolina* (New York, 1911), p. 147; Records in British Public Record Office Relating to South Carolina (hereafter BPRO), microfilm, Charleston Library Society, Charleston, S.C., 6: 287.

5. For the cultivation and manufacture of indigo, see *SCG*, October 22 and 29, 1744; C. W. [Charles Woodmason], *Gentleman's Magazine* (May, 1755), pp. 201–3 (June, 1755), pp. 256–59; Alexander Hewat, *Historical Account of South Carolina and Georgia*, 2 vols. (London, 1779), 2: 138–45; Francis P. Porcher, *Resources of the Southern Fields and Forests* (Charleston, S.C., 1863), 205–15; Harriott Horry Ravenel, *Eliza Pinckney* (New York, 1896), pp. 102–3; Samuel G. Stoney, *Plantations of the Carolina Low Country* (Charleston, S.C., 1938), p. 28.

6. Letterbook, pp. 8, 16, 22, 50; Eliza Pinckney to [Charles Cotesworth Pinckney], September 10, 1785, MS Collection, Charleston Library Society, Charleston, S.C. (hereafter MC/CLS). A covering letter of C. C. Pinckney explains that he had

Seed from the West Indies and from the previous Carolina planting went into the 1742 indigo crop at Wappoo. Eliza had to report
to her father, however, that none of his recently forwarded seed had
taken. But, she added, we "shall save enough of our own to make a
Crop next year."[7] The 1743 crop, however, was not satisfactory and
it was not until 1744 that indigo from Wappoo proved that Carolina
lands could grow a promising grade, one that could sell in a com-
petitive market. Patrick Cromwell, the second professional sent by
Colonel Lucas to carry out the complicated procedure of dye-
making, made "seventeen pounds of very good Indigo" at Wappoo
that year.[8] Six pounds of the season's product, sent to England "to
try how 'tis approved of there" were received with enthusiasm. *The
South-Carolina Gazette* carried an excerpt of a letter from London
of December 3, 1744: "I have shown your INDIGO to one of our most
noted Brokers in that Way, who tried it against some of the Best
FRENCH, and in his opinion it is AS GOOD. . . . When you can in some
measure supply the British Demand, we are persuaded, that on
proper Application to Parliament, a Duty will be laid on Foreign
Growth, for I am informed, that we pay for INDIGO to the French
£200,000 per annum."[9] Another unidentified English correspon-
dent quoted in the same issue of the *Gazette* wrote: "the Sample of
Indigo sent here . . . has been tried and found better than the French
Indigo."

Most of the valuable 1744 crop at Wappoo was saved for seed,
part of which, with true public spirit, was generously given away
"in small quantities to a great number of people." A local supply
of seed was essential, for within a few years the French so begrudged
their Carolina competition that the exportation of indigo seed from
their islands was made a "Capital Crime."[10]

requested his mother's reminiscence of her indigo experiments in order to give it
to Dr. David Ramsay.
   7. Letterbook, p. 56.
   8. Eliza Pinckney to George Lucas, 1744, in Ravenel, *Eliza Pinckney*, pp. 104–5.
   9. *SCG*, April 1, 1745.
   10. Eliza Pinckney to C. C. Pinckney, September 10, 1785, MC/CLS; James
Crokatt to Board of Trade, January, 1748, BPRO, 23: 51; also letterbook, p. 28.
By 1744 indigo was recognized as a possible money crop by many planters within
the colony. As Robert Pringle reported: "We are now in a fair way to have a New
Produce & better than Rice Vizt. Indigo, some of which has been made & accounted
by those that understood it to be very Good, a pritty many Persons are goeing upon
it to make it, & it [is] likely that next year a pritty deal may be produc'd, it is

In 1745, Lucas, after five years of investing in indigo experiments in Carolina, was at last able to realize a considerable income from this crop. Although the family had moved by then and the heavily mortgaged small plantation at Wappoo had been put on the market, accounts of the overseer at Garden Hill for this year show that he shipped to Lucas's London agent indigo valued at more than £225.[11]

Others who successfully planted a 1745 indigo crop can be identified by their seed advertisement in the *Gazette*. Among these were Charles Hill, Richard Lake on the Ashley, John Rivers on Wappoo Creek, Charles Pinckney, and Andrew Deveaux.[12] Deveaux was an elderly neighbor of Eliza's and an experienced planter, whom she mentions as giving her advice in her early agricultural experiments. He twice petitioned the General Assembly for a bounty in return for his endeavors in the culture of indigo but was refused.[13]

Indigo culture spread quickly, for the gold-leafed plant pointed the path to plantation affluence. The blue dye-cakes soon established the kind of credits in London banking houses that supported South Carolina in style during the decades before the Revolution. More than 135,000 pounds were produced for export in 1747, and good seasons were soon to produce more than a million.[14] Thus, in the

planted and made easier & with fewer hands than Rice, & very easily done, & the Weed it is made of grows & thrives very well. Intend to send you some of it from the Person who is the first projector & maker of it here." Robert Pringle to Andrew Pringle, Charleston, September 21, 1744, Robert Pringle Letterbook, 1737–1745, SCHS. Also Ravenel, *Eliza Pinckney*, pp. 104–5.

11. Murray's Account Sheet, PP/LC. Since no month is indicated, the entry might reflect sales of the 1744 crop. An item dated 1748 shows five barrels of indigo valued at £925, Carolina currency. Ravenel, "Notes on John and George Lucas," pp. 188–89. For Nicholas Cromwell's return to indigo making at Garden Hill, see George Lucas to Charles Pinckney, July 12, 1745, Middleton Collection, PP/SCHS; and George Lucas's Accounts, August, 1745; Henry Hyrne to Charles Pinckney, May 13, 1747; Nicholas Cromwell to Charles Pinckney, May 27, 1749, all in PP/LC.

12. *SCG*, December 2 and 9, 1745, January 20, 1746, February 1 and 10, 1746.

13. Smith, "Old Charles Town and Its Vicinity," pp. 13–14; Eliza Pinckney to C. C. Pinckney, September 10, 1785, MC/CLS; *SCG*, December 2, 1745. According to his own statement, Deveaux did not begin to plant indigo until 1743 and did not have success until two years later, being "a Stranger to the Difficulties attending the manufactureing of this commodity." By 1745 he was devoting twenty-nine acres to the weed in different soils "to try which will produce best" and advertising in the *Gazette* that he would "teach the making of Indigo *gratis* to all that buy Seed of me." J. H. Easterby, ed., *Journal of the Commons House of Assembly, 1745–1746* (hereafter *JCHA*), pp. 93, 98–99; *JCHA, 1748*, pp. 204–5, 218–19; *SCG*, December 2, 1745. Also George Lucas to Charles Pinckney, September 23, 1745, Book E, Ravenel Papers, SCHS.

14. Governor James Glen's address to the Assembly, December 5, 1745, *JCHA*,

product that Eliza Lucas had pioneered with vision, industry, and perseverance, she provided at a critical period an export staple invaluable to Carolina's economy.

Meanwhile there had been radical changes in the personal life of the young planter, for on May 27, 1744, she had married Charles Pinckney, a widower forty-five years of age. Carolina's first native attorney, Charles Pinckney had studied law in England. On his return to Charleston he had served as advocate general of the Court of Vice-Admiralty, justice of the peace for Berkeley County, attorney general, member of the Commons House of Assembly and Speaker of that body intermittently from 1736 to 1740, and member of the Royal Council.[15]

Eliza came to know Charles Pinckney when his first wife was still living, a lady Eliza found helpful and congenial. But Mrs. Pinckney died in January, 1744, after a long illness. Prior to her death Colonel Lucas, prevented from returning to Carolina by his administrative and military duties, had made plans for his son to journey to Wappoo to escort Mrs. Lucas and the two girls back to the West Indies. "We expect my brother George very shortly," wrote Eliza to a friend on December 14, 1743. "His arrival will, I sopose, determine how long we shall continue here." Far different, however, was the factor determining Eliza's stay. In less than six months' time she had be-

1745–1746, p. 12; *SCG*, February 1 and October 24, 1748, June 21, 1773; James Glen, "Description to the Board of Trade, 1749," in Chapman J. Milling, ed., *Colonial South Carolina: Two Contemporary Descriptions* (Columbia, S.C., 1951), p. 60; "A Table of Indigo Exported from Charleston and Savannah for Fiscal Years 1747–1748 to 1800–1801," in Lewis C. Gray, *History of Agriculture in the Southern United States to 1860*, 2 vols. (New York, 1941), 2: 1024; Philip M. Hamer, ed., *The Papers of Henry Laurens, 1746–1755* (Columbia, S.C., 1968), 1: 11, 37–38, 66–67, 83, 114, 287, 342; *SCG*, March 12 and 26, April 2, 1753. An enlightening discussion of indigo production in South Carolina is found in Lawrence Henry Gipson, *The British Isles and the American Colonies: The Southern Plantations, 1748–1754* (New York, 1960), pp. 134–38.

15. "Register of St. Andrew's Parish, Berkeley County, South Carolina," *SCHM* 14 (1913): 29; Anne King Gregorie, ed., *Records of Court of Chancery of South Carolina, 1671–1779* (Washington, D.C., 1950), p. 345; Alfred E. Jones, *American Members of the Inns of Court* (London, 1924), p. 170; [Mabel L. Webber, ed.], "Historical Notes," *SCHM* 8 (1907): 51, and 11 (1910): 187–88; Edward McCrady, *History of South Carolina Under the Royal Government* (New York, 1901), p. 473; William Bull to the Duke of Newcastle, May 22, 1741, in South Carolina Historical Society *Collections*, 2: 274; *SCG*, February 13–20, 1742; *JCHA, 1739–1741*, p. 347; Maria Henrietta Pinckney, *A Notice of the Pinckneys* (Charleston, 1860), p. 6; Mabel L. Webber, "Thomas Pinckney Family of South Carolina," *SCHM* 39 (1938): 15–26.

come Mrs. Charles Pinckney, the wedding undoubtedly precipitated by the imminent departure of the Lucas family from Carolina.[16]

Soon after the wedding Mrs. Lucas, with her son and younger daughter, returned to Antigua, and Charles Pinckney began to build a mansion of his own design in Charleston for his young bride. Overlooking the harbor, this handsome house was occupied by Eliza and Charles for almost a decade. In the large yard of her town house as well as at Belmont plantation on the Cooper River, she could enjoy her pursuits of horticulture and agriculture while continuing to supervise the indigo experiments on her father's plantations. Eliza even found time to experiment with silk manufacture, an undertaking which aroused great hopes in Carolina but which was only briefly profitable.[17]

Within a few years Eliza Pinckney had four children: Charles Cotesworth, George Lucas (born and died in June, 1747), Harriott, and Thomas.[18] She assumed her new position as wife and mother with the seriousness that marked her usual approach to life. Among her personal resolutions, which she wrote down, read to herself each day, and resolved "by the Grace of God assisting me to keep," were these: "To make a good wife to my dear Husband in all its several branches; to make all my actions Corrispond with that sincere love and Duty I bear him. . . . And next to my God, to make it my Study to please him." And: "I am resolved to be a good Mother to my children, to pray for them, to set them good examples, to give them good advice, to be careful both of their souls and bodys, to watch

16. Eliza Pinckney to Miss Bartlett, c. March, 1745, Duke University Library, Durham, N.C.; letterbook, pp. 55, 69.

17. Eliza Lucas to George Lucas, May 2, 1744, and Eliza Pinckney to George Lucas, July, 1744, both printed in Ravenel, *Eliza Pinckney*, pp. 69, 97–98; George Lucas, Jr., to Charles Pinckney, October 21, 1745, PP/SCHS; D. E. H. Smith and Alice R. H. Smith, *Dwelling Houses of Charleston* (Philadelphia and London, 1917), pp. 361–74; Harriott Horry to Mrs. Thomas Waites, n.d., printed in *SCHM* 52 (1951): 112; Wallace, *History of South Carolina*, 1: 387–88; Ravenel, *Eliza Pinckney*, p. 131; George C. Rogers, Jr., *Charleston in the Age of the Pinckneys* (Norman, Okla., 1969), p. 68. Two gowns made in England from silk she manufactured are on display today, one in the Powder Magazine in Charleston and the other in the Smithsonian Institution in Washington, D.C. The approximate date of the Lucas family's departure is provided by Robert Pringle, who sent a letter dated July 2 "per Geo. Lucas jun'r Esqr. in the Brig *Rigby Hole*, by Capt Mulryne." Robert Pringle Letterbook, SCHS; and Ravenel, *Eliza Pinckney*, p. 97.

18. A. S. Salley, ed., *Register of St. Philip's Parish, 1730–1758* (Charleston, S.C., 1904), pp. 92, 139, 206; Ravenel, *Eliza Pinckney*, p. 133.

over their tender minds; to carefully root out the first appearing and budings of vice, and to instill piety, Virtue and true religion into them...."[19]

In 1752 her husband served several months as chief justice under an interim appointment by Governor James Glen. The brief tenure of the first colonial in this office ended when—to the general consternation of the province—the crown for political reasons appointed Peter Leigh, the former high bailiff of Westminster. Leigh, accused by his enemies of progovernment electoral corruption, was given this distant post as a way both to do him justice and to remove him as a political irritant. Smarting under the affront, Charles Pinckney took his wife and children for a long-promised visit to England, where he felt he would be able to give his sons the advantage of a proper education. In England he served briefly as commissioner of the colony—the agent who represented the governor and Council in Carolina before the Board of Lords of Trade and Plantations in London.[20]

For all her seriousness Eliza Pinckney had always enjoyed society, and her days in mid-eighteenth-century London as the wife of a representative of South Carolina were happy ones. The Pinckneys stayed nearly five years in England; in May, 1758, they left their two sons in school and returned to Carolina with nine-year-old Harriott. Pinckney at once devoted himself to his neglected plantations but was soon stricken with malaria. A move across the harbor for a change of air at Mount Pleasant did not cure the fever. After an illness of three weeks he died on July 12, 1758, and was buried in St. Philip's churchyard.[21]

Eliza was shocked by her husband's death and heartbroken by the necessary separation from her boys. But she quickly occupied herself with many of the pursuits she had followed in her teens. There was much to be done at Belmont: "It has gone back to woods again," she wrote. For the sake of her children she must make this plantation

19. Ravenel, *Eliza Pinckney*, pp. 115–17.
20. Pinckney, *Thomas Pinckney*, pp. 17, 18; M. Eugene Sirmans, *Colonial South Carolina* (Chapel Hill, N.C., 1966), pp. 286, 302–4; Ravenel, *Eliza Pinckney*, p. 137; Rent Roll of Estate of Charles Pinckney, January, 1753, in Rutledge Collection, PP/SCHS; H. H. Bellot, "The Leighs in South Carolina," Royal Historical Society *Transactions*, 5th Ser., 6 (1956): 166–70.
21. Mabel L. Webber, ed., "Extracts from the Journal of Mrs. Ann Manigault," *SCHM* 20 (1919): 130; letterbook, pp. 97, 104.

profitable as well as the other properties placed in her charge: the island group near Hilton Head which became known as Pinckney Island; the thousand acres on the Ashepoo River known as Auckland; and the Pinckney Plains plantation which lay west of the upper reaches of the Ashley; Marshlands on the Cooper River; five hundred acres on the Savannah River near Silver Bluff; and five hundred acres at Four Holes. The Charleston holdings which she supervised included two homes on East Bay and other property near Colleton Square.[22]

Her daughter Harriott was nineteen when she married Daniel Horry, a rice planter who lived at Hampton Plantation on the Santee River. The couple divided their time between the beautiful plantation and Mr. Horry's large house at the corner of Broad and Legare Streets. At both of these places Mrs. Pinckney spent considerable time.[23]

The coming of the Revolutionary War drastically altered Mrs. Pinckney's comfortable circumstances. While her sons and son-in-law participated in campaigns of the war, Mrs. Pinckney was intermittently in the battle areas, at Charleston, Belmont, and Hampton. To an English friend she described why she and other South Carolinians were suffering:

To find you alive and well, my dear Madam, gave me great pleasure, a Sensation I have been little acquainted with of late as you will perceive when I tell you I have been rob[b]ed and deserted by my Slaves; my property pulled to pieces, burnt and destroyed; my money of no value, my Children sick and prisoners. . . .

Such is the deplorable state of our Country from two armies being in it for near two years; the plantations have been some quite, some nearly, ruined—and all with very few exceptions great sufferers—their Crops, stock, boats, Carts gone, taken or destroyed; and the Crops made this

22. Eliza did not see Charles Cotesworth until he was twenty-three, Thomas until he was twenty-two. Thomas Pinckney to James H. Ladson, January 4, 1824, printed in Joseph Johnson, *Traditions and Reminiscences of the American Revolution* (Charleston, 1851), pp. 87–88; Pinckney, *Thomas Pinckney,* pp. 21–23; Ravenel, *Eliza Pinckney,* pp. 189, 211, 247; M. H. Pinckney, *A Notice of the Pinckneys,* p. 13; J. H. Easterby, ed., "C. C. Pinckney's Plantation Diary," *SCHM* 41 (1940): 135, 150; Henry A. M. Smith, "Landgrave Ketelby's Barony," *SCHM* 15 (1914), pp. 157–58 and map. Charles Pinckney's will is deposited in Somerset House, London. An abstract is printed in *SCHM* 8 (1907): 217–19.

23. Ravenel, *Eliza Pinckney,* pp. 231–44; Jones, *American Members of the Inns of Court,* p. 100.

year must be very small by the desertion of the Negroes in planting and hoeing time. Besides their losses the Country must be greatly impovrished by the death of slaves as the small pox was in the British camp.[24]

Years of anxiety and personal loss passed before the family could be united in safety and begin restoration of its damaged property. After the Revolutionary War Mrs. Pinckney was often at Hampton Plantation, where Harriott Horry—soon to be widowed herself—proved competent in directing a plantation.

Charles Cotesworth Pinckney, a brigadier general at the conclusion of the war, returned to public life and was elected to the General Assembly in 1782. Soon recognized as one of the state's most distinguished lawyers, he was sent as one of South Carolina's delegates to the national Constitutional Convention in 1787. That same year Thomas had been elected to a term as governor, and the following year he presided at the State Convention which ratified the federal Constitution. Both sons became leaders and national candidates of the Federalist party.[25] The political importance of her sons led to one picturesque event which colored Mrs. Pinckney's declining years. In 1791, when President Washington made a tour of the South to rally support for the new national government, he stopped one May morning at Hampton for an "elaborate breakfast."[26]

Within a year after this happy occasion Eliza Pinckney realized that she was stricken with cancer, a disease that would soon prove fatal to her. Eliza's condition, painful and at the mercy of eighteenth-century medical practices, continued to grow worse, and in April, 1793, she traveled to Philadelphia to consult one Dr. Tate, famous for his supposed cancer cures. She died there on May 26, 1793. The following day she was buried in St. Peter's churchyard. President Washington, at his own request, served as one of the pallbearers.[27]

Eliza Lucas Pinckney had completed three score years and ten.

24. The manuscript of this letter, obviously a first draft, is endorsed: "To Mrs. R. E[vance], to be left at the Carolina Coffee House," PP/LC. See letterbook, p. 177, n. 56, regarding the Carolina Coffeehouse.

25. Webber, "Thomas Pinckney Family of South Carolina," pp. 23–25; Rogers, *Charleston in the Age of the Pinckneys*, pp. 126–30; Marvin R. Zahniser, *Charles Cotesworth Pinckney: Founding Father* (Chapel Hill, N.C., 1967), pp. 71ff.

26. Ravenel, *Eliza Pinckney*, pp. 311–12.

27. C. C. Pinckney to Thomas Pinckney, April 16, 1793, PP/LC; Ravenel, *Eliza Pinckney*, pp. 316, 317. See also C. C. Pinckney to Thomas Pinckney, May, 1792, September, 1792, and January 7, 1793, PP/LC; and C. C. Pinckney to same, August 27, 1792, Frank C. Pinckney Collection, PP/SCHS.

Her children too were remarkably long-lived for their era: Thomas died at age seventy-eight, Charles Cotesworth at eighty, and Harriott at eighty. In the political and cultural services rendered to their country the sons reflected the cosmopolitan tradition of their parents as well as the benefits of their own education abroad. Charles Cotesworth was not only active politically at the state and national levels but also played a major role in advancing educational and cultural institutions within South Carolina. Thomas is best known for his diplomatic mission to England as minister and for the treaty concluded with Spain that bears his name, a treaty which gave the United States free use of the Mississippi River and a favorable boundary settlement in the Southwest where American lands were adjacent to Spanish territory.[28]

"I was very early fond of the vegetable world," Eliza wrote. "My father was pleased with it and incouraged it." This affinity for agriculture was characteristic of her children also. Charles Cotesworth, who spent increasingly more of his time on Pinckney Island after 1800 was one of the early planters of sea-island cotton, a high-grade cotton used in the manufacture of quality goods. Like his mother, Thomas was an experimental planter. An engineer he imported from Holland developed the van Hassel system of embankment, making salt marshes along the Santee into profitable rice lands. Later, from his newly settled farms in the Pendleton area, Thomas encouraged his fellow planters to adopt scientific farming methods.[29]

Eliza Lucas Pinckney was thus not only notable in her own right, but her drive and talents were extended through the lives of her outstanding sons. It is unfortunate that there is no extant portrait of Mrs. Pinckney. Still, we do have a verbal sketch of her, given in her obituary in the Charleston *City Gazette*:

... Her manners had been so refined by a long and intimate acquaintance with the polite world, her countenance was so dignified by serious contemplation and devout reflection, and so replete with all that mildness and complacency which are the natural results of a regular uninterrupted habit and practice of virtue and benevolence that it was scarcely [possible] to behold her without emotions of the highest veneration and re-

28. Pinckney, *Thomas Pinckney*, pp. 131–33; Zahniser, *Charles Cotesworth Pinckney*, pp. 261–80; Samuel F. Bemis, *Pinckney's Treaty: America's Advantage from Europe's Distress, 1783–1800*, rev. ed. (New Haven, Conn., 1960).

29. Eliza Pinckney to C. C. Pinckney, September 10, 1785, MC/CLS; Pinckney, *Thomas Pinckney*, pp. 214–15.

spect. Her understanding, aided by an uncommon strength of memory, had been so highly cultivated and improved by travel and extensive reading, and was so richly furnished, as well with scientific, as practical knowledge, that her talent for conversation was unrivalled. . . . Her religion was rational, liberal and pure. The source of it was seated in the judgment and the heart, and from thence issued a life, regular, placid and uniform.[30]

The most careful portrait of Mrs. Pinckney was, of course, drawn by herself. Through the letters penned in her copybook we are best able to see those qualities of mind and character which endeared her to family and friends and which mark her as one of eighteenth-century America's distinguished women.

30. *City Gazette*, July 17, 1793, reprinted in *SCHM* 21 (1920): 158–59.

Preface

ɷ

The Letterbook of Eliza Lucas Pinckney is among the valuable collections of the South Carolina Historical Society at its library in the Fireproof Building in Charleston. At first glance, the manuscript with its dry parchment covers and faded brown ink on fragile pages little indicates the warmth and color of the story it tells from more than two hundred years ago. But within the letterbook are recorded the varied activities, hopes, and fears of an energetic, intelligent, and imaginative eighteenth-century woman. In keeping a copybook of her letters Eliza was following the practice of many businessmen and private correspondents of the time. Her letterbook thus served as a place to draft outgoing communications and to record memoranda or to copy a finished letter.

For an eighteenth-century lady in private life Eliza Lucas Pinckney preserved an impressive number of papers, many of which survived the hazards of fire, flood, and war. In addition to the letterbook and a few miscellaneous letters of Eliza Lucas Pinckney in the South Carolina Historical Society there are several letters and a copybook (*c.* 1759) in the Pinckney Family Papers, Manuscripts Division, Library of Congress. The National Society of the Colonial Dames of America in the state of South Carolina owns her recipe book, which it has published; and her letter describing the family's visit to the Princess of Wales is at the Powder Magazine, the Colonial Dames' museum in Charleston. Duke University Library has several of Mrs. Pinckney's letters of the 1740s, apparently pages from a letterbook; the Charleston Library Society has one.

The writer of these letters has frequently been treated by historians and has as well caught the imagination of popular writers. Since David Ramsay first published his *History of South Carolina* in 1809, most historians of South Carolina have devoted a paragraph or two to Eliza Pinckney. In 1850 selections from the early pages of the letterbook, edited by Harriott Pinckney Holbrook, were printed in a slim folio, *Journal and Letters of Eliza Lucas*. The biography of *Eliza Pinckney* by her great grand-daughter, Harriott Horry Rutledge Ravenel, published in 1896 as one of Scribner's series on *Women of Colonial and Revolutionary Times*, illustrated the growing recognition of Mrs. Pinckney's contribution to the economic and cultural life of South Carolina. Among more recent writings there is a perceptive chapter on Mrs. Pinckney in Edward Nicholas's *The Hours and the Ages* (New York, 1949), and an appealing biography for young people, *Plantation Patriot* (New York, 1967) by Frances Leigh Williams.

Scholars may be interested in the editorial techniques and standards herein adopted. For convenience letterbook entries have been divided into three parts. Items have been arranged in as accurate a chronological order as the editors could determine. Dates have been supplied where possible from internal evidence and indicated in brackets. In general the consecutive order of the entries has been maintained; however, the early part of the letterbook has posed problems of sequence. Not only are many items undated but Eliza apparently left spaces—even pages—which she subsequently filled in. Some of these entries may be the memoranda and abstracts of correspondence recorded in another "coppy book" to which she refers in one of her letters.

The textual policy in reproducing the manuscript steers between exact reproduction and complete modernization; the text is modified only to make it intelligible to present-day readers. Spelling and capitalization are preserved, with occasional exceptions where the writer did not begin a proper name with a capital. In general the punctuation of the original has been retained, but the frequent run-on sentences have been broken by full stops or semicolons. Terminal dashes have been rendered as periods, and surplus commas have been eliminated. Date lines have been elevated; scribal devices have been transcribed; the thorn, used in such forms as *ye* and *yt*, has been rendered *the* and *that*; and the ampersand has been retained only in the form *&c*. Abbreviations of proper names and honorifics have been retained, bringing down the elevated letters. In salutations and leave-takings the contractions likewise have been retained, but in the text they have been automatically expanded. For example, *wch* becomes *which*; *do.*, *ditto*; *wt.*, *weight*; *Govern't*, *Government*; and *Lp.*, *Ladyship*. The *ed* suffix to verbs, usually indicated by a superior *d*, has been treated according to modern usage.

The editor acknowledges the kindness of many people in assisting in the preparation of this volume. The Publications Committee of the South Carolina Historical Society have improved the manuscript with their broad experience in the field of historical publications. The present committee chairman, Mrs. W. Hampton Logan, has been instrumental in many ways in bringing this manuscript to press. Dr. Joseph I. Waring, both as Publications Committee chairman and as president of the society, contributed many specific suggestions.

For the committee member the late Samuel G. Stoney there is special recognition for his repeated helpfulness as well as his position as "gadfly" for continued research.

We are grateful for the frequent help of Miss Helen G. McCormack, George C. Rogers, Jr., St. Julien R. Childs, and Mrs. S. Edward Izard.

The staffs of the South Carolina Historical Society and the Charleston Library Society have been unfailing sources of help in the preparation of the manuscript. We are also indebted to the editorial and production staffs of the University of North Carolina Press.

Mrs. Granville T. Prior, the director of the South Carolina Historical Society, has been important in such a multiplicity of ways in bringing this work to completion that it would be impossible to enumerate them. The publication of this volume has been a project to which she has dedicated so much of her talent that rather than thanking her for her assistance it seems more fitting for Mr. Zahniser and myself to express appreciation to her for the privilege of assisting her in this project.

E. R. P.

The Letterbook of
Eliza Lucas Pinckney
1739-1762

Part One

·

Early Letters from Carolina

1739-1746

ᘉᘈᘉ

The lands of Wappoo Plantation from which the letters in this section were written lie today between Wappoo Creek and the busy traffic of Highway 17. Aging oaks with their flowing moss make it easy for the historian or traveler to envision Wappoo Plantation much as it looked two centuries ago. It was at Wappoo that young Eliza first made her home in colonial America: a place which may strike the modern reader as one of solitude and agricultural simplicity. But it must be remembered that the plantation bustled with activity and was usually plagued with knotty problems of personnel and finance. Especially was this true for Eliza, who had burdensome responsibilities placed upon her at a youthful age. She mentions at one point that she had "the business of 3 plantations to transact, which requires much writing and more business and fatigue of other sorts...."

Eliza responded to these duties with a maturity beyond her years. Her letters from Wappoo are sterling evidence not only of this maturity but of her desire to widen her circle of friends and to make a place for herself in the social and cultural life of colonial South Carolina. We gain insight as well into the standards and pleasures of polite society. Practiced courtesy, deference to age and position, and a sense of responsibility for community welfare are nicely demonstrated in these letters to family and friends.

Eliza's concern to study music, to read systematically, and to work in her "garden" likewise illustrated eighteenth-century standards for the cultured person. And her cultural concerns make clear that the practices and standards of colonial culture were shaped largely by English and Continental society. As she noted to her friend Mrs. Boddicott, "The people live very Gentile and very much in the English taste." Eliza's care to measure her actions and thoughts by Christian standards demonstrates the pietistic strain in eighteenth-century Carolina. Although she avoided the "enthusiasm" so characteristic of evangelist George Whitefield's followers, she was careful to cultivate the kind of thought, life, and beauty of character that Whitefield himself would certainly have applauded.

This section of Eliza's letterbook is doubly interesting to those acquainted with the lives of her children, Charles Cotesworth, Harriott, and Thomas. The standards she espouses relating to proper conduct in private and public and her attitudes toward religion, education, and family are later distinctly echoed in the lives of her children well into the nineteenth century.

May 20th. 1739
Wrote to Mr. Boddicott and sent the Deeds to him that my Papa left, after recording them.[1]

1740

March 1740
Wrote to my father on business of various sorts desiring he will not insist on puting my sister[2] to school. I will undertake to teach her French. Also gave him an account of my poor Cousen Fanny Fayweather's meloncholy and her bad state of health. Also of Colo. Pinckney's friendly offices with her Uncle when he was in New England with regard to her.

March 17, 1740
Wrote to Othniel Beal, Esqr., in answer to his obliging enquiry after my father, and begging the favour of him to send up the box that came for me from London.[3]

[To Colonel Lucas]
Hond. Sir
Your letter by way of Philadelphia which I duly received was an additional proof of that paternal tenderness which I have always

1. Colonel George Lucas's business agent in London. During her school days in England Eliza had stayed at the Boddicotts', where her two brothers, George Jr., and Thomas, were presently living.

2. Mary Lucas, called Polly. She was baptized in St. Paul's Parish, Antigua, November 4, 1735, and is probably the same Mary Lucas whose marriage to John Atkinson is recorded in the Register of St. John's Parish, Antigua, March 13, 1762. Vere Langford Oliver, *The History of the Island of Antigua*, 3 vols. (London, 1894–99), 2: 201.

3. Othniel Beale (1688–1773) was a leading merchant of Charleston. He served in various offices: justice of the peace, commissioner of fortifications, and member of the Royal Council. His wharves were across the street from his house, which still stands at 101 East Bay. Alexander Hewat, *Historical Account of South Carolina and Georgia*, 2 vols. (London, 1779), 1: 311–12. Aspects of Beale's career are discussed in M. Eugene Sirmans, *Colonial South Carolina* (Chapel Hill, N.C., 1966), pp. 253–54, 341.

Experienced from the most Indulgent of Parents from my Cradle to this time, and the subject of it is of the utmost importance to my peace and happiness.

As you propose Mr. L. to me I am sorry I can't have Sentiments favourable enough of him to take time to think on the Subject, as your Indulgence to me will ever add weight to the duty that obliges me to consult what best pleases you, for so much Generosity on your part claims all my Obedience, but as I know tis my happiness you consult [I] must beg the favour of you to pay my thanks to the old Gentleman for his Generosity and favourable sentiments of me and let him know my thoughts on the affair in such civil terms as you know much better than any I can dictate; and beg leave to say to you that the riches of Peru and Chili if he had them put together could not purchase a sufficient Esteem for him to make him my husband.

As to the other Gentleman you mention, Mr. Walsh, you know, Sir, I have so slight a knowledge of him I can form no judgment of him, and a Case of such consiquence requires the Nicest distinction of humours and Sentiments. But give me leave to assure you, my dear Sir, that a single life is my only Choice and if it were not as I am yet but Eighteen, hope you will [put] aside the thoughts of my marrying yet these 2 or 3 years at least.

You are so good to say you have too great an Opinion of my prudence to think I would entertain an indiscreet passion for any one, and I hope heaven will always direct me that I may never disappoint you; and what indeed could induce me to make a secret of my Inclination to my best friend, as I am well aware you would not disapprove it to make me a Sacrifice to Wealth, and I am as certain I would indulge no passion that had not your aprobation, as I truly am

Dr. Sir, Your most dutiful and affecte. Daughter
E. Lucas

To my good friend Mrs. Boddicott
Dear Madam,   May the 2nd [1740]

I flatter myself it will be a satisfaction to you to hear I like this part of the world, as my lott has fallen here—which I really do. I prefer England to it, 'tis true, but think Carolina greatly preferable to the West Indias, and was my Papa here I should be very happy.

We have a very good acquaintance from whom we have received much friendship and Civility. Charles Town, the principal one in this province, is a polite, agreeable place. The people live very Gentile and very much in the English taste. The Country is in General fertile and abounds with Venison and wild fowl; the Venison is much higher flavoured than in England but 'tis seldom fatt.

My Papa and Mama's great indulgence to me leaves it to me to chose our place of residence either in town or Country,[4] but I think it more prudent as well as most agreeable to my Mama and self to be in the Country during my Father's absence. We are 17 mile by land and 6 by water from Charles Town—where we have about 6 agreeable families around us with whom we live in great harmony.

I have a little library well furnished (for my papa has left me most of his books) in which I spend part of my time. My Musick and the Garden, which I am very fond of, take up the rest of my time that is not imployed in business, of which my father has left me a pretty good share—and indeed, 'twas inavoidable as my Mama's bad state of health prevents her going through any fatigue.

I have the business of 3 plantations to transact, which requires much writing and more business and fatigue of other sorts than you can imagine. But least you should imagine it too burthensom to a girl at my early time of life, give me leave to answer you: I assure you I think myself happy that I can be useful to so good a father, and by rising very early I find I can go through much business. But least you should think I shall be quite moaped with this way of life I am to inform you there is two worthy Ladies in Charles Town, Mrs. Pinckney and Mrs. Cleland,[5] who are partial enough to me to be always

4. In addition to his plantations Colonel Lucas owned property in Charleston. An advertisement in the *Gazette* mentions his house "next door to Mr. Harvey near White Point"; another refers to his property "near Conselliere's at upper end of Tradd street." *South-Carolina Gazette* (hereafter *SCG*), Charleston, S.C., August 25–September 1, 1739, December 29–January 5, 1740.

5. Elizabeth Lamb Pinckney (d. January 23, 1744), first wife of Charles Pinckney (*c.* 1699–1758). She had lived in London until she married and moved to South Carolina. The Pinckneys' Charleston house was on Union (now State) Street. Mabel L. Webber, "Thomas Pinckney Family of South Carolina," *South Carolina Historical Magazine* (hereafter *SCHM*) 39 (1938): 18. Mary Perrie Cleland was the wife of John Cleland (1700–1760), who was appointed to the Royal Council in 1750. Henry A. M. Smith, "Georgetown—the Original Plan and the Earliest Settlers," *SCHM* 9 (1908): 91, 94; Edward McCrady, *History of South Carolina Under the Royal Government* (New York, 1901), p. 801.

pleased to have me with them, and insist upon my making their houses my home when in town and press me to relax a little much oftener than 'tis in my honor to accept of their obliging intreaties. But I some times am with one or the other for 3 weeks or a month at a time, and then enjoy all the pleasures Charles Town affords, but nothing gives me more than subscribing my self

Dear Madam,

Yr. most affectionet and

most obliged humble Servt.

Eliza. Lucas

Pray remember me in the best manner to my worthy friend Mr. Boddicott.

July [1740]

Wrote my Father a very long letter on his plantation affairs and on his change of commissions with Major Heron;[6] On the Augustine Expedition;[7] On the pains I had taken to bring the Indigo, Ginger, Cotton and Lucerne and Casada to perfection,[8] and had greater hopes from the Indigo (if I could have the seed earlier next year from the West India's) than any of the rest of the things I had tryd.

6. Alexander Heron had been commissioned April 5, 1740, a major in James Oglethorpe's 42nd Regiment of Foot, the "Georgia Rangers." W. R. Williams, "British-American Officers, 1720–1763," *SCHM* 33 (1932): 188. See also A. D. Candler, ed., *Colonial Records of the State of Georgia (1732–1782)*, 26 vols. (Atlanta, Ga., 1904–16), 6: 71. This memorandum may have been used in writing the succeeding letter abstract.

7. After Great Britain declared war on Spain Oglethorpe undertook an expedition to destroy the fort at St. Augustine. The South Carolina Commons House of Assembly voted £120,000, Carolina money, for the attack and a regiment of four hundred men was raised in Virginia and the Carolinas. The land forces crossed into Florida May 9, 1740, but the inglorious expedition was over early in July. See John Tate Lanning, ed., *The St. Augustine Expedition of 1740* (Columbia, S.C., 1954), pp. ix–xii. See also Lanning's *The Diplomatic History of Georgia: A Study of the Epoch of Jenkins' Ear* (Chapel Hill, N.C., 1936), and H. Trevor Reese, *Colonial Georgia: A Study in British Imperial Policy in the Eighteenth Century* (Athens, Ga., 1963), chap. 5.

8. Lucerne is an alfalfa. "Casada" is probably *cassava*, a plant with a fleshy rootstock which was cultivated in the tropics where it was a staple food. Apparently cotton was raised on the Lucas plantations for some years. In August, 1744, Murray, the overseer at Garden Hill, wrote Eliza: "We shall have Cotten to make a good part of the cloaths but a grate deal of trouble for want of a gine." Harriott H. Ravenel, *Eliza Pinckney* (New York, 1896), p. 126.

[8]

Wrote my Father [by] the last ship a long letter consisting of 5 sides of paper concerning Mr. Bensby's talking to Major Heron about an Exchange of Commissions between Major Heron and my father. The Major asked a thousand pound in Exchange but neither he nor Mr. B. then knew that my father's regiment was augmented. Mr. Bensby will acquaint him with it and write to you about the miscarriage of the Augustine Expedition. General Oglethorp greatly blamed. The Captains of men of warr sent home their remonstrance, and the people their grievances—60 articles against him.[9]

Also concerning pitch and Tarr and Lime and other plantation affairs.

An account of a large ship, the Baltick Merchant from hence, being taken and carried in to St. Sebastians.[10] The Captain, a Quaker, would not fight. Poor Col. Braithwait undertook to fight the ship. They had not powder Enough. The Spaniards boarded her and upon inquiring and being told Col. B. fought the ship, he went in to the Cabbin where he found him comforting his wife who was greatly frighted, and shot him dead in her sight. But as soon as he arrived at St. Sebastians, the Governor of that place hanged him.

Acknowledged the receipt of things sent by my father to us in several Vessels lately. Account of Mr. Whitfield and the Ecclesiastical Court here.[11] An account of my Cousen Fayweather's going to

9. Oglethorpe responded to the charges against him by saying that he had no confidence in the provincials since they refused obedience to his orders, and had at last abandoned his camp and retreated to Carolina. David Ramsay, *History of South Carolina from Its First Settlement in 1670, to the Year 1808*, 2 vols. (Charleston, S.C., 1809), 1: 79–81. For a justification of the South Carolina troops, see McCrady, *South Carolina Under the Royal Government*, pp. 224–26. The magistrates and freeholders of Savannah had listed their grievances in a petition to the trustees in 1739. Candler, *Colonial Records of the State of Georgia*, 5: 231, 235, 244–45, 254–55. Clarence L. Ver Steeg, ed., *A True and Historical Narrative of the Colony of Georgia by Pat. Tailfer and Others with Comments by the Earl of Egmont* (Athens, Ga., 1960), pp. xxiii–xxv, 88–110.

10. Many English ships taken by privateers during the war were carried to this Spanish port. As many as forty-two were reported there during June, 1740. The *Baltic Merchant* was a ship of three hundred tons, eighteen guns. An account of her bloody capture appeared in *SCG*, August 9–16, August 30–September 6, October 16–23, 1740.

11. The famous revivalist George Whitefield, a clergyman of the Church of England and rector of the Anglican church at Savannah, was cited by the Reverend Alexander Garden, commissary of the Bishop of London, to an Ecclesiastical Court July 15, 1740, at St. Philip's Church. Garden warned the people of the "pernicious

Boston to endeavour to recover her fortune. Old Mr. Deveaux[12] very kind in instructing me in planting affairs. Shall Endeavour to get some Curiositys for the Duke of Marlborough.[13] Concerning my brothers at school.

Wrote at the same time to Mr. Wrights the Garden Hill affairs.

1740. Wrote to Mrs. Danniel an account of Mrs. Bartholomew's things. Also sent all the wearing apparel, plate, rings, &c., to her except a few things kept out which my papa is to be accountable to her for. The household goods appraised by 3 merchants, Mr. Beauchamp, Capt. Cooper and Mr. Pringle. The whole amounted to 288 pound, 5 shillings currency.

1740. Wrote to my Papa and Grandmama.

The same time Wrote to Miss Dolemott [De la Motte] to let her know her old friend my Cousen Fayweather was gone to New England and had not time to answer her letter before she went.

[To Colonel Lucas]
Hond Sir
I want words to Express the concern we are under at not hearing from you. The dangerous situation you are in terrifies us beyond

tendency of his doctrines," while Whitefield thought that when he first came "the people of Charlestown seemed wholly devoted to pleasure, polite entertainments . . . dancing masters . . . and the sin of wearing jewels." The church court suspended the evangelist, an action that widened the breach between Anglicans and Dissenters. Sirmans, *Colonial South Carolina*, p. 231; McCrady, *South Carolina Under the Royal Government*, pp. 234–39. A useful biography of Whitefield is Luke Tyerman, *The Life of the Rev. George Whitefield*, 2 vols. (London, 1930). See also William Howland Kenney, "Alexander Garden and George Whitefield: The Significance of Revivalism in South Carolina, 1738–1741," *SCHM* 71 (1970): 1–16.

12. For the Deveaux family, see Joseph G. Bulloch, *A History and Genealogy of the Families of Bellinger and De Veaux and Other Families* (Savannah, Ga., 1895).

13. Charles Spencer, third Duke of Marlborough and fifth Earl of Sunderland, accepted the colonelcy of the 38th Foot in March, 1738, and was thus commander of Major Lucas's regiment. See Gerard Le Grys Norgate, "Spencer, Charles (1706–1758)," *Dictionary of National Biography* (hereafter *DNB*).

expression and is increased by the fearful apprehensions of [your] being ordered to some place of immediate danger.

I am sorry to differ from you, dear Sir, as I must own I now do, as I am really [glad] you are not ordered to Cuba tho' I am sensible there might some advantages arise from thence such as honour and preferment and perhaps profit too, but these I esteem mere triffles when put in the balance with the life of my honoured parent. I know how ready you are to fight in a just cause as well as the love you bear your Country in preference to every other regard, and I am so farr from wishing you avoid dangers by any dishonourable or unjust means that I have Courage enough to be pleased with the asurance that you never will, though all my happiness in this life depends on your welfair. So, dear Sir, retract the thought, if you ever had so injurious a one of me, as to imagine I would wish you to do anything unworthy of you. At the same time I am to[o] honest to pretend to more Heroism than I deserve, which I should do did I conceal from you the perpetual fears and apprehensions I am in at this time concerning you.

Mama tenders you her affections, and P[olly] her Duty, and that the Almighty may always perserve you is the Constant prayer of, Hond Sir,

Yr m[ost] D[utiful] and obed[ient] Daughter
E. Lucas

Memdum.

Wrote to Miss Thomas, daughter of the Honble. Gov. Thomas[14] in Philadelphia by the Honble. Charles Pinckney Esqr., informing her I would have accepted her invitation and payd her a vizit as I had so good an opportunity of going with Mrs. Pinckney had my father been near enough to obtain his Consent.[15]

Gave her an account of the Augustine Expedition.

14. George Thomas, governor of Pennsylvania and Delaware (1738–1747), had resided in the West Indies and remained active in West Indian political affairs. See William R. Smith, "Thomas, George (c. 1695–Dec. 31, 1774)," *Dictionary of American Biography* (hereafter *DAB*).

15. *SCG*, August 23–30, 1740, reported: "By private letters from Boston in New England, we hear, that the Hon. Coll. Charles Pinckney and the Hon. Benj. Whitaker, Esq., Chief Justice of this province, and their Ladies, were all safely arrived there and in good Health." Their return was noted in the issue of October 30–November 6, 1740.

To the Honble. Crs. Pinckney, Esqr.

Sir   Febr. 6th, 1741.

I received yesterday the favour of your advice as a phisician and want no arguments to convince me I should be much better for both my good friends' company—a much pleasanter prescription yours is, I am sure, than Dr. Meads,[16] which I have just received. To follow my inclination at this time I must endeavour to forget I have a Sister to instruct and a parcel of little Negroes whom I have undertaken to teach to read, and instead of writing an answer bring it my self. And indeed gratitude as well as inclination obliges me to wait on Mrs. Pinckney as soon as I can, but it will not be in my power till a month or two hence.

Mama pays her compliments to Mrs. Pinckney and hopes she will excuse her waiting on her at this time, but will not fail to do it very soon.

I am a very Dunce, for I have not acquired the writing short hand yet with any degree of swiftness; but I am not always one for I give a very good proof of the brightness of my Genius when I can distinguish well enough to Subscribe my self with great Esteem

Sir,

Your most obed. humble Servt.

Eliza. Pinckney [sic]

To Miss F. Fairweather in Boston.   April 15th, 1741.

I have so lately wrote to my Dear Cousen I have nothing new to acquaint her with, but could not skip so good an opportunity as our old acquaintance Mr. Minott without writing to my dear Fanny.

My Papa has sent you a present of ten pistols,[17] which I should have sent you now but least you should have left Boston before it arrives have omited it till I hear from you.

16. Richard Mead, M.D., was perhaps the most famous English physician of his day. His practice, and circle of friends, included many in England's most prominent families. See Norman Moore, "Mead, Richard, M.D. (1673-1754)," DNB.

17. The pistole was a Spanish quarter doubloon, worth about four dollars in present value. Currencies of foreign powers circulated commonly in South Carolina. Colonial currency problems are discussed in Leslie Van Horn Brock, "The Currency of the American Colonies, 1700 to 1764" (Ph.D. dissertation, University of Michigan, 1941).

Mama and Polly with all your old acquaintance desire to be kindly remembered to you and beg to hear from you as soon as possible. You are frequently in my thoughts, and I long to hear you are well.

Accept of my tenderest love and believe me to be

My Dr. Fanny

Your ever Affecte. Cousen

E. Lucas

April 15th wrote to Othneil Beale, Esqr.

The same day to Capt. Cooper about the Kettle Drums.

[1741]

Wrote an answer to my Papas 2 last letters 24th of March and finished my last Coppy book[18] with a letter to him dated the 20th of April.

April 23rd, 1741

Wrote to my Father informing him of the loss of a Negroe man— also the boat being overset in Santilina Sound[19] and 20 barrels of Rice lost. Told him of our making a new garden and all conveniences we can to receive him when we are so happy to see him. Also about Starrat[20] and pitch and Tarr.

To Mrs. Boddicott.

My Dr. Madam   The 2nd of May, 1741.

'Tis one of the greatest pleasures I enjoy to hear from you, for the tenderness I have ever received from my dear friend Mrs. B[oddi- cott]—especially when a child under her care—entitles her to all the

18. This is the only reference to an earlier letterbook, apparently destroyed since then.

19. Saint Helena Sound, some forty miles down the coast from Charleston, is still pronounced by some natives the way Eliza phonetically spelled it. The boat was doubtless loaded with produce from Garden Hill on the Combahee, which flows into the sound.

20. Starrat was the overseer on the Waccamaw plantation.

regard I owe an affectionate parent. Had not your tender regard for me been sufficiently known before, your last kind letter would have proved your title to the filial appellation.

Mama joyns with me in sincere thanks for the particulars you give us of my brothers. We are much concerned for our Dear Tommy's illness, but so well satisfied of your care and tenderness of him we have no pain on that head. 'Tis as great satisfaction to us to be informed by you of my brother George's improvement. I write to both him and Miss Parry by this ship.

I received Doctor Meads prescription with the meddicines made up accordingly—have not yet begun upon them as my head has been something better, but as the hott weather advances I know it will increase and then I shall do the Doctor's prescription justice. I have had all the advice I could in this part of the world and generally found reliefe for a time. To comply with your obliging request and give you as particular an account of it as I can I am to inform you 'tis by no means perioddical. I find it rather worse in hott weather than cold and have it some times for 6 months together without a days' intermission—tho' not to a violent degree but now and then. I remember I had in England once the same acute pain for one week before I had the small pox—as I some times have here. When 'tis very violent 'tis attended with a sickness at my stomach.

I am very sorry for poor Martha. I think she has had [a] hard fate. Pray give my love to Master Boddicott. I long to see him and had I an opportunity would sing him as many French songs as ever—which I can do as I have taken some pains to keep my French. But wishing for what is not in our power is Idle. My best respects will ever attend good Mr. Boddicott and Mrs. Wilder, and I beg you will accept every affectionate regard from

Dr. Madm.

Yr. m.[ost] ob[edient] and m. ob[liged] servt.

E. Lucas

May 2nd, 1741. Wrote to my brother now 16 years old, desiring him to give us an account of publick news, any thing that passes worth Notice. And informed him of the aimable character we lately received of him from good Mrs. Boddicott.

May 3rd, 1741. Wrote to my old friend and school-fellow Miss Parry lamenting the Warr which separates us from my Dear Papa. About the Lottery, &c.[21]

June the 8th, 1741. Wrote again to my father on the subject of the Indigo, Cotton, &c. Also concerning the fall of bills of Exchange. Lamenting the death of his worthy friend Captain Fleming. Acquaint him with Mr. Manigault's great Civility with regard to Lushers taking in his goods.[22]

1741. Wrote to my Aunt on my Grandmama's death,[23] who indeed—to use the Apostle's phrase in another case—might be said to die dayly for many years past. Also on my Cousin Jacob's and Cousin Lucas's death—the latter died at a hundred years of age.

To my Father.
Hon'd Sir   June the 4th, 1741
     Never were letters more welcome than yours of Feb. 19th and 20th and March the 15th and 21st, which came almost together. It was near 6 months since we had the pleasure of a line from you. Our fears increased apace and we dreaded some fatal accident befallen, but hearing of your recovery from a dangerous fitt of Illness has more than equaled, great as it was, our former Anxiety. Nor shall we ever think ourselves sufficiently thankful to Almighty God for the continuance of so great a blessing.

21. The grand period of lotteries in South Carolina was not until the next century, but for a time they provided a popular method of disposing of goods in many of the colonies. Massachusetts, Rhode Island, New York, and Pennsylvania outlawed lotteries during the 1740s, and South Carolina passed a law on May 4, 1751, stating that a fine of five hundred pounds would be imposed on anyone conducting a lottery for any kind of property, and five pounds for anyone contributing to a lottery. Thomas Cooper and David J. McCord, eds., *Statutes at Large of South Carolina*, 10 vols. (Columbia, S.C., 1836–75), 3: 729. See also Carl Bridenbaugh, *Cities in the Wilderness* (New York, 1938), pp. 348–49.

22. Gabriel Manigault (1704–81) was a wealthy merchant, reputed to be the richest man in the province in the eighteenth century. Evidence of his wealth is cited in George C. Rogers, Jr., *The Evolution of a Federalist: William Loughton Smith of Charleston, 1758–1812* (Columbia, S.C., 1962), p. 21. The Manigault family is discussed in Huguenot Society of South Carolina, *Transactions* 4 (1897): 48–84.

23. Mrs. Lucas's mother's death. Letterbook, p. 16.

I simpathize most sincerely with the Inhabitance of Antigua in so great a Calamity as the scarcity of provisions and the want of the Necessarys of life to the poorer sort. We shall send all we can get of all sorts of provisions particularly what you write for. I wrote this day to Starrat for a barrel [of] butter.

We expect the boat dayly from Garden Hill when I shall be able to give you an account of affairs there. The Cotton, Guiney corn, and most of the Ginger planted here was cutt off by a frost. I wrote you in [a] former letter we had a fine Crop of Indigo Seed upon the ground, and since informed you the frost took it before it was dry. I picked out the best of it and had it planted, but there is not more than a hundred bushes of it come up—which proves the more unluckey as you have sent a man to make it. I make no doubt Indigo will prove a very valuable Commodity in time if we could have the seed from the west Indias [in] time enough to plant the latter end of March, that the seed might be dry enough to gather before our frost. I am sorry we lost this season. We can do nothing towards it now but make the works ready for next year. The Lucern is yet but dwindlering, but Mr. Hunt tells me 'tis always so here the first year.

The death of my Grandmama was, as you imagine, very shocking and grievous to my Mama, but I hope the considerations of the misery's that attend so advanced an age will help time to wear it off.

I am very much obliged to you for the present you were so good to send me of the fifty pound bill of Exchange which I duely received.

We hear Carthagene is taken.[24]

Mr. Wallis is dead. Capt. Norberry was lately killed in a duel by Capt. Dobrusee, whose life is dispaired of by the wounds he received.[25] He is much blamed for querreling with such a brawling

24. The success of the English fleet at Cartagena had been erroneously reported in *SCG*, April 30–May 7, 1741. Sir Edward Vernon, who had recently become a national hero with his capture of Portobello (Spanish stronghold on the Isthmus of Darien) in November, 1739, attacked Cartagena de Indias in 1740 with a large squadron. When the harbor fortress of Boca Chica fell, Vernon sent word of victory to England. But Cartagena remained impregnable, and the English, decimated by yellow fever, finally retired to Jamaica. German Arciniegas, *Caribbean: Sea of the New World*, trans. Harriet de Onis (New York, 1946), pp. 297–301.

25. Details of this event are given in *SCG*, June 18–25, 1741, quoting a letter of May 16 from Port Frederica in Georgia: "Capt. Richard Norbury, Capt. Albert Desbrisay and several other of Gen. Oglethorpe's officers, dined together at St. Simons Camp, on Sunday the tenth of this month; there arose a dispute between Capt. Norbury and Capt. Desbrisay, the other Gentlemen interposed, and in all Appearances recon-

man as Norberry who was disregarded by every body. Norberry has left a wife and 3 or 4 children in very bad circumstances to lament his rashness.

Mama tenders you her affections and Polly joyns in duty with

My Dr. Papa

Y. m. obt. and ever D[evoted] D[aughter]

E. Lucas

June 1741. Wrote again to my father and sent the provisions he sent for.

1741. Wrote to my Aunt Concerning my dear brother Tommy's illness and my poor Cousen F. Fayweather's deep meloncholy at New England.

Wrote to Mr. Clealand about a bill of Exchange. The 4 wheeled post chaise and wine.

July 1741. Wrote to my Eldest brother upon his going into the Army. After an appoligy for a girl at my early time of life presuming to advise and urge him to beware of false notions of honour. That he makes proper distinctions between Courage and rashness, Justice and revenge. Acknowledged his letter of the 28th of October. Recommended to him upon his first entrance into life to be particularly careful of his duty to his Creator, for nothing but an early piety and steady Virtue can make him happy.

July 23rd, 1741. Wrote to my father concerning the Indigo affair. The report of his having changed Commissions with Major Heron. About Plantation affairs and other business.

ciled the two captains, and they drank several Glasses of Wine together (after the Dispute) in a friendly Way; and soon after, the Company broke up, and went different Ways; but unfortunately Capt. Norbury and Capt. Desbrisay met, upon which a fresh Dispute arose, they drew their Swords, and before any Body had time to part them, Capt. Norbury received Three Wounds, one in his Belly, the other two in his Arms; he died on the Spot. Capt. Desbrisay received Three Wounds, he was run through one Thigh, wounded in the other and in his left Hand."

[17]

July 1741. To Othneil Beale, Esqr., about Starrats affairs.

To Miss F. Fayweather in Boston
My Dear Cousen,   [c. June–July, 1741]
    'Tis a great affliction to us to hear what a bad state of health you
have in New England; on the other hand we are greatly consoled
to hear by Mrs. Pringle with what friendship and tenderness you
were received by your Uncle. Mama is very uneasy [because] she
has not heard from her dear Fanny for I let her know as little of your
illness as I can help. Papa and all our friends in Antigua were well
the last time we heard and desired to be remembered to you. Col.
Pinckney and Lady desire their Compliments to you and always
enquire of your welfair by every one from New England. Mr.
Pinckney wrote you a long letter from thence—when he was there
and you here—concerning your affairs, but which I believe you never
received. Little Polly desires her love to her Cousen and is always
talking of you; she never forgets to drink your health every day.
Mama desires to be remembered to you in the kindest manner and
beg you will let her know if you want anything.
    We are obliged to you for the Apples. Potatoes were quite out of
Season before we knew by Mr. Fayweather's letter they would be
acceptable.
    I am so much in the Country I can inform you of nothing new but
a few wedings: Mr. Middleton to Miss Williams,[26] Mr. Cooper to
Miss Molly Raven, and old Mr. Skoon is dead.
    Adieu my dear Fanny.[27] My prayers shall be constant for your
happiness. Accept the affections of
                                            Yr. Sincere friend
                                            E. Lucas

    26. Henry Middleton in 1741 married Mary, daughter and heiress of John Wil-
liams. Their daughter Sarah (1756–84) married Charles Cotesworth Pinckney in
1773. Langdon Cheves, "Middleton of South Carolina," *SCHM* 1 (1900): 240. A
good brief sketch of Middleton is John G. Van Deusen, "Middleton, Henry, 1717–
1784," *DAB*.
    27. Miss Fayweather shortly hereafter drops from the scene. She had apparently
been in Antigua, and later in Carolina with the Lucases.

To Mrs. Pinckney

Dear Madm.

To my great Comfort Mary-Ann informs me you are perfectly recovered of the indisposition you complained of when I was in town. As I then simpathized with you in your pain I would follow the scripture rule and rejoice with you on your recovery at Belmont; but I am afraid to trust myself on that agreeable spott and the Company I meet with there least it should make it too difficult for me to return at the time I ought to be at home.

At my return hither everything appeared gloomy and lonesome. I began to consider what alteration there was in this place that used so agreeably to sooth my (for some time past) pensive humour, and made me indiferent to every thing the gay world could boast; but found the change not in the place but in my self, and it doubtless proceeded from that giddy gayety and want of reflection which I contracted when in town; and I was forced to consult Mr. Lock[28] over and over to see wherein personal Identity consisted and if I was the very same self. I don't affect to appear learned by quoting Mr. Lock, but would let you see what regard I pay to Mr. Pinckney's recommendation of Authors—and, in truth, I understand enough of him to be quite charmed. I recon it will take me five months reading before I have done with him.

I am now returned to my former Gravity and love of solitude and hope you won't conclude me out of my Witts because I am not always gay. I, you know, am not a proper judge in my own Case. I flatter my self you will be favourable in your oppinion of me—tho' 'tis become so much the fashion to say every body that is grave is religiously mad. But be it as it will, those unhappy people have some times intervals, and you may be assured I am in my right Sences when I subscribe my self.

Dear Madm.
Y. m. obt. h. Sert
E. Lucas

28. A reference to John Locke (1632-1704), English philosopher and essayist and onetime confidential secretary to Anthony Ashley Cooper, one of the Lords Proprietors of Carolina. Eliza may have been reading his "Essay Concerning Human Understanding."

My Comp[liment]s wait on Colo. Pinckney.
I cant joyn Mama's; she has been abed these
two hours.

To the Honble. Crs. Pinckney, Esqr.
Sir

I think my silence requires less apoligy than my writing, especially as it has saved you the trouble of a reply, or I should beg your excuse for not answering your favour before and give you the reason which is as follows: I have had a very great cold [so] that I could not hold up my head or see out of my Eyes clear enough to write a line—and what perhaps you will think the most mortifying Circumstance of all, the power of prating was denied me for I had quite lost my tongue. This however was not all, for upon a review of Miss Blakeney's letter, found I had mistaken the time a week. I shall be at Mrs. Pinckney's disposal any day next week if 'tis not too much trouble to send to Mr. Hunt's for me.

I am not surprised you regret leaving the Country air for Town, especially as you are got to Parnassus and converse so freely with the Muses.

Mama joyns in Compts. to Mrs. Pinckney with

Sir

Your most obedt. Servt.

E. Lucas

The Honble Charles Pinckney, Esq.
Sir,

The inclosed, designed to go by Mary-Ann, was by accident left behind by which you will perceive how much out of order I was when you expected me. I might indeed have sent a verbal message afterwards had I imagined you would have given your self the trouble to go to Mr. Hunt's to meet me—a favour I had not [a] right to expect with all your politeness and friendship 'till I had answered your last.

Pray tell Mrs. Pinckney I am ready to submit to any punishment she thinks fitt to inflict if she does not think me sufficiently so by the pain I have already suffered on the occasion—which, give me leave to assure you, has not been a little. Did I know what day Mrs. P. would be in town I would put my self intirely in her power to take her revenge by waiting on her there and prevent the trouble of sending a second time to Mr. Hunts.

I am
Sir
Y. m. O. Servt.
E. Lucas

[To Charles Pinckney]
Sir,

Your letter with Mr. W's Journal[29] was an additional favour, but I am sorry you think I have so little taste to make a bribe necessary to induce me to pay Mrs. Pinckney a vizet. I shall endeavour next week to give you [a] better oppinion of my judgement.

When you receive this, I hope, Sir, you will acknowledge I am out of your debt—I mean only in the Epistolary way; for as to that profusion of Compliments you have bestowed on me, it will never be in my power to repay. As 'tis impossible for me to make you one so [I] expect you will be a merciful Creditor to

Sir
Yr. most obedt. Servt.
E. Lucas

My Papa in a letter we lately received desires his
Compt. and thanks to you and Mrs. Pinckney for
yr. kind remembrance of him.

To my Father.   September 20th, 1741.

I received a letter dated 2d July from My Honoured Papa which seems to accuse me of forgetfulness or thinking it too much trouble to write often to him. It gives me great concern that there should be even the appearance of a shadow for such a thought; for the paternal

29. Probably a reference to George Whitefield's *A Journal of a Voyage from London to Gibraltar* or *A Continuation of the Rev. Mr. Whitefield's Journal from a few days after his arrival at Georgia to his second return thither from Pennsylvania.* Both books were advertised in *SCG*, January 15, 1741, and in many subsequent issues.

tenderness I constantly experience from you must be as constant a momento to a return of every filial duty; but was Nature silent in the case and the tyes of gratitude no longer binding, surely self love would prevail and keep me from any omission towards you. But this is indeed not the motive by which I am actuated; I hope 'tis a principle more Generous and worthy [of] your daughter, and that you will do me the justice to believe your not hearing from me for some time past was purely the effect of accident, as I truely am

                        Hon'd Sir
               Yr. m. D[utiful] and obt. D[aughter]
                        E. Lucas

September 20, 1741. Wrote to my father on plantation business and concerning a planter's importing Negroes for his own use. Colo. Pinckney thinks not, but thinks it was proposed in the Assembly and rejected. [He] promised to look over the Act and let me know. Also informed my father of the alteration 'tis soposed there will be in the value of our money—occasioned by a late Act of Parliment that Extends to all America—which is to disolve all private banks, I think by the 30th of last month, or be liable to lose their Estates, and put themselves out of the King's protection. Informed him of the Tyranical Government at Georgia.[30]

October 14th, 1741. Wrote to my father informing him we made 20 w[eight] of Indigo and expected 10 more. 'Tis not quite dry or I should have sent him some. Now desire he will send us a hundred weight of seed to plant in the spring.

---

30. This colony was still under military government headed by General Oglethorpe and officers he appointed. Disturbed by questions relating to slavery, rum, and land tenure, the colonists blamed Oglethorpe, thinking that by his misinforming the trustees he was responsible for their condition. Charlestonians were particularly aware of this situation because the local printer, Peter Timothy, in 1741 published *A True and Historical Narrative of the Colony of Georgia in America* by "Three Georgia Gentlemen" who criticized Oglethorpe and wrote a satiric dedication to him. See Hewat, *Historical Account*, 1: 123; Elizabeth J. Deariso, "The Spanish War in Georgia," in *Studies in Georgia History and Government*, ed. James C. Bonner and Lucien E. Roberts (Athens, Ga., 1940), p. 30; and the 1960 edition of *A True and Historical Narrative*, pp. 123-34, 155.

October 16th. Wrote to Starrat about sending the Negroes down from Wacammaw.

October 18, 1741. Wrote to Boston to my Cousen Fanny Fayweather and sent her some of this Country potatoes.
At the same time wrote to Othneil Beale, Esqr., to forward it.

1741. Wrote to my dear brother Tommy, Ill in London.

Wrote to my brother George, 27th of October, 1741, desiring him to corrispond with me in French, and inclose him a letter to Mrs. Boddicott and one to Tommy.
At the same time wrote to Mrs. Boddicott desiring her to tell my worthy friend Mr. Boddicott [that] he certainly grows an old man tho' he was hardly forty when I left England; but he behaves like one in his grand Climatericks that a young Lady must be forced to write to him twice before he will indulge her with an answer to her letter.

Oct. 29th, 1741. Wrote to my father acquainting him that I received a letter from Mr. Boddicott with a very amiable character of my brother George. He says he is a very fine Youth.
Acknowledge the receipt of a piece of rich Yellow Lutstring[31] consisting of 19 yards for my self, ditto of blue for my Mama, and thanked my father for them. Also for a piece of Holland and Cambrick received from London at the same time. Toll him we have had a moderate and healthy summer and preparing for the King's birthday next day.[32] Toll him shall send the rice by Bullard.

31. Lustring, often called "lutestring" in the eighteenth century, is a stout, lustrous silk used in making dresses and ribbons.
32. George II's birthday, October 30, was a festive occasion throughout the colonies. SCG, October 31–November 7, 1741, reported the local celebration: "Yesterday being the Anniversary of his Majesty's Birthday, the Lt. Gov. reviewed the two Troops of Horse, and the Charlestown Regiment of Foot, which was much more numerous than ever, and performed a little Exercise with a surprising Dexterity;

Oct. 29th, 1741. Wrote to good Mr. Boddicott in answer to his letter received the day before.

1741. Wrote to my Cousen Glover informing her I received a letter from my Cousen Fanny Fayweather 10 days before by which she must be perfectly in her sences, is very cheerful and speaks very affectionately of her Cousen in New England, but says not a word of her having been ill. Hope therefore my Cousen Glover will write very tenderly to her and not mention any thing of her illness least it should affect her too much.

[Nov. 11, 1741] Wrote to Mr. Murry to send down a boat load of white oak Staves, bacon and salted beef for the West Indias. Sent up at the same time a barrel [of] salt, ½ weight salt peter, some brown Sugar for the bacon, and 6 weight sugar and a couple bottles wine for Mrs. Murry.

And desire he will send down all the butter and hogs' lard.

1742

Jan. 1741/2. Wrote my father a letter consisting of 7 sides of paper —about the Exchange with Colo. Heron, the purchasing [of] his house at Georgia, the Tyranical Government at Georgia. There went home last year a petition from a great number of sufferers for redress —with their caises and proofs. They got safe and was only answered that the majestrates that did the Injustice must make satisfaction. The people are now sending home an agent to apply for redress in another way.

Returned my father thanks for a present I received from him by Capt. Sutherland of twenty pistols, and for the sweetmeats by Capt. Gregory. Concerning Cousen F. Fayweather—she promises soon to pay her duty by letter. I have consulted Mr. Deveaux about setting a cow-pen; not yet determined.

after the Review, His Honor entertained the members of both Houses of the General Assembly, the Judges, Magistrates and all other Officers, both civil and military, with a very handsome Dinner, at which several loyal Healths were drank, and the evening concluded with an elegant Supper and Ball, at which was a very numerous and gay appearance of Ladies."

We never heard a sylible of William. Peggy went to England.

Shall send the preserved fruit as they come in Season.

Informed him I had begun to learn musick again with Mr. Pacheble, as he desired, and should endeavour to make myself mistress of the Harpsicord.[33] Begged the favour of him to send to England for Dr. Pepashe's Cantantas, Weldon's anthems, Knoller's rules for tuning.

Concerning seling off all the Cows belonging to Woppon [Wappoo] Estate. About the Jerusalem thorn; shall try deferent soils for the Lucern grass this year. The ginger turns out but poorly. We want a supply of Indigo seed.

Sent by this Vessel a Japaned waiter of my own Japaning[34]—my first essay. Sent also the Rice and beef. Sent Gov. Thomas of Philadelphia and daughter a tea chest of my own doing also.

Congratulate my father on my brother's recovery from the small pox, and having a commission.[35] An account of the Crops made at each of the Plantations.

To the Honble. C. Pinckney, Esqr.   Saturday

You justly observe a completion of happiness is not attainable in this life, to which truth I readily subscribe at all times, but especially while the disapointment we have just mett with in [not] seeing you and Mrs. Pinckney is recent. Mrs. Drayton (the bride)[36] with whom we lately spent a festal day at the Lieut. Governours told us you would as [of] this week vizet your friends at Ashley River, but your last removes the pleasing prospect. I shall however make my self all the amends I can by waiting on Mrs. Pinckney on Thursday next.

33. Charles Theodore Pachebel was one of the outstanding early musicians in Charleston. Known through concerts given in Boston, New York, and Newport, he came to Charleston by the mid-1730s. Besides giving music instruction, Pachebel served as organist at St. Philip's Church. Bridenbaugh, *Cities in the Wilderness*, pp. 455, 464; George W. Williams, "Eighteenth Century Organists of St. Michael's," *SCHM* 53 (1952): 146.

34. A popular occupation of young ladies was to decorate articles with a coat of japan or lacquer in the Japanese fashion.

35. Young George Lucas was listed in the *Gentlemen's Magazine* of August, 1741, p. 442, as an ensign in "Dalzell's Foot."

36. On November 14, 1741, John Drayton (1713–79) married Charlotte Bull, daughter of Lieutenant Governor William Bull of Ashley Hall plantation. Emily Drayton Taylor, "The Draytons of South Carolina and Philadelphia," *Publications of the Genealogical Society of Pennsylvania* 8 (March, 1921): 9; "The Bull Family of South Carolina," *SCHM* 1 (1900): 77–78.

In the meantime I entreat my friends if they would have me easey, not to give themselves too much pain on my account and assure them that there concern is much more painful to me than two or three blisters. They, you know, are but skin deep and consiquently nothing compared to those that affect the mind. I am at a loss how to return you our thanks suitable to our obligation. Mama bids me tell you she is quite ashamed of the troubles our people gave you, as is

Sir

Yr most obedt. Servant

E. Lucas

Our Compliments wait on Mrs. Pinckney.

[To Miss Bartlett]
Dear Miss B.   Jan. 14, 1741/2
'Tis with pleasure I commence a Corrispondance which you promise to continue tho' I fear I shall often want matter to soport an Epistolary Intercourse in this solatary retirement.[37] However you shall see my inclination is not in fault and the plea of wanting a subject is not an Idle excuse, for rather than not scribble you shall know both my waking and sleeping dreams, as well as how the spring comes on, when the trees bud and inanimate nature grows gay to chear the rational mind with delight; and devout gratitude to the great Author of all when my little darling that sweet harmonist the mocking bird begins to sing, etc., etc.

You asked me a question when I was in town I could not then resolve you, viz., what letter began the Tenor Cliff. I have since informed my self as follows: Wherever the Tennor cliff is marked, whether it be the first, second, third, forth or fifth line or space, that line or space is called C.

N.B. 'Tis not as in the bass or treble cliff constantly the same: g the first of the bass and E of the treble. If you are not clear in it from what I have said I will in my next give you an Example.

Our best respects wait on Colo. Pinckney and lady, and believe me to be, dear Miss

Yr most obedt. Servt.

E. Lucas

37. This is the first of many letters to Mary Bartlett, Mrs. Pinckney's niece, who was visiting from England.

[To Miss Bartlett]   [Jan. 1741/2]

'Tis paying you no Compliment, Dr. Miss B., when I say I could with more justice return all those obligeing things you are pleased to say of me in your last; but, however you have injured your judgment by what you have therein asserted, you have demonstrated the height of your good nature. But I must beg it as a favour for the future that you treat me less in the stile of Compliments or the consequence will be that I shall be very vain when I know a good judge—one of my own sex, too—has so high an oppinion of my trifleing attainments; for tho' it may proceed from an Excess of good nature in you, self love may blow the spark of vanity and make the merit her own. As to the other sex, I dont trouble my head about them. I take all they say to be words, of course, or to show their own bright parts in the art of speech-making, so they can do me no harm.

I hear the Rye Man of Warr is arrived.[38] Do they say whether the Warr is likely to continue or not? I was going to say I wish all the men were as great cowards as my self, it would make them more peaceably inclined. Now could I morralize for half an hour on the wickedness and folly of warr and bloodshed, but my letter is of a convenient length to subscribe, after paying our best respects to the Colo. and Mrs. Pinckney

Dr. Miss B
Yr. m. obedt. St.
E. Lucas

To Mrs. Cheesman[39]
Madm.   [c. March 1742]

The last time I had the pleasure of being with you, you seemed under fearful apprehensions for the Consiquence of Mr. B[ryan's] prophecy,[40] which induces me to acquaint you with the agreeable

38. *SCG*, June 14–21, 1742, reported: "We hear that Capt. Charles Hardy, in His Majesty's ship the *Rye* (which arrived here about the middle of Jan. last, from England) will sail on a cruise as soon as she has got a new Main Mast.—*Then stand clear Ye Spanish Privateers.*"

39. Elizabeth Cheesman acquired Lake Farm, a 236-acre tract of land on the Ashley River in January, 1741. Henry A. M. Smith, "The Ashley River: Its Seats and Settlements," *SCHM* 20 (1919): 76.

40. Hugh Bryan, a gentleman holding commissions in the magistracy and militia, was the most devoted Carolina disciple of the revivalist George Whitefield. As a boy Bryan had been captured by the Indians and kept in slavery, enduring suffer-

news of his being convinced of his Error. [He] is extremely concerned for what has passed and readily acknowledges he was not guided by the infalible spirit but that of delusion. Please to communicate this to Mrs. Hill,[41] and I am with Mama's Compliments

Madm,

Y. m. o. St.

E. Lucas

This may be depended upon.

[To Miss Bartlett]

Dear Miss B.

As my poetic vein comes by fitts and those short and seldom, I must desend to dull prose to tell you I am much obliged for your poetical compliment. The lines are very pretty, tho' you take the poets licence to raise your heroine much above her deserts. If this is your first attempt you will certainly be an excellent poettress in time, but let a friend advise you to chuse a subject for the future more worthy of your muse than a penejerick on

Yr humble Servt.

E. Lucas

Mama begs Mrs. Pinckneys acceptance
of a little Indigo Seed, Sorrel and
negroe pepper[42]—the last a good
Ingredient in dressing Turtle.

ings which left him eccentric. When he gathered together groups of Negroes and taught them Christian principles and also prophesied they would revolt and win their freedom, the citizens became alarmed. While the Grand Jury prepared to bring charges against him Bryan secluded himself in the woods, supposedly guided by an invisible spirit. Failure of the miracles he predicted sobered Bryan and he concluded the episode with a letter of apology to the Speaker of the Commons House of Assembly. *SCG*, January 1–8 Postscript, January 8–15, 1741; March 20–27, 1742; McCrady, *South Carolina Under the Royal Government*, pp. 238–43; Sirmans, *Colonial South Carolina*, pp. 231–32; J. H. Easterby, ed., *Journal of the Commons House of Assembly, 1741–1742* (hereafter *JCHA*), pp. 461–62.

41. Lake Farm was close to Hillsborough, which backed up to the Lucas's property and ran to the Ashley at Governor's Creek. It was the home of Charles Hill, a chief justice of the province, 1722–24, and his wife, Elizabeth Godfrey Hill. See two articles by Henry A. M. Smith: "Old Charles Town and Its Vicinity," *SCHM* 16 (1915), map opposite p. 3, pp. 57–59, and "The Upper Ashley; and The Mutations of Families," *SCHM* 20 (1919): 191.

42. Negro Pepper, also known as Ethiopian or Guinea Pepper, is a tree of tropical

[To Miss Bartlett]
Dr. Miss B   [March 1742]

I am willing you should participate of the pleasure we enjoyed
yesterday by hearing Mr. B[ryan] is come to his sences and acknowledges with extream concern he was guided by a spirit of delusion which carried him the length he has lately gone under a notion
of inspiration. Poor man! with what anguish must he reflect on making the spirrit of God the author of his weaknesses, and of disturbing
the whole community, who tho' they knew him to be no prophet
dreaded the consiquence of his prophecys coming to the ears of the
African Hosts, as he calls them. I hope he will be a warning to all
pious minds not to reject reason and revelation and set up in their
stead their own wild notions. He fancied indeed he was soported in
his oppinions by the sacred Oracles, and (as a father of our church
observes) so did all the broachers of herisey in the primitive church.
But why should we not expect to be deluded when we refuse that
assistance which the bountiful Author of our being has naturally
revealed to us and set up in every mans mind, without which 'tis
impossible to understand his will supernaturally revealed. For tho'
their may be things in the Xtian sistem above reason such as the
incarnation of our Saviour, etc., yet surely they highly dishonour
our religion who affirm there is any thing in it contrary to reason.

Dont you by this time wish my preachment at an End and repent
telling me you think my letters too short? But I cant conclude yet
till I have told you I see the Comett[43] Sir I. Newton foretold should
appear in 1741 and which in his oppinion is that that will destroy the
world. How long it may be traveling down to us he does not say; but
I think it does not concern us much as our time of action is over at
our death, the exact time of which is uncertain; tho' we may reason-
ably expect it within the utmost limits mentioned by the psalmist.

Meditateing on the shortness of life gives me no pain at present,
and I hope I have not inspired you with an unpleasing gloom, for a

Africa. The pungent aromatic fruit was long used as a spice. Acknowledgment is
due Dr. J. Hampton Hoch for this note.

43. There were two comets recorded in 1742. The first was sighted at the Cape of
Good Hope in February and in Europe and Asia in March. The second, "with a
queue having 30 degrees of length," was noted by three navigators in mid-April in
the area of the Cape. Neither of these was Newton's Comet. Alexandre Guy Pingre,
Cométographie, or traité historique et théorique des Comètes, 2 vols. (Paris, 1783–
84), 2: 47–49. Acknowledgment is due the United States Naval Observatory, Washington, D.C., for this reference.

life spent as I am persuaded yours is with innocence and that accompanied with all the good actions in your power, added to the soports the Xtian religion affords the pious mind, must prevent any great alarms at approaching death even to a lady of sixteen. I think that is the utmost you can reckon for I imagine I am your Signior by about two years. However, there is a disgust at the separation of soul and body natural to human minds, but that is in a great measure to be overcome by the soports of the Xtian religion.

What you desired of me I must now make the subject of my next, for I have spun out this to a greater length than I intended. The longer your letters the better I am pleased with them—and must inform you, when you write but two sides of half a sheet, I wont allow such large spaces between the lines as you commonly make.

Our compliments, &c. conclude me

Yr. m o S

E. Lucas

Memdam. March 11th, 1741.[/2]. Wrote a long letter to my father about the Indigo and all the plantation affairs, and that Mr. H. B. [Hugh Bryan] had been very much deluded by his own fancys and imagined he was assisted by the divine spirrit to prophesey: Charles Town and the Country as farr as Ponpon Bridge should be destroyed by fire and sword, to be executed by the Negroes before the first day of next month. He came to town—60 mile—twice besides sending twice to acquaint the Governor with it. People in general were very uneasey tho' convinced he was no prophet, but they dreaded the consiquence of such a thing being put in to the head of the slaves and the advantage they might take of us. From thence he went on (as it was natural to expect when he gave him self up intirely to his own whims) from one step to another till he came to working mirracles and lived for several days in the woods barefooted and alone and with his pen and Ink to write down his prophecies till at length he went with a wan[d] to divide the waters and predicted he should die that night. But upon finding both fail—the water continued as it was, and himself a living Instance of the falicy of his own predictions —was convinced he was not guided by the infalible spirrit but that of delusion and sent a letter to the speaker upon it, which I here inclose you.

Shall send by Capt. Gregory, if it can be got ready in time for him, the Turpintine and neats foot oil.

[To Miss Bartlett]
Dr. Miss B   [c. March–April, 1742]
By your enquiry after the Comett I find your curiosity has not been strong enough to raise you out of your bed so much before your usual time as mine has been. But to answer your querie: The Comett had the appearance of a very large starr with a tail and to my sight about 5 or 6 foot long—its real magnitude must then be prodigious. The tale was much paler than the Commet it self and not unlike the milkey way. 'Twas about a fortnight ago that I see it.

The brightness of the Committ was too dazleing for me to give you the information you require. I could not see whether it had petticoats on or not, but I am inclined to think by its modest appearance so early in the morning it wont permitt every Idle gazer to behold its splendour, a favour it will only grant to such as take pains for it—from hence I conclude if I could have discovered any clothing it would have been the female garb. Besides if it is any mortal transformed to this glorious luminary, why not a woman.

The light of the Comitt to my unphilosophical Eyes seems to be natural and all its own. How much it may really borrow from the sun I am not astronomer enough to tell.

Your letter was too long by one sentence, and only one—and that was desireing me to blott out part of your letter.

I now send you the patern of a Cap. 'Tis quite new—which makes me send it to you—and called a whim. You will think the lady that sent it me—who was also the inventor—made a very ill choice when I had so many whims before, more than I could well manage I assure you. But perhaps she thought the head should be all of a peice, the furniture within and the adorning without the same. But as I am of a diferent oppinion I send it to you who have as few as any lady at your time of life.

Our best Compliments attend the Col. and Mrs. Pinckney. I received Mr. Pinckneys favour, but 'tis to[o] late to answer it now. Mrs. P. has been very kind in transacting my little matters. I am most sincerely theirs and

Yr. m o St
Eliza. Lucas

[To Miss Bartlett]
Dr. Miss B   [c. March 1742]

All your letters pronounce the contrary of what you lately aserted and I insist you injure my Corrispondant no more with unjust reflections or I shall be greatly offended.

I did not receive your letter in time or should certainly have come to town to hear the Sermon, on a subject so new to me. I am, however, much obliged to you for remembering me on the occasion.

I must beg leave to say the rest to Col. Pinckney. My thanks are due to you also, Sir, for your very obliging invitation to your grand festival. Give me leave now to congratulate you on your Second Prætorship.[44] A Gentleman of your connection informed me you was to be chosen for the ensueing year.

I am with Mamas and my best respects to Mrs. Pinckney, Miss B. and

                                          Yr. m o h St.
                                          E. Lucas

[To Miss Bartlett]
Dr. Miss B   [c. March–April, 1742]

I admire your resolution of conquering the Lazey deity Somnus you talk off. I asure you the sight of a commit is not the only pleasure you lose if you lie late a bed in a morning; for this, like every other pernisious custome, gains upon us the more we indulge it. I cant help calling it pernicious, and I devide it into heads like a Sermon: 1st, because by loseing so much of our time we lose so much of life; 2dy because 'tis unhealthy; 3dly and lastly, because we lose by farr the pleasenest part of the day. From all which I could draw some useful inferences, but whether it will be so agreeable to you to hear preaching any where but in a pulpitt I am in doubt.

44. "The Right Worthy and Amicable Order of Ubiquarians . . . the first convened in America," was established in Charles Town in March, 1741. According to a notice in the *Gazette*, "The Roman Constitution in its most perfect state is the settled Policy of this most worthy order," and its governing praetor and senators were elected every six months. The notice of the "Festival" in March, 1742, announces that Charles Pinckney was elected praetor at the meeting at Jacob Woolsord's on the Bay, and that the company "proceeded in a very decent and regular manner to Dinner, at the Council Chamber, where an elegant entertainment was provided for them, and the Day concluded in a very agreeable Manner with the greatest Chearfulness, Order and Decency." See *SCG*, March 19–26, September 12–19, 1741; March 27–April 3, 1742; March 21–28, 1743. The late Samuel G. Stoney of Charleston supplied the above reference.

An old lady in our Neighbourhood is often querrelin with me for riseing so early as 5 o'Clock in the morning, and is in great pain for me least it should spoil my marriage, for she says it will make me look old long before I am so; in this, however, I believe she is mistaking for what ever contributes to health and pleasure of mind must also contribute to good looks. But admiting what she says, I reason with her thus: If I should look older by this practise I really am so; for the longer time we are awake the longer we live. Sleep is so much the Emblem of death that I think it may be rather called breathing than living. Thus then I have the advantage of the sleepers in point of long life, so I beg you will not be frighted by such sort of apprehensions as those suggested above and for fear of your pretty face give up your late pious resolution of early rising.

My Mama joyns with me in Compliments to Mr. and Mrs. Pinckney. I send herewith Colo. Pinckneys books and shall be much obliged to him for Virgils works; notwithstanding this same old Gentlewoman (who I think too has a great friendship for me) has a great spite at my books and had like to have thrown a volume of my Plutarchs lives into the fire the other day. She is sadly afraid, she says, I shall read my self mad and begs most seriously I will never read father Malbrauch.[45] With this request I believe I shall comply for 'tis very probable I never may. I cant help runing a parrellal between the above lady and my valueable and worthy friend Mrs. Woodward, who I know has as much tenderness for me as any woman in the world, my own good Mama hardly excepted, but she incourages me in every laudable pursuit.

A letter I received yesterd[ay] from my dear papa says their last news from England was that the Czarina of Moscovy was dethroned and princess Elizabeth, daughter of Peter the great, has got the crown through the councils and interest of the French court.[46]

I am

Dr. Miss B
Y m o h St
E. Lucas

45. Nicolas Malebranche was a French philosopher of the Cartesian school. "Malebranche, Nicolas (1638–1715)," *Encyclopedia Britannica*.

46. Early in December, 1741, Princess Elizabeth, apparently with the support of French Ambassador La Chétardie, engineered a *coup d'état*, overthrowing the regency of Anna Leopoldovna. The international significance of the coup is discussed briefly in Sidney Harcave, *Russia: A History* (New York, 1952), pp. 117–18.

[To Miss Bartlett]
Dr. Miss B

I was much concerned to hear by our man Togo Mrs. Pinckney was unwell, but as you did not mention it in your letter I am hopeful it was but a slight indisposition.

Why, my dear Miss B, will you so often repeat your desire to know how I triffle away my time in our retirement in my fathers absence. Could it afford you advantage or pleasure I should not have hesitated, but as you can expect neither from it I would have been excused; however, to show you my readiness in obeying your commands, here it is.

In general then I rise at five o'Clock in the morning, read till Seven, then take a walk in the garden or field, see that the Servants are at their respective business, then to breakfast. The first hour after breakfast is spent at my musick, the next is constantly employed in recolecting something I have learned least for want of practise it should be quite lost, such as French and short hand. After that I devote the rest of the time till I dress for dinner to our little Polly and two black girls who I teach to read, and if I have my paps's approbation (my Mamas I have got) I intend [them] for school mistres's for the rest of the Negroe children—another scheme you see.[47] But to proceed, the first hour after dinner as the first after breakfast at musick, the rest of the afternoon in Needle work till candle light, and from that time to bed time read or write. 'Tis the fashion here to carry our work abroad with us so that having company, without they are great strangers, is no interruption to that affair; but I have particular matters for particular days, which is an interruption to mine. Mondays my musick Master is here. Tuesdays my friend Mrs. Chardon (about 3 mile distant) and I are constantly engaged to each other, she at our house one Tuesday—I at hers the next and this is one of the happiest days I spend at Woppoe. Thursday the whole day except what the necessary affairs of the family take up is spent in writing, either on the business of the plantations,

47. The suggested method of having Negroes teaching Negroes was very advanced for this time. For the Reverend Alexander Garden's plan to train Negro teachers, see: *SCG*, March 14, 1743; George C. Rogers, Jr., *Charleston in the Age of the Pinckneys* (Norman, Okla., 1969), p. 91; McCrady, *South Carolina Under the Royal Government*, pp. 245–47; Frederick Dalcho, *An Historical Account of the Protestant Episcopal Church in South-Carolina* (Charleston, S.C., 1820), pp. 148–49, 156, 158, 178.

or letters to my friends. Every other Fryday, if no company, we go a vizeting so that I go abroad once a week and no oftener.

Now you may form some judgment what time I can have to work my lappets. I own I never go to them with a quite easey conscience as I know my father has an aversion to my employing my time in that poreing work, but they are begun and must be finished. I hate to undertake any thing and not go thro' with it; but by way of relaxation from the other I have begun a peice of work of a quicker sort which requires nither Eyes nor genius—at least not very good ones. Would you ever guess it to be a shrimp nett? For so it is.

O! I had like to forgot the last thing I have done a great while. I have planted a large figg orchard with design to dry and export them. I have reckoned my expence and the prophets to arise from these figgs, but was I to tell you how great an Estate I am to make this way, and how 'tis to be laid out you would think me far gone in romance. Your good Uncle I know has long thought I have a fertile brain at schemeing. I only confirm him in his opinion; but I own I love the vegitable world extremly. I think it an innocent and useful amusement. Pray tell him, if he laughs much at my project, I never intend to have my hand in a silver mine and he will understand as well as you what I mean.

Our best respects wait on him and Mrs. Pinckney. If my Eyes dont deceive me you in your last [letter] talk of coming very soon by water to see how my oaks grow. Is it really so, or only one of your unripe schemes. While 'tis in your head put it speedily into execution and you will give great pleasure to

Y m o s
E. Lucas

Memdm. Wrote in haste to my father in April 1742.

[To Miss Bartlett]
Dr. Miss B

I have got no further than the first volume of Virgil but was most agreeably disapointed to find my self instructed in agriculture as well as entertained by his charming penn; for I am pursuaded tho' he wrote in and for Italy, it will in many instances suit Carolina. I had never perused those books before and imagined I should imediately enter upon battles, storms and tempest that puts one in a maze and makes one shudder while one reads. But the calm and pleasing diction of pastoral and gardening agreeably presented themselves, not unsuitably to this charming season of the year, with which I am so much delighted that had I but the fine soft language of our poet to paint it properly, I should give you but little respite till you came into the country and attended to the beauties of pure nature unassisted by art. The majestick pine imperceptably puts on a fresher green; the young mirtle joyning its fragrance to that of the Jesamin of golden hue perfumes all the woods and regales the rural wander[er] with its sweets; the daiseys, the honysuckles and a thousand nameless beauties of the woods invite you to partake the pleasures the country affords.

You may wonder how I could in this gay season think of planting a Cedar grove, which rather reflects an Autumnal gloom and solemnity than the freshness and gayty of spring. But so it is. I have begun it last week and intend to make it an Emblem not of a lady, but of a compliment which your good Aunt was pleased to make to the person her partiality has made happy by giving her a place in her esteem and friendship. I intend then to connect in my grove the solemnity (not the solidity) of summer or autumn with the cheerfulness and pleasures of spring, for it shall be filled with all kind of flowers, as well wild as Garden flowers, with seats of Camomoil[48] and here and there a fruit tree—oranges,[49] nectrons,[50] Plumbs, &c., &c.

We are much concerned to hear of Mrs. Pinckneys illness. I have lately found benefit for the pain in my head by keeping my feet a little while every night before I go into bed in hott water. I dare say it would give her present ease if not cure her, but whether it may be

48. Camomile, or "chamomile," with its strong-scented foliage, had been cultivated in gardens since the middle ages; and the medicinal tea from its flower heads was a folk remedy for various ills.

49. Oranges were grown successfully in Carolina for several years, and figures for 1745 show that they were an export item that year. The severe freeze of February 7, 1747, damaged the industry, but it was revived so that increasingly greater quantities were exported into the 1760s. J. Hampton Hoch, "Pre-Revolutionary Commerce in Crude Drugs in Carolina," *Journal of the American Pharmaceutical Association* 27 (1938): 716.

50. Although there is a similarity to the word *nectarine*, Dr. J. Hampton Hoch believes that this trinomial had not been established by 1742. The identity of the fruit tree "nectron" is uncertain.

hurtful for the spleen or not I can't say. I wish she would mention it to Dr. C.[51]

Pray make our compliments and conclude me

Yr. m. o. St.
E. Lucas

[To Miss Bartlett]
Dr. Miss B.

That we were disapointed of seeing you as I expected I hope proceeded from any thing rather than an increase of Mrs. Pinckneys disorder—on whose account we are much concerned.

I suspect David blundered egregiously in delivering his message. Mine was that I would wait on Mrs. Pinckney if I knew when Col. Pinckney left town, to spend a little time with her during his absence. But as my coming depended on that event, I could set no time till I heard from Mrs. Pinckney when he set out. But I have now reason to think David has fixt a time for me and prevented your coming here, and thus we are disapointed both ways—which indeed I deserve for sending verbal messages.

I here inclose you the words of a new song. The tune cant be purchased with any thing but your company. As 'tis past ten o'Clock Saturday night you will give me leave to conclude sooner than usual.

Yr. m o h St
E. Lucas.

[To Miss Bartlett]

I am sorry I cant wait on Dear Miss B. on Monday for two reasons: first, the loss I shall have of all your agreeable companies; and the other is my curiosity which you have very much raised must remain unsatisfied. I have so much business on my hands at present I hardly know which to turn my self to first, and most of it such as cant be defered. But pray, cant this important affair be commited to writing, for woman like I shall not rest till I know it. In pity then take penn in hand.

51. Dr. Lionel Chalmers, a Scottish physician, practiced in Charleston for more than forty years, c. 1737-77. Joseph Ioor Waring, *History of Medicine in South Carolina, 1670-1825* (Columbia, S.C., 1964), pp. 188-97.

Pray pay my compliments to Col. Pinckney and tell him the ladies of merit have my consent to believe as much as they please of the fine things the Gentlemen say to them, but in this case I claim the previledge of judging for my self, as I do when [I] subscribe my self

Yrs. &c.,

E. Lucas

[To Miss Bartlett]

Dr. Miss B.

The contents of your last concerns us much as it informs us of the accident to Col. Pinckney. I hope Mrs. Pinckney dont apprehend any further danger from the fall than its spoiling him for a horsman. If it only prevents him riding that dancing beauty Chickasaw for the future, I think 'tis not much to be lamented, for he has as many tricks and airs as a dancing bear.

Wont you laugh at me if I tell you I am so busey in providing for Posterity I hardly allow my self time to Eat or sleep and can but just snatch a minnet to write to you and a friend or two now. I am making a large plantation of Oaks which I look upon as my own property, whether my father gives me the land or not; and therefore I design many years hence when oaks are more valueable than they are now—which you know they will be when we come to build fleets.[52] I intend, I say, 2 thirds of the produce of my oaks for a charity (I'll let you know my scheme another time) and the other 3rd for those that shall have the trouble of putting my design in Execution. I sopose according to custom you will show this to your Uncle and Aunt. "She is [a] good girl," says Mrs. Pinckney. "She is never Idle and always means well." "Tell the little Visionary," says your Uncle, "come to town and partake of some of the amusements suitable to her time of life." Pray tell him I think these so, and what he may now think whims and projects may turn out well by and by. Out of many surely one may hitt.

I promised to tell you when the mocking bird began to sing. The

52. The live oak was valued in shipbuilding. Robert Johnson had reported to the Board of Trade, January 2, 1729, that it "is much wanted in his Majesty's Docks and is the best Oak in the World for that Service, and of all his Majesty's Dominions in America, only grown in Carolina." Records in British Public Record Office Relating to South Carolina (hereafter BPRO), microfilm, Charleston Library Society, Charleston, S.C., 16: 29, 30.

[38]

little warbler has done wonders; the first time he opened his soft pipe this spring, he inspired me with the spirit of Rymeing, and [I] produced the 3 following lines while I was laceing my stays:

> Sing on thou charming mimick of the feathered kind
> and let the rational a lesson learn from thee,
> to Mimick (not defects) but harmony.

If you let any mortal besides your self see this exquisite piece of poetry, you shall never have a line more than this specimen; and how great will be your loss you who have seen the above may jud[g]e as well as

Yr. m. obedt. Servt.
Eliza. Lucas

I hope you never forget to pay my
Mamas and my best respects to Colo.
Pinckney and Lady.

[To Thomas Lucas]   May 22nd, 1742
I am now set down, my Dear Brother, to obey your commands and give you a short discription of the part of the world I now inhabit. South Carolina then is a large and Extensive Country Near the Sea. Most of the settled parts of it is upon a flatt—the soil near Charles Town sandy, but further distant clay and swamplands. It abounds with fine navigable rivers, and great quantities of fine timber. The Country at a great distance, that is to say about a hundred or a hundred and fifty mile from Charles Town, [is] very hilly.

The Soil in general [is] very fertile, and there is very few European or American fruits or grain but what grow here. The Country abounds with wild fowl, Venison and fish. Beef, veal and motton are here in much greater perfection than in the Islands [West Indies], tho' not equal to that in England; but their pork exceeds any I ever tasted any where. The Turkeys [are] extreamly fine, expecially the wild, and indeed all their poultry is exceeding good; and peaches, Nectrons and mellons of all sorts extreamly fine and in profusion, and their Oranges exceed any I ever tasted in the West Indies or from Spain or Portugal.

The people in general [are] hospitable and honest, and the better sort add to these a polite gentile behaviour. The poorer sort are the most indolent people in the world or they could never be wretched in so plentiful a country as this. The winters here are very fine and pleasant, but 4 months in the year is extreamly disagreeable, excessive hott, much thunder and lightening, and muskatoes and sand flies in abundance.

Charles Town, the Metropolis, is a neat pretty place. The inhabitants [are] polite and live in a very gentile manner; the streets and houses regularly built; the ladies and gentlemen gay in their dress. Upon the whole you will find as many agreeable people of both sexes for the size of the place as almost any where. St. Phillips church in Charles Town is a very Eligant one,[53] and much frequented. There are several more places of publick worship in this town and the generallity of people [are] of a religious turn of mind.

I began in haste and have observed no method or I should have told you before I came to Summer that we have a most charming spring in this country, especially for those who travel through the Country for the scent of the young mirtle and Yellow Jesamin with which the woods abound is delightful.

The staple comodity here is rice and the only thing they export to Europe. Beef, pork and lumber they send to the West Indias.

Pray inform me how my good friend Mrs. Boddicott, my Cousen Bartholomew and all my old acquaintance doe.

My Mama and Polly joyn in Love to you with

My dr. brother
Your most affectionately
E. Lucas

Memdm
Wrote to my brother in French.

[To Miss Bartlett]
Dr. Miss B.   [c. June, 1742]

After a pleasant passage of about an hour we arrived safe at home as I hope you and Mrs. Pinckney did at Belmont. But this place appeared much less agreeable than when I left it, having lost the agreeable

53. This splendid church, on the same site as the present St. Philip's, was built between 1711 and 1733 and burned in 1835. A perceptive discussion of Charleston, and South Carolina, in this period is in Rogers, *Charleston in the Age of the Pinckneys*, chaps. 2–4.

company that then enlivened it. The Scene is indeed much changed for instead of the easey and agreeable conversation of our friends I am engaged with the rudiments of the law to which I am yet but a stranger. And what adds to my mortification, I soon discovered that Doctor Wood[54] wants the politeness of your Uncle, who with a graceful ease and good nature peculiar to himself is always ready to instruct the ignorant. But this rustic seems by no means to court my acquaintance for he often treats me with such cramp phrases I am unable to understand him; nor is he civil enough to explain them when I desire it. However, I hope in a short time with the help of Dictionarys French and English we shall be better friends, nor shall I grudge a little pains and application if that will make me useful to any of my poor Neighbours. We have some in this Neighborhood who have a little Land and few slaves and Cattle to give their children that never think of making a will till they come upon a sick bed and find it too expensive to send to town for a Lawyer. If You will not laugh too immoderately at me I'll Trust you with a secrett. I have made two wills already. I know I have done no harm for I coned my lesson very perfect and know how to convey by will Estates real and personal and never forget in its proper place, him and his heirs for Ever, nor that 'tis to be signed by 3 Witnesses in presence of one another. But the most comfortable remembrance of all is that Doctor Wood says the Law makes great allowance for last Wills and Testaments presumeing the Testator could not have council learned in the law. But after all what can I do if a poor creature lies a dying and their family takes it in to their head that I can serve them. I cant refuse; but when they are well and able to employ a lawyer, I always shall.

A Widdow here abouts with a pretty little fortune teazed me intolerable to draw her a marriage settlement, but it was out of my depth and I absolutely refused it so she got an abler hand to do it. Indeed she could afford it. But I could not get off from being one of her trustees to her settlement and an old Gentleman the other. I shall begin to think my self an old woman before I am well a young one having these weighty affairs upon my hands.

54. Eliza must have been studying Thomas Wood's two-volume *Institute of the Laws of England*. This work, first published in 1720, was printed in as many as ten editions and remained the leading work on English law until superseded by William Blackstone's *Commentaries* in 1769. Edward I. Carlyle, "Wood, Thomas (1661–1722)," *DNB*.

I have just heard the moloncholy and shocking storry of Mrs. Le Brasures shoting her self.[55] It surprizes me so much I must conclude

Yr. m. o. st

E. Lucas.

Mama and Polly desire their Compliments
to Colo. Pinckney and Lady and [are] much
obliged to them for their friendly vizet.

To my Dr. friend Mrs. Boddicott.
My Dr. Madm.   June 29th, 1742.

I shall make no appoligy for not sooner answering your very obliging favour of the 20th of Nov.—every paragraph of which carries the most pleasing marks of sincere friendship—as I am persuaded you will do me the justice to believe nither my inclination was wanting nor that respect which I so justly owe you. Tis your too great tenderness for me makes you imagine I am too thoughtful for I have the pleasure to assure you I indulge no meloncholy apprehensions but endeavour cheerfully to resign to the Devine appointments; and as I make this a rule it enables me to keep up an habitual cheerfulness of temper which makes me happy my self and those connected with me, and at this time to soport with less pain the mortifying account we lately received of my much loved brothers being given over by the Phisicians. The loss of so promising a child is a real affliction to us all. But what shall we say! There is an Almighty Being infinitely Wise who governs all Events and consiquently knows what is best for us. Tis then the wisest as well as most dutiful step we can take patiently to submit, however hard the tryal may appear to us.

Mama begs you will accept her most grateful acknowledgments for your friendly care of him.

We have an account of my brother Georges safe Arrival in Antigua and Expect him shortly here.

I am much concerned for Mrs. Crabs misfortune as well as for

55. "Mrs. *Anne LeBrasseur*, a Widow Gentlewoman of considerable Fortune; a prime Disciple of Mr. Whitefield's, and who, since his Appearance amongst us, had shifted into a Third Communion, shot herself with a Pistol, loaded with a Brace of Balls, through the Body; and expired in an Hour or two after, professing her full Assurance of her Salvation, and that she longed to be in the blessed mansions which she knew were prepared for her. She recommended the Care of her Child to the Rev. Mr. Garden." *SCG*, June 14–21, 1742.

poor Mrs. Goddards loss of her mother and husband. Pray remember me to them and all my old acquaintance.

I am afraid poor Martha has a very bad debtor in William Decon. He has left us a great while; he first went and Enlisted himself under Colo. Vander-Dussen but was released upon the Colo. hearing he was our Servant. His roveing disposition continued and he soon after left us without saying a word, and where he is gone is quite uncertain. My Papa let him have some mony before he left London to pay some demands upon him there; what the sume was I don't know. He has also had mony here that, I apprehend, if there is any thing at all coming to him, 'tis a very triffle; but be it what it will, I will take care and send it as soon as I can learn what it is.

My Cousen Fayweather went to pay her Uncle a vizet a year ago at New England. She is not yet returned; she is much delighted with that Country.

I hope soon to hear from Master Boddicott and beg his acceptance of a kegg of Sweetmeats by this opportunity. My best respects wait on Mr. Boddicott, Mrs. Wilder and Miss Parry, and pray accept them your self from

Dr. Madm.

Yr. most obliged and Affecte. humble Servt.

E. Lucas

June 29th, 1742. Wrote a long letter to Miss Parry congratulating her on being fixt in a part of the world she is so fond off, and condoleing with her on her Mamas death and informed her I wrote to Mrs. Person, my old governess, by this opportunity.

[To Thomas Lucas]
My Dearest brother   June 30, 1742
The ill state of health you have so long laboured under gives us inexpressible concern. If there is the least probability of the recovery of my much loved brother it will be the greatest satisfaction we can enjoy to be acquainted with it from your self. 'Tis a great comfort to us in the midst of our affliction on your account to know you have all the care and tenderness from Mrs. Boddicott which you could possible have were you with us.

I know the goodness of your temper too well to be under any fear of your not bearing your misfortune with patience and resignation to the Devine will and being easily persuaded to any thing that may be of Service to you. Mama's blessing attends her dear little Tommy and longs to hear from him, and joyns in best respects to Mr. and Mrs. B, Mrs. Wilder, Mr. Gren, Miss Parry and Master Boddicott; and little Polly [joyns]in love to you with

My Dr. Brother
Yr. most affectionate Sister
E. Lucas

To my former Governess Mrs. Pearson.
Dear Madm   June 30th, 1742

As I always retain a grateful sence of the obligation I am under to you for your care of my Education so it will be ever a pleasure to me to acknowledge it and asure you of the pleasure it will always give me to hear from you.

My best respects wait on Mr. Pearson and Mrs. H. Miss Parry has been so obliging often to inform me of the wellfair of your family.

You will expect, Madam, I should say something of the part of the world I am now fixt in. 'Tis South Carolina, a large and plentiful province. Charles Town, its metropolis is a gentile, agreeable place, and its inhabitants a polite set of people. Our Winters are generally fine, but three or four months in the Summer excisive hott. My Papa has been obliged to leave us to attend his post in the West Indias, and my Cousen Fayweather [is] gone to pay her Uncle a Visit in New England.

Pray pay my Compliments to Mr. Evans, Mr. Horwood, Miss Martin who I hear is married but know not even her name. Miss Clark, Miss Portlock and all the young ladies I had the pleasure of being known too. Be so good to accept of a kegg of Sweet meats with this and my Mama's Compliments added to those of, Madam,

Yr. affecte and obedt. Servt.
Eliza. Lucas

Pray remember me to Mrs. Manlove.

[To George Lucas]
My Dear brother

The account my father lately gave us of your going soon on service has been the subject of my thoughts almost ever since. Among that variety of objects which press upon the mind in its most serious intervals this never fails to make one. I cant help reflecting on the dangerous situation of a soldiers life, continually exposed to accidents and fatigue, and the meloncholy consideration of a beloved father and brother being in great danger depresses me to the greatest degree and prevents my proceeding any farther—

I have recollected my self and will endeavour to banish a train of thinking fitter for a Sceptick than a Xtian. But what subject shall I write on. I am quite at a loss. Apropo, I was lately thinking how valueable a Virtue fortitude is and I stand in great need of it just now my self, and have also a mind to indulge the vanity of dictateing to you.

Remember then, My dear brother, that fortitude, a Virtue so Necessary in all stations of life and to all people, seems more particularly so to a Soldier, and I believe the generallity of that profession think so; but I doubt the younger sort dont always distinguish rightly between true fortitude and that which too often passes for it, and often decieves even the possesors them-selves. I mean heat of temper and a certain fierceness to encounter an Enemy which, as I said, often passes under the name of courage, but in which some of the brute Creation Equals if not exceeds the greatest Hero of you all. But, how deferent from that is the truely aimable Virtue fortitude or Strength of mind, which is hardened against evil upon rational principles, that is so guarded with reason and Consideration that no outward event is able to raise any violent disturbance in it, that has such a Constant power over its passions as not to be very timerous in danger, Envious in want, impatient in suffering, or revengeful under injuries. This composed [state] of mind in the midst of dangers and evil accidents is what I would have my dear brother endeavour to attain in as great a degree as this state of imperfection will permit.

Pardon my dear brother the liberty I take with you. I am a little older than you are and therefore asume on that account, or advise rather from the tenderest regard for your happiness, as I am truely

Your most affecte Sister
E. Lucas

Mama desires I will tell you her blessing and prayers attend you wherever you go.

[45]

To Miss B. at the Honble. Crs. Pinckney, Esq., in Crs. Town

This, Dear Miss Bartlett, is a proof of the obedience I pay to all your Commands or I could never have chose a worse time to write to you, with a mind less at ease or more clouded with meloncholy Ideas.

I am just returned from paying a Vizet to my poor friend Mrs. Chardon[56] whom I found quite out of her Sences, an object that must greatly move a stranger that had not lost every spark of humanity; what then must it be to an intimate friend! who loves, esteems and admires her even now that her charming intellects are so much disordered, for through the meloncholy veil her goodness of heart still appears. She was ever as good as women could be, but fain would have been an angel before her time and in the attempt ceased to be rational, and is now inferior to her own species of which she was so lately an ornament.

When I consider the many hours [of] agreeable conversation I have had with her; the many happy times we have read, worked, walked together in friendly Converse with her whose mind I know to be incapable of any disguise, I am greatly affected. When I see her worthy Parent lamenting this only, this darling child, the joy of her life, thus lost before she is arrived at the prime of her age, what do I not feel; but when I reflect on her cheerful temper, good sence, natural and pleasing vivacity now changed to inconsistant laughing, sighing, singing and incoherent discourses, I am shocked beyound what I am able to express. Surely there cannot be a more dismal prospect in nature than man, the master piece of this our world, deprived of the noblest principle of his nature and laid on a level with the beast that perrish and even inferior in some respects to those.

I will pursue no longer this meloncholy theme and ask pardon for having wrote so much on one that can convey nothing but gloom and distress except that lively gratitude which must always attend reflections like these to the bountiful Authour of our being and well being for continueing to us that blessing, the want of which we

---

56. Mary Woodward Chardon was the daughter of Eliza's neighbors, Colonel and Mrs. Richard Woodward. In 1735 she married Isaac Chardon, who died the following year; she later married the Reverend Richard Hutson of the Independent Church in Charleston. Joseph W. Barnwell, "Dr. Woodward and Some of His Descendants," *SCHM* 8 (1907): 34 and *passim*.

lament in another. I am with Compliments to Mr. and Mrs. Pinckney in which my Mama joyns

Dear Madm.
Yrs. &c.
E. Lucas

To Miss Bartlett

Dr. Miss Bartlett

I send by the bearer my compliments to Mrs. Pinckney and the last volume of Pamela.[57] She is a good girl and as such I love her dearly, but I must think her very defective and even blush for her while she allows her self that disgusting liberty of praising her self, or what is very like it, repeating all the fine speeches made to her by others when a person distinguished for modesty in every other respect should have chose rather to conceal them or at least to let them come from some other hand; especially as she might have considered those high compliments might have proceeded from the partiallity of her friends or with a view to encourage her and make her aspire after those qualifications which were ascribed to her, which I know experimently to be often the case. But then you answer she was a young Country Girl, had seen nothing of life and it was natural for her to be pleased with praise and she had not art enough to conceal it. True, before she was Mrs. B. it be excuseable when only wrote to her father and mother, but after she had the advantage of Mr. B's conversation and others of sence and distinction I must be of a nother oppinion.

But here arises a dificulty; we are to be made acquainted by the Authour of all particulars, how then is it to be done. I think by Miss Darnford or some other lady very intimate with Mrs. B. Here you smile at my presumption for instructing one so farr above my own level as the Authour of Pamella (whom I esteem much for the regard he pays to virtue and religion throughout the whole piece) but, my Dear Miss Bartlett, contract your smile into a mortified look for I acquit the Authour. He designed to paint no more than a woman, and he certainly designed it as a reflection upon the vanity of our sex

57. The novel by Samuel Richardson, published in 1740.

that a character so compleat in every other instance should be so greatly defective in this; defective indeed, for when she mentions that poor Creature Mr. H. Applusees it puts me in mind of the observation in Done Quixott How grateful is praise though it be from a madman. I have run thus farr before I was aware for I have nither capacity or inclination for Chritisism tho' Pamela sets me the example by critisizeing Mr. Lock and has taken the librty to disent from that admirable Author.

One word more and I have done, and that is I think the Authour has kept up to nature (one of the greatest beauties in the whole piece) for had his Heroin no defect the character must be unnatural, as it would be in me to forget my respects to your worthy Uncle and Aunt Pinckney and that I am

Yrs. &c.
E. Lucas

To Mrs. H.
Madam

Tho it appears too asumeing for my age and little experience to determin a point of such consiquence as this is in the early part of life especially which you desire of me, your importunity wont permit me to delay any longer giving you my sentiments on those divertions commonly called innocent ones and which under proper restrictions are so.

That there is any real hurt in a pack of Cards or going a suet[58] figure round the room, etc., no body I believe are obsurd enough to think, but tis the use we make of them. The danger arises from the too frequent indulging our selves in them which tends to effaminate the mind as it takes it of of pleasures of a superior and more exalted Nature as well as waists our time; and may at length give it a disrelish for them. For where these airry pleasures have taken intire posession of the mind the rational faculties are more and more unactive and, without doubt, for want of use will degenerate into downright dulness so that 'tis not playing a game at Cards or going to a ball now and then to relax the mind—but the immoderate love of them is sinful.

They should be matters quite indeferent, and we should very carefully observe the effect they have upon our own temper if that is not

58. An archaic form of *sweet*. Sir James H. Murray, *et al.*, eds., *A New English Dictionary on Historical Principles* (Oxford, Eng., 1919), s.v.

ruffled or too much pleased with them. If it does not indispose us to those dutys which we are indispensibly bound to as rational creatures related to God and one another, we may safely go; for under these two heads is comprehend[ed] every Virtue. I have said nothing of my own darling amusement Musick and which I indulge in more than in any other. This, methinks, has something of a devine original and will, as Mr. Addison observes, doubtless be one of the imployments of Eternity, and oh! how ravishing must those strains of musick be in which exerted the whole power of harmony, when as Milton discribes it, speaking of the angels

> Their golden harps they took
> harps ever tuned that glittering by their side
> like quivers hung and with preamble sweet
> of charming symphony they introduced the lasting song.[59]

By the help of a fine quotation I am come to an end, but shall never cease to be

Dr. Madm.
Yrs. &c.
E Lucas

[To Colonel Lucas]
Hond Sir   [*c*. June 1, 1742]
Your letter giving us an account of my dear little brothers being given over by his phisicians is an inexpressible concern to me as well as to my poor Mama. So engageing a child must be lamented by all that [k]new him. Our friend good Mrs. Boddicott expresses the most tender concern for him. What then must those feel that are related to him by blood as well as friendship! But what shall we say! There is an all Wise Being that orders Events, who knows what is best for us and determins accordingly; and we ought (if 'tis not in our power cheerfully) at least patiently to submit to his will. But in spite of my reason, nature pleads, and I find we are too nearly allied for her to cease her complainings when that tye is disolved.

My Cousens part of the mony you sent I conveyed to her some time ago by a safe hand, Mr. Coopers Nephew.

59. This quotation from Book III of "Paradise Lost" may have been written from memory, as the last line is misquoted. The 1688 edition, as well as subsequent ones, reads: "they introduce / Their Sacred song."

The quantity of Indigo I mentioned was produced of half an acre or rather more. The works being new and not dry enough in time the Indigo stood till many of the leaves droped. We shall be glad of the seed as soon as possible.[60]

Colo. Cook, his son and two daughters called upon us a fortnight since in their way from Georgia to Charles Town.[61] The ladies told me their papa had met with cruel treatment from Genl. Oglethorpe. When he was so ill they dispaired of his life, the Genl. would not give him leave pursuant to the doctors advice to leave Fredirica and stay a short time at Savanah for the change of air. He had all his letters intercepted and could nither send nor receive any, and when by Mrs. Cooks going to England her self she procured leave for her husbands return to England some of Mr. O[glethorpe's] creatures contrived to keep it in the Secretary of warrs office a month, and his son was obliged to come at last to fetch him. They sail from hence in about ten days for London. I hope Colo. Cooks representation of his conduct and this change of the ministry—with the Enquiry about to be made how the publick mony has been applyed for some years past, among which those large sumes that has been given for Georgia must be accounted for—will produce some good effects, and from the expected alterations at Georgia we draw some hopes of seeing my dear papa settled with us once again.[62]

Our Council and assembly are petitioning for 6 Indipendant companys for Carolina.[63]

You complain of my letter of the 21st of Oct. and account for its shortness by my prepareing for the then approaching birth Night.

60. Processing indigo on a South Carolina plantation is illustrated in Henry Mouzon's *Map of the Parish of St. Stephen in Craven County* [1773].

61. In a notice dated May 19 the *SCG* for May 22–29, 1742, reported that "The Honorable Col. Cook and several other Officers of General Oglethorpe's Regiment are arriv'd in Town in order to embark for England."

62. Lieutenant Colonel William Cook's nineteen charges against Oglethorpe's moral and military character were heard in a court-martial in June, 1744, after Oglethorpe had returned to London. The general was completely exonerated and Cook dismissed from service. Eliza's sympathies remained entirely with Cook. She wrote her brother George [January, 1745]: "Poor Col. Cook is broke on account of his complaint against Mr. Oglethorpe; the last mentioned carryed many of his own Creatures home with him which did the business and thus we find a man of Col. Cook's fair character ruined by this wrech who has a superior interest at court." Hewat, *Historical Account*, 1: 122–23; Walter Cooper, *The Story of Georgia*, 4 vols. (New York, 1938), 1: 256; Candler, *Colonial Records of the State of Georgia*, 2: 213, 229, 239; 23: 327. Eliza's letter is in the Duke University collection.

63. See *JCHA*, 1741–42, pp. 514, 554.

Give me leave, Sir, to asure you I had a much better excuse than going to a ball for not writing more fully to you and such a one as I am sure you would be glad I should be without, as 'tis no other than having on at that time a blister[64] to my Neck and one to each temple for a pain in my head, and from which I have found some benefitt.

I am greatly obliged to good Mr. and Mrs. Pinckney for their partiality to me, and, was it not on account of leaving my Mama too much alone and neglecting some affairs that require my attention at home, the friendly and pressing invitation they continually give me to give them as much of my company as I can would induce me to be much oftener in town than I am.

Mrs. Woodard and Mrs. Chardon, Colo. Pinckney, Mr. Graham, Mr. Cleland and their ladies desire their best respects to you. Mama tenders you her affections and says she begins to grow uneasey at not having a letter from you for some time paste.

Polly joyns in duty to you and my Aunt and love to my Cousens with

Hon'd Sir

y m o and ever Dutiful Daughter

E. Lucas

[To George Lucas]

I have been thinking, My Dear brother, how necessary it is for young people such as we are to lay down betimes a plan for our conduct in life in order to living not only agreeably in this early season of it, but with cheerfulness in maturity, comfort in old age, and with happiness to Eternity; and I can find but one scheme to attain all these desireable ends and that is the Xtian scheme. To live agreeably to the dictates of reason and religion, to keep a strick gaurd over not only our actions but our very thoughts before they ripen into action, to be active in every good word and work must produce a peace and calmness of mind beyond expression. To be consious we have an almighty friend to bless our Endeavours and to assist us in all difficulties, to be consious We have to the utmost of our power and ability endeavoured to please him, and shall finally injoy Him for ever, who is infinite perfection it self, gives rapture beyond all the

64. Poultice.

boasted injoyments of the world—allowing them their utmost extent and fulness of joy.

Let us then, my dear Brother, set out right and keep the sacred page always in view. You have entered into the Army and are not yet sixteen years of age. Consider then to how many dangers you are exposed, (I dont now mean those of the field) but those that proceed from youth, and youthful company, pleasure, and disipation. You are a Soldier, and Victory and conquest must fire your mind. Remember then the greatest conquest is a Victory over your own irregular passions. Consider this is the time for improvment in Virtue as well as in every thing else, and tis a dangerous weakness to put it off till age and infirmities incapacitates us to put our good designs in practise. But old age, you will say, is a long way off from you and me. True, and perhaps we shall never reach it. 'Tis then an additional reason why we should make use of the present and remember no time is ours but the present—and that so fleeting that we can hardly be said to exist.

Excuse my fears, my much loved brother, and believe they are excited by the tenderest regard for your wellfare, and then I will inform you I am in some pain (notwithstanding your natural good sence, for the force of Example is great) least you should be infected with the fashonable but shameful vice too common among the young and gay of your sex. I mean pretending a disbelief of and ridiculeing of religion; to do which, they must first Enslave their reason. And then where is the rule of life? However it requires some degree of fortitude to oppose numbers, but cherish this most necessary virtue; tis so to all mankind, particularly to a soldier. Stand firm and unshaken then in what is right in spite of infidelity and ridicule. And you cant be at a loss to know what is right when The Devine goodness had furnished you with reason, which is his natural revelation, and his written word supernaturally revealed and delivered to mankind by his son Jesus Christ.

Examin carefully and unprejudicedly, and I am persuaded you will have no doubts as to the truth of revelation. For my own part I am so happy in the belief of the Xtian scheme that I cant help adopting an expression I have some where mett with, that if 'tis a delusion tis so pleasing a one that I would not be undeceived for the whole world. For if we lead a life of piety here, 'tis a life of all others the most pleasing and agreeable. And if there is no future state we are in as happy a situation as the irreligious. But if there should! with what dreadful astonishment must they cry out in Solomons words, we fools counted his life madness and his end to be without honour. How is he numbered among the children of God and his lott is among the saints. But say these wise heads, these pretenders to reason, how can we believe the scriptures when there are things contained therein contrary to reason! Were it really so the objection would be just, but upon examination you will find reason in the manner they use it is but another name for their prejudices.

God is Truth it self and cant reveal naturally or supernaturally contrarieties. The Christian religion is what the wisest men in all ages have assented too. When I speak of religion I mean such as is delivered in the scripture without any view to any particular party with exclusion of all the rest. It has been acknowledged by the greatest men of our nation and many others that revealed religion is consonant to the most exact reason tho some things may appear at first sight contrary to it. But you must observe there may be things above, tho' not contrary to reason.

Give me leave to show you how Mr. Boil[65] illustrates it by the following comparison. If a diver should ask you what you can see on a deep sea, You would answer you could see the depth of some yards and no further. If he should ask further if you could see what lay at the bottom of the sea, You would answer no. If then the Diver should bring up mussels or Oysters with perls in them, you must acknowledge they lay beyound your sight—and consiquently must argue a common tho' not personal imperfection—and that the perls have the genuin coulour and luster of such gems. But if the diver should pretend each of these perls as big as a Tennis ball or larger than the shell it was inclosed inn, not round but cubical, and not white and orient but black or scarlet, you would conclude his assertion undesernable by your Eyes; and would therefore deny what he asserted because it would argue your sight imperfect and false, though the organ was qualified to receive its proper object.[x]

If I dont hasten to conclude you will certainly think I have a plott against you and have a mind by this long Epistle to try in what degree you posess those valueable virtues, patience and humility. The first

65. Robert Boyle (1627–91), natural philosopher and chemist. A standard work is Louis T. Moore, *The Life and Works of the Honourable Robert Boyle* (London, 1944).

I doubt has given way and you are quite tired, and the last struggles to soport the receiving advice from one inferior to you in understanding and not much more than a year your senior. But let her triumph! for 'tis a Virtue that adds loveliness to all the rest, and is the characteristical mark of a great mind; 'tis a dificult one to attain indeed, and there requires much pains to posess it, and to use the words of the above mentioned great authour: It is more heroic to overcome Virtues when they act united than to contend only with vices (passions are open Enemies) which a man must do to be humble, for 'tho other virtues assist one another they all conspire to overthrow humility. But while I am inculcateing this doctrine upon you, dont let me forget to practise it my self by asking your pardon for thus presumeing and hope you will receive it as a testimony of the tenderest regard from

Your most affectionate Sister
E. Lucas

My Mamas blessing attend you.
We have not heard very lately from my Papa.
ˣ Thus farr Mr. Boyle and I can perceive.

July 2nd, 1742. Wrote to my father acknowledging the receipt of the money and other things sent by Mr. J. Boon; concerning imploying Mr. Garvey on part of the Garden Hill tract. Informed him that the 30th of June an express arrived from Georgia that 12 hundred Spainyards were landed at a small Island near Friderica.[66]

 Wrote to Murry upon the least alarm or apprehension of danger imediately to bring down the Negroes. Informed him also of Capt. Franklands taking 4 Vessels, one said to be worth 10 thousand pound sterling.[67]

66. Oglethorpe had built the fort and small town of Frederica, surrounded by a pentagonal rampart on St. Simon's Island, near the present town of Brunswick. The Spanish squadron from Havana and St. Augustine comprised fifty ships and three thousand men. The fleet anchored at St. Simon's bar, then proceeded up the Altamaha beyond the reach of Frederica's guns to make landings. The Spanish were defeated in an engagement called the Battle of Bloody Marsh, and soon boarded ship and sailed away. E. Merton Coulter, *Georgia: A Short History* (Chapel Hill, N.C., 1947), pp. 47–49; Hewat, *Historical Account*, 1: 110; Ramsay, *History of South Carolina*, 1: 81 and *passim*.
67. Four Spanish prizes were brought into Charleston harbor. One was the man-

Aug. 29th. Wrote to my Cousen at New England giving her some hopes of my brothers paying her a vizet. Sent her by this opportunity—Capt. Breeding—a barrel [of] Rice and another of potatoes. Informed her of my Papas coming soon to us or sending for us to him. Polly desires her acknowledgments to Miss Fayweather for the present of flowers she was so good to send her.

Sept. 8th, 1742. Wrote to Miss Mary Fayweather in Boston.

The same time Wrote my Father a full and long account of 5 thousand Spainyards landing at St. Symons. We were greatly alarmed in Carolina. 80 prisoners now in Charles Town. They had a large fleet but were scattered by bad weather. Our little fleet from Carolina commanded by Capt. Hardy could not get to the General's Assistance;[68] the Enemy now sailed to St. Wanns.[69] 'Tis said Capt. Hardy, instead of cruising off St. Augustine barr where it was probable he would find them, returned with all the men to Charles Town—which has greatly disgusted the Gov. and Council as well as the rest of the Inhabitance.[70] There is sent now 3 men of War and 4 provincial Vessels under the Command of Capt. Frankland.[71]

of-war *St. John Baptista*, whose captain, Don Juan de Lean Fandeno, had "taken 38 English vessels" and "commanded at the taking of Captain Jenkins ship when his Ears were cut off." *SCG*, June 14–21, June 28–July 5, 1742. Captain Thomas Frankland's exploits are discussed briefly in Rogers, *Charleston in the Age of the Pinckneys*, pp. 31–32.

68. The Carolina fleet of three ships could not cross the St. Simon's bar because of contrary winds. Georgians were bitter against South Carolina for helping so little, so late. As one observed, the South Carolinians came only "after the Spaniards had been chased quite out of the Colony." Quoted in Coulter, *Georgia: A Short History*, p. 50. See also Hewat, *Historical Account*, 1: 118–19; Ramsay, *History of South Carolina*, 1: 80–83.

69. The St. Juan or St. John's River which forms a wide bay at Jacksonville, Florida.

70. Captain Hardy gave orders for the Carolina vessels to return to Charleston even though the governor and council had advised him before his departure to pursue the enemy and "destroy them even in the Harbour of St. Augustine." *SCG*, July 26–August 2, 1742.

71. *SCG* for August 2–9, 1742, reported: "Capt. Thomas Frankland in his Majesty's ship the *Rose* arrived here with a Dutch Snow prize and a fine Spanish Privateer Sloop. . . . When Capt. Frankland was coming up he was saluted by the four Vessels (one after another) which were fitted out by this Government against the Spaniards and ordered back by Capt. Hardy. . . . Inhabitants upon the several wharfs . . . gave him Three Huzza's. . . . All the Vessels belonging to this Government were accordingly put under his command, as Commodore of all His Majesty's Ships now in these Parts."

The last Indigo seed sent not good. None of it came up. We shall save enough of our own to make a Crop next year.

Sent my father his kettle Drums; informed him of Mr. Smiths seling the rum he sent us and giving away the preserved sorrel, tho' he assured us it was by mistake put on board a vessel going to Barbados and carried there. Sad wretch. Wrote on plantation affairs. Payed the compliments of all his friends who treat us with great friendship and respect. Sent for west India Concumber seed.

Sept. 1742. Wrote to Miss Bartlet who pressed me to come to town; excused my self by haveing many affairs to inspect both within and without doors. The box from England she mentions for me wont tempt me. I imagine 'tis materials for Japaning; the weather got to hott for that warm work.

Wrote to my Brother at Antigua complaining of his not writing oftener.

Sept. 24th, 1742. Wrote to my father informing him the Council had pe[ti]tioned for a regiment instead of 4 Independant companys since the Spainyards had been a[t] Georgia.

Also that I had prevailed on Mama to send Polly to school.

Nov. 1742. Wrote to my father giving him an account of the Arrival of the fleet from Jamaica. The number of men have not yet heard; I am told there is fifty officers.

To my father
Hond. Sir   Novr. 11th, 1742
Since my last the fleet is returned to Jamaica. Their orders were such that, if the Spainyards were gone and we under no apprehensions of their returning, to return to Jamaica with the whole detachment. They were very desirous to stay longer, and the Carolinians as desireous to have them stay. They were very well received here and took great pleasure in acknowledging it upon all occasions. They

are quite enamoured with Carolina; nor is it to be wondered at after coming from Jamaica, a place of which they give a most horrible character. The character they give of the women there must, I think, be exaggerated and therefore I wont enlarge on that head.

The Gov. gave the Gentlemen a very gentile entertainment at noon and a ball at night for the ladies on the Kings birthday at which was a Crowded Audience of Gentlemen and ladies. I danced a minuet with your old acquaintance Capt. Brodrick, who was extreamly glad to see one so nearly related to his old friend. I promised to pay his compliments to you and asure you how extreamly glad he would be to see you. A Mr. Snell (a very talkative man) desires his best respects and says many obliging things of you for which I think my self obliged to him and therefore punish my self to hear a great deal of flashy nonsense from him for an hour together.

I am Dr. Sir

Your most obedt. and ever Dutiful Daughter

E. Lucas

Dec. 1742/3. To my Cousen in Boston acknowledging her letter and present and that of Miss M. Fayweather promising to Corrispond with them both.

1743

Wrote on new years day to Miss Bartlett after her having been at Wappo.

Jan. 7th, 1742[/3]. Wrote to my father concerning my brother Tommy, his Nurse, his pretty stile in writing, &c. Inform him of some negroes detected going to Augustine.[72] They accused Mol[att]o Quash.[73] I was at his tryal when he proved him self quite Innocent.

72. The South Carolina Council *Journals* have repeated references to the Spaniards at St. Augustine encouraging Carolina slaves to escape to that garrison. By 1749 the problem was so serious that Governor Glen declared to the Assembly: "Unless a stop be put to this Practice it may . . . prove . . . destructive to the Province." Governor Glen's speech of November 23, 1749, *JCHA, 1749-1750*, p. 286.

73. He can be identified as the same "Mullatto Quash" listed among the twenty working slaves at Wappoo included in Eliza's dowry, and also referred to as

The ring leader is to be hanged and one Whyped.[74]

       That we rejoyce in the prospect of seeing my papa this spring.

       Mr. Glen not yet arrived; 'tis imagined he is detained by p——y.[75]

       Polly gone to school at Mrs. Hick's at 140 pound per annum.[76]

Feb. 3rd, 1743/4.[77] Wrote to my Aunt concerning Mr. Smith.

The same day wrote to my father concerning his affairs in England and of my brother Tommy.

    Thanks for all the things he sent. Sent him by the return of the Vessel. 2 barrels Rice, ditto Corn, 3 ditto peese, 1 pickled pork, 2 keggs Oysters, one of Eggs by way of Experiment put up in salt; in case they answere, my scheme is to supply my fathers refineing house in Antigua with Eggs from Carolina.

    Concerning settleing a plantation to the North with the Woppo slaves, &c., &c.

To My Father   Feb. 10, 1742/3

    I am at a loss where to write to my Dear and Honoured Father, but am determined not to omit this pleasing duty while I am able to perform it. I shall therefore send this to my brother to forward it to you. Possibly the expedition may be over and you returned in safety. Happy indeed shall I be when this grateful news reaches us; suffi-

"Quashy, a Carpenter" (1746) and "Quash, a Carpenter, since baptized by the name of John Williams" (1749). "Wills and Miscellaneous Records, Charleston County," 100 vols. (typescript of manuscript), Charleston, S.C., County Library, 75A: 95–106; 75B: 373–74; 78A: 250.

74. The Court of Justices and Freeholders, of which no records remain, conducted trials of slaves. David D. Wallace, *History of South Carolina*, 4 vols. (New York, 1934), 1: 279.

75. James Glen, the new (and impecunious) governor, although he had been commissioned more than five years before, did not reach Charleston until December 17, 1743. He delayed leaving England until salary arrangements were satisfactory. *SCG*, December 19–26, 1743; Sirmans, *Colonial South Carolina*, p. 195.

76. The reference may be to Mary Hext, who gave notice in the *SCG* of August 15–22, 1741: ". . . that young Misses might be boarded and taught Needle Work, of all sorts. . . . That Writing, Arithmetick, Dancing and Musick is also taught by Masters well qualified." Eliza also wrote to her father, April 22, 1742: "Mama's indulgence now makes her [Polly's] going to school necessary." Pinckney Family Papers, Manuscripts Division, Library of Congress (hereafter, PP/LC).

77. Later references indicate the date is 1743.

ciently thankful I never am to the great Author of all my happiness for a blessing like this, for more than the utmost gratitude I can pay is due.

I received the friendly congratulations of Miss Dunbar on your being made Lieut. Col. and Gov. of Antigua with a very gentile present to Polly and another to myself. My brother seems mortified at being left behind and not suffered to attend you on this expedition. His going would doubtless have improved him in millitary affairs, but I hope his staying will be no disservice to his morrals as it may teach him to bear disapointments and curb too ambitious aspireings in his young tho' good mind—a useful piece of knowledge in human life and perhaps requires as much true fortitude as faceing an enemy.

But to cease morrallizing and attend to business. The [rice] crop at Garden Hill turned out ill, but a hundred and sixty barrels; and at Wappo only 43. The price is so very low as thirty shillings per hundred. We have sent very little to town yet for that reason. People difer much in sentiment about the number of ships we are still to have.

We have not heard from England for more than three months. What can keep the shiping? We conjecture 'tis an imbargo.

In my letter of the 3rd of Feb. I desired to know if you aproved of settleing a plantation to the North near Major Pawly. Please to let us know in your next if we have your approbation and it shall be done in the fall.

We expect a Vizet from the Spainards this Summer. Mr. Oglethorp harrases them much at their forts at St. Augustine. He has lately killed some and took two prisoners.

Mama tenders you her affections, and blessing to my brother, and I am

Hond. Sir

Y. m. o[bedient] and D[utiful]

D[aughter]

E. Lucas

March 17, 1743. Wrote to my Cousen in Boston by Mr. Pelham recommending him as a musick master and beging the favour she would recommend him to all her acquaintance; that I had learned of him my self.

Sent her some peach trees and our Country patatoes.
The same day wrote to Miss Fayweather.

April 11, 1743
To Miss Dunbar at the Honble. Charles Dunbars, Controuler of the Customs at Antigua.

My acknowledgements are due to Dear Miss Dunbar for her favour of the 16th Feb., as well as for Mrs. Dunbars and your obliging congratulation and present. The hopes of seeing you is an additional pleasure to what I promise my self in haveing again my Papa and brothers company, and indeed nothing but this satisfaction can atone for the regret with which I shall leave Carolina, a country for which I shall always have the greatest regard.

I am quite angry at your finding fault with your penmanship and shall be very severe upon every one that presumes to injure my young and agreeable corrispondant. I know I am obliged to Mrs. Dunbar for this first Epistle. I hope your next need not be in proof of your obedience but of your inclination to give pleasure to

Dear Miss Grace

Yr. m. obedt. and affecte.

humble Servt

E. Lucas

Mama and Polly joyn with me in best respects
to Mr. and Mrs. Dunbar. Pray pay my Complts.
to Mrs. Crump and Miss Barks.

To Miss Bartlett in St. Pauls Church Yard, London
Dr. Miss Bartlett   [c. May 1743]

I am determined to extort a pardon from you for my breach of promise by accusing your good Uncle and Aunt as the Cause. You already know how happy I am in their friendship and how much they study to make my papa's absence easey to me by a thousand obliging ways. In consequence of this benign disposition they lately contrived a most agreeable tour to Goose-Creek, St. Johns, etc. to show me those parts of the Country, in which are several very hansoume Gentlemens Seats, at all [of] which we were entertained with the most friendly politeness. The first we arrived at was Crow-field, Mr. Wm. Middletons seat where we spent a most agreeable week.[78] The house stands a mile from, but in sight of the road, and makes a very hansoume appearance; as you draw nearer new beauties discover themselves, first the fruitful Vine mantleing up the wall loading with delicious Clusters; next a spacious bason in the midst of a large green presents itself as you enter the gate that leads to the house, which is neatly finished; the rooms well contrived and elegantly furnished. From the back door is a spacious walk a thousand foot long; each side of which nearest the house is a grass plat ennamiled in a Sepertine manner with flowers. Next to that on the right hand is what imediately struck my rural taste, a thicket of young tall live oaks where a variety of Airry Chorristers pour forth their melody; and my darling, the mocking bird, joyned in the artless Concert and inchanted me with his harmony. Opposite on the left hand is a large square boleing green sunk a little below the level of the rest of the garden with a walk quite round composed of a double row of fine large flowering Laurel and Catulpas which form both shade and beauty.

My letter will be of an unreasonable length if I dont pass over the mounts, Wilderness, etc., and come to the bottom of this charming spott where is a large fish pond with a mount rising out of the middle —the top of which is level with the dwelling house and upon it is a roman temple. On each side of this are other large fish ponds properly disposed which form a fine prospect of water from the house. Beyond this are the smiling fields dressed in Vivid green. Here Ceres and Pomona joyn hand in hand to crown the hospitable board.

Thus I have given you a very languid discription of a delightful place; the Laguire Expedition[79] has damped every gay Idea, and

78. Crowfield truly was one of the handsomest estates in colonial South Carolina. It is now completely destroyed, but a drawing of the grounds, based on remains and this letter, may be seen in Samuel G. Stoney, *Plantations of the Carolina Low Country* (Charleston, S.C., 1938), pp. 54–55, 119.

79. La Guaira, the port for Caracas, Venezuela, was a strong Spanish fortress. The elaborate British naval expedition ended in disaster. At the approach of the British fleet the Spaniards at the forts of La Guaira opened fire. "Hulled us every shot," reported an eye-witness. And "seeing three of our best ships that we had going out of the Line upon the Careen and their masts shot away, they began to fire much brisker than before." Colonel Lucas commanded the ill-fated landing party, which consisted of his own regiment, all the marines of the squadron, and four hundred

faded every flow'ry expression; nor would the silvan scenes or even Arcadia it self charm till my dear fathers safe return.

I take some pains, you see, to let you know my genius is not defective; any thing rather than that. Oh, vanity of female Youth!

How came it into your head to ask me to write a poem on Virtue for you; into mind to give you any hopes that I would attempt it. I am sure I could as well read Homer in the Original as write a piece of good poetry on any subject whatever; that on Virtue I own always gives an Alacrity to my mind, and was I equal to it, would Celebrate each branch of it in Numbers suitable to the high sence I have of the Sacred theme. But tis too exalted for my diminutive pen and I must admire in silence.

I am quite tired of writing as I sopose you are of reading, and cant say one word on the other seats I saw in this ramble, except the Count's large double row of Oaks of each side the Avenue that leads to the house—which seemed designed by nature for pious meditation and friendly converse. I wont say a Syllible of the Conquest I made of the old Gentleman, the owner of this mansion; not because I imagine you will think me vain, but because I know your Uncle who is much pleased with it will send you a full account.

Compts. etc. conclude me
Yr. affecte. humble Servt.
E. Lucas

Miss Writ [Rhett] is married to Capt. Frankland.[80]

[To Miss Livingston]
Dr. Miss L.

Tis with blushes I accept your obliging offer to assist me in finishing my head which nothing but your repeated importunity could effect. I am really ashamed of being so troublesome. The Flute would be, I am persuaded, much better imployed with you. Notwithstanding the eagerness of my temper to lern whatever I take in my head

seamen from the warships. *SCG*, April 11–18, May 9–16, and June 13–20, 1743; Frances Leigh Williams, *Plantation Patriot* (New York, 1967), p. 138.

80. The *SCG* of May 30, 1743, reported that on Friday, May 27, 1743, Captain Thomas Frankland of the *Rose* man-of war was married to Miss Sarah Rhett, "a beautiful and accomplished young lady, with a large fortune."

I have made very little progress. I have however got through my Gamutt and can Tumble over one little tune which will be at your Service when I see you.

Mama's Compliments to Mrs. Livingston with those of

Madm.
Y. m. obdt. St.
E. Lucas

[To Thomas Lucas]

I was much concerned at not hearing from my Dear brother by the last ship; I have now more reason to be so since my Cousen B. informs me of a dangerous illness which you have hardly over-come. That heaven may preserve you long a blessing to all your family is the sincere prayer of a sister that esteems and values you as she ought and hopes for much happiness from you.

Surely one of the greatest—if not the very greatest—of human evils is the seperation of Dearest friends, but it is one that must certainly happen for as sure as we are born we must dye. You have lately, my dear brother, had a memento of the Universal truth. Let us then endeavour to familiarize the awful change to our minds; but death at Eighteen, you will say, appears more tremendously gastly; leave then the gloomy grave, the Mattock and the spade and turn the bright side of the prospect; and let us triumph in a blessed immortality amid scenes of endless bless and never fading joy. Why then should we not talk of changing a mortal for an immortal habitation with the same pleasure as of any other great happiness we have in view. Guilt indeed adds horror to the grave and makes the king of terrors appear more terrible; nay, even to the virtuous there is something in the disolution of soul and body at which nature recoils. But the great support which the principles of Christianity affords will enable us to meet the grisly monarch with a fortitude superior to what is natural. How I shall conclude this last action of human life God only knows, but 'tis a scene that has been often acted over in my imagination. Oh, may that important hour be no more dreadful to my apprehension than the thoughts of it has been. Then shall I resign this breath with ease and Comfort and sleep in peace with my kindred Earth till the great and Auful change.

I am not, my dear brother, out of humour with the world or any of my fellow mortals that I can talk with ease of leaving it so early. No, I have still some tender engagements to it; fillial and fraternal affection, sincere and disenterested friendships have charms that bind me to it.

Mama desires her blessing and Polly her love with

My dr. brother
Yr. truely affecte. Sister
E. Lucas

To Mrs. Pinckney
Dear Madm

I herewith beg you will accept an offering of the first fruits of my Vines. They are not equal to what I could wish them to present to you, but would fain have the fruit of my labours honoured by your acceptance. The pious heathens used to offer the first of their Vintage to Bacchus the God of riot; I have made a better Choice by being born in a more enlightened age, and make mine to Xtian temperance by offering them to you. You see, my dear Madam, the subject of my Epistle is quite equal to my present; the whole of both consists of a bunch of grapes, nor will what I can add give any flavour to the juice of the grape, which is that I am

Madam
Your most affecte. and
obedt. Servt.
E. Lucas

To Mr. Boddicott in London
Worthy Sir

My Dear brothers languishing condition which your last gave an account of is an allay to the pleasure your letters always give me when they inform me of the welfair of yourself and family, of whom I always think with the utmost gratitude.

I think you cant make the least doubt of my papa's aprobation in your not sending the child over in so week a condition. His last letter was dated the 5th of April in the latitude of 16[81] after the battle at

81. He was nearing his home port at Antigua, which is on the 17th degree.

La-guira.[82] Their next design is against Port Cavalla which I hope is by this time happily over.[83] Our exchange is seven for one.
Memdum.
Not time to coppy the rest.

Wrote to my Brother on his disappointment in not going to La-guire and his concern thereon; Endeavoured to pursuad him [to] a resigned disposition, and haveing our passions in due subjection to our reason is the greatest Victory that can be acquired, and perhaps tis a leason the easier learned for being early taught. If among the Romans he had a Civel crown that saved the life of a citizen what reward will he deserve that has won many from Vice to Virtue by his example, &c.

To Mrs. Pinckney
Dr. Madm
If you are not yet provided I have heard of a horse I believe will suit you at £140 and shall be proud of your commands if I can be any ways serviceable therein. The owners are no further from me than James Island.

Please to make my Compts. to Colo. Pinckney. The book he lent me I now return with thanks. I mett with a paragraph in it which gave me a good deal of pleasure because 'tis exactly similiar to my papa's Case at Cavalla; 'tis in a letter from Prince Eugene to an Eminent Minister in vindication of my Lord Albermarls conduct at the battle of Denain. The words which I mean are these "But when they (the soldiers) run as soon as they have given one fire and cannot be rallied, no General in the world can help it."[84] This declaration from so great a General as Prince Eugene must have great weight had it been read by a less partial eye than that of a daughter.

82. See note 79 above.
83. Port Cavallo is about one hundred miles west of La Guaira. SCG, July 18–25, 1743, reported that the fleet "was returned to Antigua, after having met with much the same treatment in their Attack on Port Cavallo, as at Laguira."
84. The famous Austrian general, Prince Eugene of Savoy (1663–1736) refers in his memoirs to the victory of the French at Denain in July, 1712, during the War of the Spanish Succession. The Earl of Albemarle, who was in command of Dutch battalions, was captured while trying to rally his troops. The Prince wrote of Albemarle: "He had conducted himself as a man of honour, but I defy the most able general to extricate himself, when his troops, after a bad discharge, shamefully take to flight." Memoirs of Prince Eugene, trans. William Mudford (New York, 1811), p. 159.

I have had too many Instances of your friendship to doubt your pardon for this impertinence. The morn approaches and my drowsiness calls me to rest and secures you from any more at present from

Dr. Madm.

Yr. affecte. and obdt. Servt.

E. Lucas

To the Honble Charles Pinckney, Esqr.

Sir

The penance you have enjoyned is equal to an Egyptian task for I take it to be full as hard for me to repeat Docr. Parnels Hermit[85] to you having never read it more then twice, as it was to them to make brick without straw; but if you will be so good to lend me the book I'll promise to repeat it to you some time in Sept. next which is the soonest I can promise my self the pleasure of waiting on Mrs. P.

We are much obliged to Mr. Dart for the Mocking birds.[86] My papa will be very much pleased with them. To secure them from their mortal foe the Catt I have putt them in my own Closet where they afford me a thousand useful reflections: here the nigard that eats his morsel alone and the mean suspicious wrech whose bolted door nev'r moved in pity to the wandring poor, may learn a leason of hospatality from the birds of the air. The little Chirpers has drawn to the window an old bird that has a nest in a tree in the garden with 3 young ones in it. These 6 imploy her morning in providing for and feeding them. I was one day seting in the room viewing them perched, and as I soposed, expecting their warbleing Benefactress, when she came to the window from whence I imagined the sight of me must soon fright her (it was impossible for me to move); but even that could not prevent her generous purpose to the little strangers, but she flew close by me and perching on the cage droped in what her bounty had before provided. This thing pleased me more than you can imagine. I communicated it to some of my neighbors and beged their company next day to be witnesses of the fact, for I really thought it would appear incredible. They were so obliging to say

85. "The Hermit," the best-known poem of Thomas Parnell (1679–1718), is a moral *conte* in heroic couplets—some 250 lines.

86. The reference is possibly to John Dart, a member of the Commons House of Assembly from St. Philip's Parish in 1742 and later commissary general. *JCHA, 1742–1744*, pp. 32, 393.

they could never doubt my varacity upon any subject what ever tho'
what I attested might appear extreamly improbable; but in this case
there was nothing extraordinary, for it was very common to hang a
Cage of young mocking birds in a Garden to be raised by the old
ones if there was one near, but this I was a stranger too.

I see you smile while you have be[en] reading this to Mrs. Pinckney, and she replys, the dear girl forgot she was not writing to little
Polly when she indulged her descriptive vien and that the subject of
her birds is too triffling a one to engage your attention. Be it so, but
tis your own faults you will have me write and as my Ideas are
triffling my subject must be conformable to them.

Now to a subject which will please you better. Two young ladies
in Boston desire me to make their Compliments to you and Mrs.
Pinckney, and insist you will give me your opinion in writing which
is the prettiest of the two Cousens, Miss Molly or Miss Fanny Fairweather. Fanny has heard you said she was like her Cousen but not
quite so pretty. Their is a dispute between them. They compliment
one another but I know each of them in her heart thinks her self the
hansomest but the important decision lies upon you. How you will
do to please them both is too great a dificulty to be attempted by
Sir
Your most obedt. Servt.
E. Lucas

Mama desires her best respects to Mrs. Pinckney.
Pray, is there no account of Miss Bartlets arrival.

To the Honble. C[harles] P[inckney], Esqr.
Sir
I stand corrected. Your reasoning is convincing and unanswerable,
and your reproof more obliging than the highest compliment you
could have made me. I did not, however, stand in need of great
strength of argument to convince me 'twas a great weakness to an-
ticipate the ill I so much dreaded; nor was I ever satisfied with my
own conduct in this point. But when nature, gratitude, and every
tender engagement joyned with my own weakness to tempt me to
rebel against religion and reason, those powerful pleaders were too
strong for me. My utmost endeavours shall not be wanting for the

[67]

future to attain a greater firmness of mind. I suspect my own weakness and shall therefore be on my gaurd; but as you are not my Confessor you shall never discover any which I can conceal from you.

My compliments to Mrs. Pinckney concludes

Sir

Yr. m. obliged and obedt.

Servt.

E. Lucas

To Mrs. Chardon.

Dear Madam

The meloncholy contents of our letters from England deprives us of the pleasure of waiting on you this morning as we promised. The languishing condition my brother Tommy is in is almost insupportable to so tender and indulgent a mother as my poor Mama; and indeed if there could be any excuse for such an excess of grief as hers it might be pleaded on this occasion for if 'tis alowable to do justice without suspition of partialality to a brothers character, I can say I hardly ever knew more good qualities centered in one person than in this unfortunate child. He has an understanding, grave turn of thought, and a just way of thinking rarely to be mett with at his time of life, and these are joyned to the most compasionate and benificent disposition of mind. What then must be our concern for so promising a child; and yet flattering to our hopes as his life might be, our greatest affliction is that he lives in such extream pain, and it would be an allay to our grief to hear he is removed out of the misery he endures in this Vale of tears. May the Souvreign disposer of all events enable me to follow the example set me by my dear brother, who asures us he is intirely resigned to that Almighty Being in whoos hands are life and death.

Our best respects attend good Mrs. Woodward and Mr. H.

I am

Dr. Madm.

Unalterably

Your sincere friend and affecte.

humble Servt

E. Lucas

[68]

Sept. 15, 1743. Wrote to my father a very long letter informing him I had received his relating the whole of that unfortunate and ill conserted expedition at Laguira. About plantation affairs: We made very little Indigo this year—the reasons why. Just received a letter from Mrs. Boddicott [on] my dear brother Tommeys Illness. Capt. West would not take any freight for the things he brought. Wrote to him on the Independant companys. On Mr. Cooks having droped his claim to the Southward lands. About settleing the Woppo slaves. Acknowledged the receipt of his letter dated at Port Cavalla with the papers of all the transactions there and at Laguira inclosed.

[To Mrs. Boddicott]
Dear Madm.   Decr. 14th, 1743
    Yesterday I recieved your favour dated the 20th of August which gave me information that never fails to bring me sincere pleasure: that of your and Mr. Boddicott's being perfectly well, but my dear brothers illness is a real affliction. I know my papa must approve your conduct in every thing relating to him and am pursuaded he would not have ordered him over had he imagined it so much against his inclination; and as the thoughts of a voyage is so painful to him I am sure you would not force him nor tire him with persuasions nor will my papa desire it when he knows it.[87]

    My poor Mama (who is under the greatest affliction on this occasion) desires her best respects to you and Mr. B. and her thanks for your tender care of him, of which she is perfectly satisfied.

    We are at a loss what to say in this affair. We would leave no means untryd if we were sure of his reaching here. This Air might be of Service to him. But in his situation we are at a loss what to do. You and Mr. B are the best judges.

    I wrote to my good friend Mr. B. the 27th of July; that you mention from Mr. B. junior I never gott.

    We expect my brother George very shortly. His arrival will, I sopose, determine how long we shall continue here.

    The inclosed to Miss Pary has been wrote some time. I must beg the favour of you to forward it. I am concerned she dont like the country as her Uncle is fixt there. I hope she will be better reconciled

87. Tommy Lucas made the trip to Antigua a few months later. George Lucas to Charles Pinckney, June 14, 1744, PP/LC.

to it for she has good sence and I think a little reflection must make things of this nature easey. For our happiness must be very precarious while we lie at the mercy of every accident to interrupt our tranquillity. To be happy we must have one steady rule for our conduct in life. We must consult reason and follow where that directs.

Mr. Boon is recovered from a dangerous fitt of illness. I always put him in mind to write to you when I see him and shall deliver your message.

Pray, Madam, give me the satisfaction of hearing from you as often as you are at leasure and pay my Compliments to Mr. B, Mrs. W. and all my old acquaintance. I remain

Dr. Madam.
Yr. m. obliged and affecte
humble Servt.
E. Lucas

[To Thomas Lucas]
My dear brother

Your long and incurable illness is a proof that unmingled happiness is not the portion of mortals. What joy did I not promise my self in seeing my much loved brother, when he arrived at the state of manhood, answer the pleasing expectations all his family entertained of him. Those quick parts and that amiable person promised all we could wish, but, alass, how is the prospect changed. How has our joy been turned into grief and anguish—but hush, 'tis the almighty's will, and may we indure it with that submision that is due upon all occasions from the creature to their infinitely Wise Creator.

The pleasure with which I read that part of your letter where you say you do not quite dispair of being cured was very great, but 'tis a satisfaction of a higher nature still to find you—so young—perfectly resigned to the Devine apointments. You have, my brother, made a wise choice in giving yourself up to Him who is our chief and ultimate happiness. Still implore his assistance to enable you to bear up under every effliction with that fortitude and resignation the great principles of Christianity inspire. To be cut of so early, to those whose mind and thoughts lie groveling here below, must be an event almost insoportable; but to a mind that has a relish for immortal joys, death is not that king of terrors as is commonly represented. Nature indeed may shudder at the approach of the grisly monarch, but there is a soport superior to nature in which I hope you will ever confide.

Tis guilt, my dear Tommy, that makes the contemplation of death frightful and heightens the horrors of the grave. But to those that have a well grounded hope of a blessed immortality to come, the prospect brightens and all beyond the grave is gay and Serene. There we shall bid adieu to sorrow and imperfection. There we shall have our faculties enlarged and enjoy as much happiness as a creature is capable off.

Adieu, my dear brother. I hope (still) not for ever. While I think of it nature pleads, and my heart bleads at the thoughts of our seperation. But let us submit. If we meet no more in this world, we shall meet again in the realms of everlasting bliss and amity.

I am truely My dr brother
Yr. affectionate Sister
E. Lucas.

Mama gives her blessing to her dear
Tommy. You will receive a letter from her
by this ship. Pray pay our best respects to
all Mr. Boddicotts worthy family.

1745–46[88]

Memdm.: Wrote last week to Mrs. Allen Concerning the Rebellion.[89]

To Mrs. Clifford excusing Mr. P[inckney] not writing at that time and the reasons.

Octr. Wrote to Mrs. Allen concerning Indigo.

88. These three brief items, the only ones in the letterbook between 1743 and 1753, begin the sequence of entries at the back of the volume.
89. Charles Edward Stuart, the Young Pretender, landed on Eriskay Island on July 23, 1745, and shortly thereafter raised the standard of rebellion against George II and the Hanoverian line. Though he enjoyed a few brief weeks of success as Scotland rallied to his call, the Young Pretender's army was crushed in mid-April by English forces under the generalship of William Augustus, Duke of Cumberland. Basil Williams, *The Whig Supremacy, 1714–1760* (London, 1952), pp. 238–44.

Part Two

·

Letters from England

1753-1757

૮ુરૂ

Marriage to Charles Pinckney in 1744 brought a deep and continuing happiness to Eliza. Her gratification with the marriage and her delight in the children that soon followed seemed to make her life even more challenging and satisfying.

Charles Pinckney, successful, ambitious, and forward-looking, decided early in the 1750's that he must take his family to England in order to provide the quality of education his sons would need as upper-class colonials. Accordingly, they sailed in April, 1753. The Pinckneys first settled in Richmond but later bought a home near Ripley where Pinckney could commute quickly to London yet still enjoy the beauty of Surrey. Pinckney's employment as commissioner representing South Carolina to the Board of Trade provided him suitable employment and social contacts in London.

With Charles Cotesworth and Thomas soon placed in public schools, Eliza found herself relatively free to enjoy the stimulating entertainments of a cosmopolitan city. Museums, the theater, recitals, and the company of lively and sophisticated friends made Eliza reluctant to sympathize with her husband's determination to return to Carolina within three years. As young Peter Manigault observed in December, 1753: "The Coll. sticks to his Resolution of

[73]

Continuing but three Years in England; and I believe all that his Lady will be able to say, will not put honest Carolina out of his Head."

Events early in 1756 convinced Pinckney that the Great War for the Empire would soon spread and become more violent. It therefore seemed prudent to return to Carolina, dispose of his property there, and seek safer areas in which to invest. Eliza's adieu to England and her sons was necessarily both hasty and reluctant. But with her usual steady judgment she concluded that her husband's decision was sound and that the family welfare depended upon their presence in Carolina. To Carolina she returned, however, with the warm memories of five exciting and satisfying years. Her granddaughter recorded that Eliza "always spoke with pleasure of the gayeties in which she had participated during her second visit to England, of the celebrated actors and actresses whom she had seen, and that she never missed a single play when [David] Garrick was to act."

[To Mary W. Wragg?]¹   [c. May 20]

Tis so great a happiness to us, Dear Madam, to have a share in your Esteem, which you have so obligingly demonstrated not only on the other side [of] the water but on this also, that you must give me leave to indulge my self with the pleasure to think you will be glad to hear from us [by] the first opportunity.

We are now, I thank God, safely sett down in South-hampton Street where we arrived pretty late last night. We had the pleasure of Seeing Mr. and Mrs. Winchester this morning. The first inquiry I made was after your dear little ones and Sisters and had the pleasure to hear they were all well. I shall see them as soon as possible. Mr. Pinckney inclosed your letter to Mr. Winchester before we went on shore—and very luckily for all the rest of our letters were carefully put up in the Desk and sent round with the rest of our baggage by water. We expected they would have been in London before us, but they are not yet arrived.

I gave a wistful look at your house when we left Charles Town but did not dare venture in to take my leave. I observed punctually your desire not to open your letter till over the barr. The first thing I did when at liberty was to read it, but with what tender simpathy and concern is not easey for you to conceive much less for me to express. Was I to say any thing on that interesting subject—for such I am sure it is to me—Mr. W[ragg] might look grave, and I have so great a regard for him that the loss of his smiles would be a very particular mortification to me.

We arrived at Portsmouth the 29th April where we intended to stay 10 or 12 days, but were alarmed with the small pox being at Portsmouth, Gasport and South-hampton; and therefore Mr. P. wrote to Mr. W[inchester] before he went on shoar, inclosed your letter and wrote to him about the innoculation,² a house for us, etc.

---

1. Probably Mrs. Mary Wood Wragg (d. December, 1767), the wife of William Wragg, a member of the Royal Council. Mabel L. Webber, ed., "Extracts from the Journal of Mrs. Ann Manigault," *SCHM* 20 (1919): 259; Henry A. M. Smith, "Wragg of South Carolina," *SCHM* 19 (1918): 123 and chart.

2. Inoculation, which had been used in England since 1732 and in Carolina since 1738, was still considered a dangerous measure. Joseph Ioor Waring, "James Killpatrick and Smallpox Inoculation in Charlestown," *Annals of Medical History* 10 (1938): 301–8. Peter Manigault wrote from London to his mother Mrs. Gabriel Manigault in Carolina, May 16, 1753: "Last night I had the pleasure of Mr. and Mrs.

We arrived in 25 days after we left Crs. Town barr. Never poor wretch suffered more that escaped with life than I; notwithstanding we had so fine a passage. Be so good to excuse me to Mrs. Glenn.[3] I promised to write to her upon my arrival, but am so weak and so much hurried am not able now expecially as the ship sails to-morrow.

Pray pay our best respects and Compliments to our good friend Mr. W. &c.

> I am with great truth
> Dr Madm.
> Yr affecte. humble Servt.
> E. Pinckney

Memdm. Since my arrival
wrote to good Mrs. Manigault.

Wrote to Mrs. B. on Tuesday and inserted a fine quotation from Thompson.

To
My dr Polly

I must write you if but 2 lines in hopes they will produce two more which I do asure you will be as acceptable and about as great a rarity as a cake of Ice would be from your warm regions of perpetual summer.

I am extreamly sorry to inform you of the death—the sudden death —of our old and valuable friend Mr. Boddicott. He was well in the morning and dead at night of an apoplexy. (The Lord preserve us from such sudden calls.) Poor Mrs. Boddicott! How shocking a stroak to her, much greater than what befell her 18 months before when she was suddenly struck with a fitt of the Palsey.

We have not time to finish Coppying the rest of [it] to my sister.

Pinckney . . . to spend in the Evening with me. . . . Mr. Pinckney was just returned from the Ceremony of Inoculation performed upon the Children." Mabel L. Webber, ed., "Peter Manigault's Letters," *SCHM* 32 (1931): 176.

3. Governor and Mrs. James Glen now occupied the Pinckney's new house on East Bay.

Memdm. Wrote to Lady Nisbet from Richmond[4] to acquaint her (as her Ladyship was so obliging to make me promise her I would inform her as soon as possible) how our Children got through the Innoculation.

Performed my promise also to Mrs. Glenn by writing to her as soon as I was able after my arrival.

Wrote to Miss Wilhelmina King[5] in answer to a letter she wrote to Harriott which did not arrive till she was gone from home.

Wrote to my Mother by Colo. Talbott who was so obliging to give me a months notice of his sailing. At the same time to both my brothers and my Sister.

Memdm.
Wrote to my Lady Carew[6] upon our Coming from Bath to put her in mind of her promise to pay us a vizet at our return from Bath; beg she would bring Miss C. and Miss S. with her and Sir Nicholess. Tell her we have two spair beds, it will not put us to the least inconveniency.

Told her of our Vizet to Studly, Mr. Hugerfords—our friendly and polite treatment there; our Peregrination from thence to see what ever was curious in Wiltshire, Stone Henge, Old Sarum, Salsbury Cathedral; to Pembroke at Wilton and Lord Folkstons at Longford, &c., &c. Returned again to Mr. Dakes near Lake, then to Studly again, then to Bath again and Bristol.[7]

4. Mr. and Mrs. Pinckney rented a house in Richmond, then a suburb of London.
5. The daughter of Mrs. Pinckney's friends, Lord and Lady King at Ocham Court, near Ripley in Surrey. Harriott H. Ravenel, *Eliza Pinckney* (New York, 1896), p. 159.
6. Eliza and Lady Carew, the former Miss Martin, became friends during Eliza's earlier stay in England. Beddington, the beautiful home of Sir Nicholas and Lady Carew, was near Ripley. Ravenel, *Eliza Pinckney*, pp. 92, 159.
7. Highlights of this delightful tour included palace wings designed by Inigo Jones and Hans Holbein, art galleries filled with Italian sculpture, and paintings by Renaissance masters. For an account of another tourist's adventures through Wiltshire (about 1775) see William Gilpin, *Observations on the Western Parts of England* (London, 1797), pp. 54-71, 77-80, 96-108.

[To Mrs. Gabriel Manigault]
Dearest Madm. [c. December–January, 1753–1754]

I received your favour with extream pleasure and should reproach my self had I neglected answering it the first opportunity that afforded to Carolina had it not been occationed by my being out of London that I had such short warning of ships sailing that I have not till now had time for more than a mere How-doe letter; and such, though more agreeable as they relieve my friends from more tedious Epistles, I cant with any satisfaction bring my self too at a distance of near 4 thousand miles.

Before I proceed any further I must congratulate Dear Mrs. Manigault on the near prospect of having the Child of her heart return to her, a Child who I dare assert—and not only from mine but better judgments—will make her amends for all her cares and answer all her hopes. Was I writing to any body but Mr. Manigaults Mama I could indulge my self with a better grace in speaking my sentiments of so deserving a young Gentleman, and must beg leave to say thus much even to you: that quite abstracted from the merit of his worthy family his own desert, his polite and obliging behaviour which we have experienced intitles him to all the returns his friends can make.[8]

While I am pleasing my self with the happiness of one worthy family, my heart achs for another. How sincerely do I pity the good father who has neglected nothing for the advantage of an inconsiderate and thoughtless son. I mean our venerable friend Mr. Garden.[9] His son is now prisoner at a spunging house in London. He some time since left his Master, had got a wild scheme in his head of taking a house in the Country and giving up all thoughts of the Law, of which he seemed to have a contemptable oppinion. Mr. Pinckney heard of this by accident, informed Mr. Corbet[10] of it and beged the

8. Peter Manigault (1731–73) was studying in England. He returned to Charleston in December, 1754, and assumed his place among the Charleston oligarchy. Webber, "Peter Manigault's Letters," *SCHM* 31 (1930): 171; *SCG*, December 5, 1754.

9. Young John Garden (1733–55) was the son of the Reverend Alexander Garden, commissary of the Bishop of London in Charleston. *SCHM* 31 (1930): 35. For Peter Manigault's letters about Garden, see Webber, "Peter Manigault's Letters," *SCHM* 32 (1931): 270, 275; 33 (1932): 58.

10. Thomas Corbet, formerly an attorney in Charleston, moved to London in 1750 and became high bailiff of Westminster. Peter Manigault lived in his London home, where Corbet courteously received the young Carolinians at school or the Inns of

favour of him to assist him in finding him out, which they did; and after some time brought him to a better way of thinking and to consent to go back to his Master, an Eminent attorney, provided he would receive him.

Mr. P. went to Mr. Waldo who he was acquainted with through Mr. Gardens recommendation and he had behaved with great politeness to us on our arrival in England—but all Mr. P. could say and write, (and several letters passed between them on the subject) could not prevail. He absolutely refused to take him. But while these matters were about Mr. Garden was arrested by his Taylor for upwards of 100 £. His relations here refused to joyn Mr. P. to bail him tho' they profess great regard for his father; (people here take great care of their mony) but when Mr. P. and Mr. C. came to bail him they found more actions against him. Mr. Corbet very readily joyned Mr. Pinckney, as would Mr. Watson have done if there had been occasion. They went to the house where he was a prisoner and found more actions against him and cant tell where they will end, so that he is still in Custody. He was to have been carried to Newgate but upon some proposals they made to see matters made up that step was prevented and he continued where he was.

His Master and some of his friends were for having him carried to prison. A fine school for the reformation of youth! to be a companion to the wickedest and vilest of wretches, the very dregs of mankind, and in a loathsome and infectious Jail. Surely these people want feeling hearts, but how can fathers want bowels! I fear I tire you, but I am really affected with the fate of this unhappy young man. If Mr. Garden and the rest of the family dont hear any thing of this from other hands, I know you will be so good to make it a secret; but if they do, be so good to aprize them of the real truth. Mr. Pinckney dont write to Garden because he expects he will be imbarked before this reaches Carolina.

I am very glad you have had so healthy a summer as I share largely in every felicity that attends Carolina. I thank God we have been all perfectly well; Mr. Pinckney and the children have not had even a common cold and the winter is much more moderate than we expected.

Court. *SCG*, April 23, 1750; Webber, "Peter Manigault's Letters," *SCHM* 31 (1930): 172n.

We have been chiefly at Richmond since in England, where we vizet 10 or a dozen agreeable familys. The most disagreeable thing here to me is the perpetual card playing. It seems with many people here to be the business of life.

We have traveled about seven hundred mile by land this summer. 'Tis a very pleasant but expensive way of spending time.

We spent the last Season at Bath where we were so Luck'y to meet with several of our acquaintance; we thought our selves particuarly so in meeting with Mr. and Mrs. Baker, Dear Mrs. Wraggs brother and Sister there. Was I to live at a distance from London I dont know any place so agreeable as Bath. They have an exceeding good market every day in the greatest perfection and cheaper than any part of England that I have been inn. We spent some time most agreeably at two Gentlemans Seats in Wiltshire—one of Major Luttrells relations, a very antient and Rich family. They treated us with great friendship and politeness and showed us every thing that was curious and Elegant in that County, of which there is not a few.

We go to London next week for good. We have been at a great loss for a house there, and—would you think it—have not been able to get a tolerable unfurnished house from Temple Barr to Charing Cross so that we are obliged to take a furnished one. 'Tis however a very hansome one and gentilely furnished in a very good street and in the Center of every thing. With these conveniences and an Extensive good acquaintance I hope Mr. P. will be quite reconciled to England for the time he proposes to stay here. At present he is not quite satisfied with it and has many [y]earnings after his native land,[11] tho' I believe never strangers had more reason to like a place every thing considered than we have. But still I cant help applying a verse in the old song to him some times, "Thus Wretched Exiles as they roam

11. From London, Peter Manigault wrote to his mother of Pinckney's discontent with England: "He already seems to have some desire to return to Carolina and I daresay he will, sooner than he at first talked of. . . . His wife is an excellent Woman and I venture to say would chuse to pass her days in England: however she is too good a Wife ever to thwart her Husband's Inclination" (June 24, 1753); "He seems a little better reconciled to England, but can't bring himself to play at Whist for Crowns" (September 27, 1753); "The Coll. sticks to his Resolution of continuing but three Years in England; and I believe all that his Lady will be able to say, will not put honest Carolina out of his Head" (December 8, 1753); "Coll. Pinckney is just now recovering from an Indisposition of the same kind [rheumatism] which I dare say will be a new cause for Dislike to England, as he never was attacked in that way before" (February 26, 1754). Webber, "Peter Manigault's Letters," *SCHM* 32 (1931): 179, 192, 270, 277.

find favour every where but languish for their native home, ["] etc.

I have been particuarly happy in renewing an old friendship with my Lady Carew, a friendship begun at a very early time of life and now renewed with great affection and condesention on her part (as she is greatly my superior in every thing) and with great sincerity on mine.

Memdm. Not time to coppy it fully but mentioned Master Wrights, Compliments, &c.

To Mrs. Figg
Dear Madm.   [c. December–January, 1753–1754]

Impute my long—I am ashamed to say, very long—silence to any thing rather than disregard or forgetfulness of you and my dear Cousens for whom I have most justly a very great Esteem. It would run my letter to too great a length to give you all the reasons why I have not before wrote to you since you have been in the North. The principle ones however has been my having been such a Gossip from home and the trouble we have had to get a house in London. Would you believe that from Temple Barr to Westminster we could not get an unfurnished house but one and that at a hundred a year; but so it is, and we are obliged to be in a furnished one for we dont think of continuing at Richmond after our term in this house is up. The house we have taken is a very good one in a very good street. 'Tis the last house but one on the left hand in Craven Street[12]—where we shall always be extreamly glad to see dear Mrs. Figg and the young ladies.

A journey into the North in the spring we at present think off. We were so luckey to be in the same house with Mrs. Stubbs at Bath, a good natured agreeable woman. I was much obliged to you for introduceing me to Mrs. Woodrough. Mr. P. and I were very much pleased with the old Lady. She was extreamly friendly and cheerful. She came to Bath some time after us. We have agreed if ever we return to that Place to let her know it that we may be there together.

N. B. Have not patience to coppy this long letter in which I gave my Cousen Figg a discription of Bath.

12. Peter Manigault wrote to his mother on December 8, 1753: "I went to Richmond on purpose to see them, which by the Bye was no small Compliment, as it cost me seven Shillings in Chaise Hire. They have taken a furnished House in Craven St. at £120 a year, which is Tip-Top Rent." Webber, "Peter Manigault's Letters," *SCHM* 32 (1931): 270.

[81]

[To Lady Carew]

I have just received My Dear Lady Carew['s] most affectionate and friendly letter and had I words to express the sense I have of her friendship and kindness to me should thank her as I ought. You make me very happy in the expectation of Mrs. Haberdons acquaintance, for which I am greatly indebted to your partiality. I wish I could take the liberty to ask the favour of that Ladys company with you on Wednesday if she is at Beddington at that time.[13] I am interrupted and must hasten to conclude.

Our Compliments, etc., to Sir N[icholas] and Miss S[anders]. We impatiently wait for Wednesday till when and Ever, I am

> My dearest friend
> Yr. Ladyships most affecte.
> and obliged
> E. Pinckney

[To Lady Carew]
My dr. Madm.

Be so good to give me one line to let me know how you got home. You cant conceive the Anxiety we have been under on your going 12 mile (though in a Coach and six) on so dismal a Night. It rained excisive hard and the wind blew a perfect storm soon after you left us. A hundred whimsical (I hope I may call them so) apprehensions came into my head. I try'd what the new books Boadicea and Sir Charles Grandison[14] just receive[d] could do to put you for that night out and bring my mind to a settled frame, nor could I get to sleep till past one when I hoped you might be well at home. Confirm me my hopes were well founded and make me happy as soon as you can.

We beg you will accept our acknowledgments in a particular man-

13. Mr. and Mrs. Pinckney had bought a house at Ripley and settled there. Ravenel, *Eliza Pinckney*, p. 159.

14. Richard Glover's play *Boadicia* is listed in the Annual Register of the Theatre-Royal in Drury Lane for 1753. Benjamin Victor, *History of the Theatres of London and Dublin from 1730*, 2 vols. (London, 1761), 1: 128. Samuel Richardson's novel *The History of Sir Charles Grandison* was published in 1753. Richardson's reputation as a novelist had been established by his eight-volume *Clarissa Harlowe* (1747–48). See Leslie Stephen, "Richardson, Samuel (1689–1761)," *DNB*.

ner for this last favour tho' be at the same time asured, My Dear Lady C, that I would always deprive myself of a pleasure, even the great one of seeing you, than you should run the least risk by gratifying me; and I was so very uncourtly I was about to desire your Ladyship to defer the favour you intended till the weather was more moderate, but hesitated so long till it was too late.

Mr. Pinckney and my most affectionate regards attend Sir N, etc.

I am Dr Madm.

Your Ladyships etc.

E. Pinckney

To My Lady Carew at Beddington

Your letter, my Dearest friend, gave me great pain as it gave so bad an account of your health. I have had the pleasure since to hear you are much better from Mrs. Haberdone. I am much obliged to your Ladyship for so agreeable an acquaintance which I shall do all my utmost to cultivate. Your reason for my not hearing of you from Miss Saunders was extreamly friendly and tender; I should indeed have suffered much pain had I known you had been so much indisposed. However, pray conceal it not from me for the future. I always love to know the best and worse of all that concerns me.

I think Sir Nicholass (to whom pray pay our best regards) judges very right to keep you out of town this hott weather. I cant say I wish to see you here at this time.

If I thank you for every Instance of your goodness to me I shall make my letter of an Enormous length. The last Instance however I most gratefully remember: your calling upon my little rough school boy, who I sopose you found as I generally do, a very school boy.

1755

[To] My Lady Carew

My Dearest friend   [c. August–September 1755]

Your Ladyship has been very happy to have escaped thus long being persecuted with my impertinence, but the time of your repose is expired and like the rest of your fellow mortals you must experience the uncertainty of Earthly tranquility. You will perhaps wonder I have let you rest so long; to put an end to your surprize then I

[83]

will inform you that it was not out of any great tenderness to your Ladyship—as well as I love you, and without flattery that is not a little—but a variety of circumstances has prevented me. I expect your acknowledgments for my ingenuus confession though not for your long repose. I now really long to know how you do and those most dear to you, to pray pay Mr. P.'s, and my affectionate Compliments &c.

E. Pinckney

Instead of this We intended to have done our selves the pleasure of Breakfasting with your Ladyship this week at B[eddington] but Mr. Pinckneys time has been wholly ingaged in prepareing papers and attending on the Lords Commissioners for Trade and Plantations on the late alarming accounts of the strides the French are making on the backs of the English Colonys in North America[15]—and which may too soon very materially affect that province to which we are so neerly related.

[To Lady Carew]

The day after I received My dear Lady Carews favour of the 4th June I took up my penn in order to write to her but was really so much affected when I began upon recolecting the many repeated tryals you have had for the last 2 years and which led me also to reflect on the unstableness and uncertainty of all human happiness that I was lost in the gloomy contemplation and threw aside my penn as utterly uncapable of giving the least consolation to my afflicted friend. Soon after our dear little boy who had got a small swelling in his face some time before—occasioned by a construction of the glans by a cold [from] standing too long upon damp ground in an Easterly wind, and which the Surgeon thought would be very trifleing at first—increased so much as to alarm us and induced us to carry him up to London for further advice tho' we had had two surgeons in the Country. His cheek mended apace after we got to London and in a

15. Mrs. Pinckney probably refers here to the Battle of the Wilderness, where the troops of General Edward Braddock were defeated on July 9, 1755, by a mixed force of nine hundred French and Indians. Braddock, who intended to attack Fort Duquesne, was instead mortally wounded. George Washington led the remnant forces back to Fort Cumberland. The defeat was significant because the Indians of the Northwest now chose the French side, thus exposing the western regions of Virginia, Pennsylvania, and Maryland to a series of devastating attacks. See L. K. Koontz, *The Virginia Frontier, 1754-1763* (Baltimore, 1925), pp. 59-71.

fortnight was very near well, and we then returned into the country with him again where he was seized with a severe fever, which has reduced him very much, but I thank God he has now lost his fever some time and his Cheek [is] near well.

This has prevented my writing to your Ladyship sooner as well as prevented our indulging ourselves with the long intended gratification of our wishes to spend a few days with you at Beddington; for were they less ardent than they are, the very obliging invitations you and Sir N. are so good to make us would make it irresistable.

Mr. Pinckney made me very happy by teling me he saw Sir Nicholass well at Guilford at the Sessions, who informed him all the family were better and in particular Miss Carew, and that she was well Enough to move for the change of air. I know you lose no time much less throw it away or I should say, the first hour you throw away, let it be on your humble Servant; but I will change the expression and beg to hear from you as soon as you can conveniently give me a line. I shall be very glad to hear good Mrs. Martin and all the family are well, who must have suffered equally with you in the loss of Dr. Haberdones Son. A very sharp affliction the death of the dear Infant must indeed have been to all his relatives, expecially as he was almost all the remains of a much loved child and Sister.

I most sincerely hope your afflictions will now have a period and that the father of Mercies will restore your dear Daughter to you beyond your most sanguine expectations.

I can by no means consent to your silence least you give me pain by what you suffer. 'Tis a faulty tenderness, my dear madam, for though they must be void of tenderness and humanity as well as friendship that dont feel for those in affliction yet there are advantages to be reaped from it, also, I do asure you what you have suffered was a Check to my impatience in my dear Childs late Illness, and bad as it was it seemed much lighter upon a Comparison with what poor Miss Carew had suffered who was still alive and like to get the better of a distemper so very painful and dangerous as well as tedious.

I am with mine and Mr. Pinckneys Compliments, &c.

Memdm. Wrote to My Lady Carew in answer to hers of the 26th last month; fix'd upon Thursday for Mr. Pinckney and self to wait

[85]

on them at Beddington.; joyn with her Ladyship in lamenting the distance between Riply and Beddington; must endeavour to make it up by a more constant Epistolary intercourse.

[To Lady Carew]
Dr. Madm.   [c. November, 1755]
Both my sleeping and waking thoughts reproach me for not inquiring after dear Miss Carew this very bad weather for I have dreamed of you for two Nights past all night long and though I am not superstitious enough to regard dreams in any other way I think we may admit them as monitors to reform our errors or as incentives to Laudable actions.

I was about to write to your Ladyship soon after your friendly vizet to Riply to know how you got home and to pay our thanks for that most obliging Instance of your regard tho' with so much inconveniency and danger to your self, but my little boy was taken with a fever and ingrossed my whole attention. This I know to so tender a parent as your Ladyship will be thought a sufficient excuse. I beg now, tho' late, you and Miss Saunders and good Sir N[icholas] for permiting you will accept my best acknowledgments.

I now see you so seldome that this is almost the only way I have of conversing with you, and therefore should be glad [if] I could make my letters consist of more than mere How d'oos, but except the action done by the New England forces under Gen. Johnson.[16]

Memorandum. Not time to Coppy it fully that wrote upon the Earthquake at Lisbon.[17] Mr. P. desires his best respects may be acceptable to Sir N with those of, My Dr. Madam
                              Yr. Ladyships Most obliged and
                              affectionate humble Servant
                              Eliza. Pinckney

16. William Johnson, with a 3,500-man mixed force of New Englanders and Indians defeated Baron Dieskau's 1,400-man force at the Battle of Lake George on September 8, 1755. Max Savelle places this battle in its proper context in *The Origins of American Diplomacy: The International History of Anglo-America, 1492–1763* (New York, 1967), p. 418. Lawrence Henry Gipson's masterly multivolume series on *The British Empire Before the American Revolution* covers all aspects of the Seven Years' War. See especially Volume 7, *The Great War for the Empire: The Years of Defeat, 1754–1757* (New York, 1946).

17. On November 1, 1755, in a quake felt from Scotland to Asia Minor, the greater part of Lisbon was leveled. A tidal wave and fire completed the destruction. An

[To Lady Carew]   Febr. 7th, 1757

Is it possible I can have a letter by me unanswered from My dear Lady Carew ever since Octr? I find 'tis really so! and am quite ashamed to say your Ladyship is not mistaken though it gives me fresh proof of your indulgence and goodness to me by your kind letter received yesterday, of which I should be very little deserving had I not something to plead in my own excuse for the omission. When I received the first mentioned favour we designed to have spent our Winter at Bath where several of our friends I found were to be, and being informed by your Ladyship you were to be there also confirmed us in our intention—when the frequent opportunities I should have in conversing with my much valued friend Lady C. was the principal pleasure I promised my self in being there.

I delayed writing to you then till we had fixed the time for seting out, but before that was determined the bad accounts we had from abroad and the many repeated ones afterwards turned the tide of pleasure we had in prospect to gloomy anxiety[18] and made me neglect all Epistolary intercourse with my friends ever since. For upon our continual alarms from abroad Mr. Pinckney came to a resolution to return to Carolina for two Year and wait an opportunity to dispose of the greatest part of what he has there and fix it in a more secure tho' less improvable part of the world. And as I can by no means think of staying behind him, you can judge, My dear Madam, what I have suffered and do still suffer in the expectation of parting with all my dear children for 2 or 3 year—and considering the uncertainty of life, perhaps for ever! These, my dear friend, are too interesting considerations not to be sensibly felt by us. A long sea Voyage as

estimated forty thousand persons were killed. See J. M. Queiroz Veloso, *Lisboa Atráves de história portuguesa* (Lisbon, 1942). Bahngrell W. Brown, "The Quake that Shook Christendom—Lisbon," *Southern Quarterly* (July, 1969).

18. The years 1756–57 generally were disastrous ones for Britain and Prussia. In India the British lost Calcutta. On the Continent Frederick the Great was defeated by the Austrians and French and the Duke of Cumberland surrendered his English and Hanoverian army to the French. The irresolute new commander in chief of the British forces in America, John Campbell, Earl of Loudoun, let the French capture Forts Oswego and George in August, 1757. This series of disasters led military experts to predict that England and Prussia would soon be forced to make a humiliating peace and that France would then gain control of all North America west of the Alleghenies. L. H. Gipson, *The Great War for the Empire: The Years of Defeat*, is the best treatment of those trying years.

well as the danger of being taken, and what hardships we may suffer in an Enemys Country at this time are apprehensions that also excite pain but of a less affecting nature than leaving the dear creatures for whose advantage we are content to undergo all inconveniences.

How uncertain are human dependancies! Four years ago we left a fine and flourishing Collony in profound peace, a Collony so valuable to this nation that it would have been looked upon as absurd to have the least doubt of its being protected and taken care of in case of a warr, tho' a War then seemed a very distant contingency. And indeed I looked upon an Estate there as secure as in England, and on some accounts more valueable—especially to those who have a young family. But how much reason we have had to change our sentiments since the commencement of this warr is too plain to every body ever so little acquainted with American affairs.

We first had thoughts of carrying our little girl with us, but considering the danger to which she must be exposed have thought better of it and leave her as well as her brothers.[19]

We think of leting our house at Riply with the furniture standing till our return and shall be some time in London before we Embark, as we intend to wait for a man of War if there should be any prospect of one in the Summer or fall of the year going that way.

I wont lengthen my letter by apoligizing to your Ladyship for troubleing you with my own little concerns; it might be necessary to a Lady of more ceremony and less tender sentiments than yours. But I have been too long acquainted with the goodness of your heart to imagine you prefer the form and distance (with your friends) to which your station in life entitle you (if you chose it) to the friendly simpathy and tender feelings of humanity, which prompts you to indulge a repetition that may ease the mind of a friend at present much engaged with its own meloncholy apprenhensions.

Be so good to make my compliments acceptable to Miss Martin. I think my self greatly obliged to her for her kind intention and your Ladyship will make me very happy in bringing me acquainted with her.

Poor dear Miss Carew! I am very sorry her journey to Bath has been of so little affect. We have had dreadful weather for her complaints. I long much to see her, and we shall certainly wait on your Ladyship and Sir N[icholas] before we leave England.

19. Harriott did return to America with her parents.

My best wishes attend Miss Sannders. I am much concerned for any misfortune to her.

Mr. Pinckney has been in town near a fortnight. I am still quite in the dark as to the fate of the unhappy Admiral Byng. People differ widely in their sentiments whether he will die or not. If, as the Court marshal think, his miscarriage was only owing to want of judgment 'tis hard to suffer Death for an Error of that kind; but if otherwise, as the generallity of the world think, justice is certainly due to the nation which has been such great sufferers by his misconduct. With your Ladyship I most sincerely pity his relations, but as the people is so strongly posessed with his being guilty heaven only knows what may be the consiquence if mercy should take place at this time. But by delaying his execution I think it looks very like a pardon ensueing.[20]

'Tis time to draw to a conclusion when I have payed my best respects to Sir N. who I hope long ago recovered from his lameness got by his fall. I hope you drank the waters at Bath, which must certainly be very proper after your indisposition in the fall of the year.

Adieu, My dear Madam, and be asured what ever part of the world Providence alots me I shall ever retain the most affectionate regard for you. Your own merit and the constancy of my disposition will make you ever dear to me, and I shall rejoyce and share in every felicity that attends you be the distance between us ever so great.

You perceive I am loath to conclude while I have any paper to write on tho' I intended it before; and indeed 'tis high time for I must have tired you as well as my own Eyes. And though I write very fast I find my thoughts flow so much faster than my pen moves I shall make this page unintelligible by omissions and interlinings.

Once more adieu and believe me, dear madm,

> Yr. Lp., etc.
> E. Pinckney

Riply.

20. John Byng, British admiral, was severely condemned by British public opinion when he failed to do all in his power to secure Fort St. Philip on Madagascar against French attack. Byng was tried by court-martial, condemned to death, and shot on March 14, 1757. See John Charnock, *Biographia Navalis*, 6 vols. (London, 1794–98), 4: 145–79. Charnock's account must be read with caution, as must most of the literature on Byng. A good brief account is John Knox Laughton, "Byng, John (1704–1757)," *DNB*.

Part Three

·

Later Letters from Carolina

1758-1762

As their vessel sailed up the Cooper River in May, 1758, the Pinckneys could see through the fringe of masts along the waterfront their own handsome house, still occupied by the royal governor. Settling in his modest house on Ellory Street, Colonel Pinckney turned his attention to his plantation properties. His brother William, who had supervised the estates, had been incapacitated that same year by a paralytic stroke. Colonel Pinckney therefore found much to be done on the lands he had not visited in five years.

Just a month after their arrival Pinckney contracted malaria, fought the fever for three weeks, and then died on July 12. Eliza was nearly overcome by grief, as the following letters show. But she was strengthened by her unshaken conviction that "all things work together for good to them that love the Lord" and by the knowledge that the family's welfare depended primarily upon her efforts and wisdom.

Her fight to perpetuate the family, its wealth, and its standing within the community required all her energies. On the one hand she became guardian of the Pinckney properties. Eliza's earlier training in managing the estates of Colonel Lucas was now put to good use. But her real battle was for the hearts and minds of her two sons, still in England and exposed to the temptations of a notoriously dissolute city. At almost every opportunity through the years Eliza impressed upon Charles Cotesworth and Thomas their late father's love and hopes for them and their duty to work hard and live morally orthodox lives for the sake of the family. Duty, piety, moral virtue, filial reverence—these were the concepts Eliza pressed upon her sons from a distance of several thousand miles.

This was Eliza's greatest battle—save her last one for life—and her most successful one. In later life she often expressed gratitude to her Creator for her exemplary sons, frequently in the words of her favorite hymn, Joseph Addison's:

> When all thy mercies, O my God
> My rising soul surveys,
> Transported with the view, I'm lost
> In wonder, love and praise.

To the Right Honble. Lady Mary Drayton[1]

Dr. Madm.   [c. June–July, 1758]

I have long intended my self the pleasure of writing to Your Ladyship since your going into the Country but a Succession of interven-
ing circumstances has from time to time prevented me, and now
sleepless nights and an aching heart occationed by poor Mr. Pinckneys severe illness makes me very unfitt for this imployment as I
have such a tremor upon my nerves I can but just hold my penn. But
weak and low as Mr. Pinckney is, when he has an interval of ease he
cant help interesting himself in the welfair of his friends.

Master McKenzies disappointment has a good deal concerned
him. He has therefore desired me to pay his Compliments to your
Ladyship and Mr. Drayton and to let you know that as it must be
very disagreeable to Master Mackenzie to be wholly unimployed
that he shall be extreamly welcome to become one of our family in
town untill my Lord and Lady C['s] pleasure is known how to dispose of him. And Mr. Pinckney will put him into a Course of reading Law which may be of use to him as a Gentleman, though he may
not intend to practise the Law as a Lawyer. This Mr. P. offers as an
inducement to your Laying aside the thoughts of your so soon sending him home again as this summer. And in the mean time 'tis not
improbable some thing more imediately in the way his parents intended he should set out in life may happen before the insueing
spring.

If upon your Ladyship and Mr. D. considering it you aprove of
this scheme, be pleased to let me know by a line and as soon as Mr. P.
is better and we settled at home—we have taken a house which will
be ready to receive us in a few weeks—will be very glad of Mr. Mc.
company and shall take all the care of him in our power.

Mr. P. desires me to say further he is sorry he cant make him the

1. Lady Mary, the daughter of Archibald MacKenzie, Earl of Cromartie, and
widow of Captain Clarke, married on August 4, 1757, Thomas Drayton of South
Carolina, a member of the Royal Council and of the Commons House of Assembly.
They lived at Magnolia on the Ashley, which had been in the family since 1700.
After Drayton's death in November, 1760, she married John Ainslie and in January,
1776, she was again remarried, this time to Henry Middleton. She died at sea in
November, 1788. Emily Drayton Taylor, "The Draytons of South Carolina and
Philadelphia," *Publications of the Genealogical Society of Pennsylvania* 8 (March,
1921): 5–8.

offer, in case of his liking the Law and his parents aproving his being of that profession, to take charge of him altogether for that purpose on account of his bad health as well as it being too late in life for him to enter into such an ingagement.

Memorandum. Have not time to coppy any more of this letter.

To My dear Children Charles and Thomas Pinckney

How shall I write to you! What shall I say to you! My dear, my ever dear Children! but if possible more so now than Ever, for I have a tale to tell you that will peirce your tender infant hearts! You have mett with the greatest loss, my children, you could meet with upon Earth! Your dear, dear father, the best and most valueable of parents, is no more!

God Almighty soport your tender minds in this terrible distress, and enable you to put your whole trust and confidence in Him, enable you to rely on him that he will be your father, your comfort, and soport. Endeavour to submit to the Will of God in the best manner you can, and let it be a comfort to you, my dear babes, as long as you live that you had such a father! He has set you a great and good example. May the Lord enable you both to follow it, and may God Almighty fulfill all your pius fathers prayers upon both your heads. They were almost incessant for blessings both spiritual and temporal on you both. He never mentioned you but with repeated blessings, and with up lifted Eyes and hands to heaven; God bless them, God bless them was his constant prayer when ever he named you, and that was very often. His affection for you was as great as ever was upon Earth! And you were good children and deserved it. He thought you so; he blessed and thanked God for you, and had most comfortable hopes of you. And he left you in the care and protection of the Great and Good God, who had been his merciful Father and Guide through life, and whom he truely loved and served with sincerity—whose merceys to him had been without number through all his life, and did not forsake him when he stood in most need of soport: in the hour of Death!

His sick bed and dying moments were the natural conclusion of

2. Charles Pinckney died July 12, but it is the next month before Mrs. Pinckney is able to write to her sons in school at Camberwell.

such a life as his was; for that God whom he had served, enabled him to put the firmist trust and confidence in him. His patience was great and uncommon, and he had the most perfect resignation to the Will of his God that ever man had. He met the king of terrors without the least terror or affright, and without agony, and went like a Lamb into eternity, into a blessed Eternity! where I have not the least doubt he will reap immortal joy for Ever and Ever. Such was the end of this Good man, this pius Christian, your father—the best of husbands and of fathers, and equally good in every relation and connection in life; and this treasure was ours!

We have, my dear children, mett with the greatest of human Evils, but we must drink of the cup it has pleased God to Give us, a bitter Cup indeed! but aloted us by Infinite Wisdom, and let us ever remember, terrible and grievous as the stroke is, we have still reason to thank the hand from whence it comes for all his mercys to him, through life and through death, and to us for having given us this inestimable blessing, for having spared him so long to us, for all the Graces and Virtues he endowed him with, for the goodness of his understanding, and the soundness of his judgement, for all his aimable qualities, for one of the best hearts that ever informed the human body, for all he was and had; he and we are indebted to the infinitely wise and good God, and above all for the most comfortable and joyous hope that we shall meet in Glory never never more to be seperated!

This hope, This expectation, is the soport and comfort of my life, a life which I will endeavour as much as is in my power to preserve, not only as a duty to the God that gave it, but as a duty due from me to the remains of your dear dear father, to you and your dear Sister; and I hope the Almighty will enable me to do my duty in every instance by you, and that all my future life may be spent to do you good, and in showing to you, the dear pledges of the sincerest affection that ever was upon Earth, how much, how truely, I loved and honoured Your dear father by my affection and care of you.

Adieu, my beloved children! God Almighty bless, guide and protect you! Make you his own children, and worthy such a father as yours was, and comfort you in this great affliction is the fervent and constant prayer of Your ever affectionate tho' greatly afflicted Mother

Eliza. Pinckney

who feels most exquisitely for you what you must suffer upon the receit of this letter. God Almighty soport your tender spirrits.

Amen. Amen.

To Mr. Gerrard[3]

Sir

This informs you of the greatest misfortune that could have happened to me and my dear children on this side Eternity! I am to tell you, hard as the task is, that my dear, dear Mr. Pinckney, the best of men, of husbands and of fathers, is no more! Comfort, good Sir, Comfort the tender hearts of my dear children. God Almighty bless them, and if he has any more blessings for me in this world may He give it me in them and their sister.

The inclosed for the dear boys be so good to give them when you think it a proper time. What anguish do I and shall I feel for my poor Infants when they hear the most afflicting sound that could ever reach them!

I remember poor Tommy, upon the first talk of our coming to Carolina early one morning as he lay abed, and I alone with him, without any discourse leading to it, told me he had a favour to beg of me, which was: If we went to Carolina and his dear papa should dye there that he might never know it, and that he would ask his papa the same favour if I dyed there. I think my poor dear Charles has expressed something of the same sentiment, and I am sure he has not less filial affection and sensibility than his brother. I therefore submit it to you and Mrs. Evance whether to let them know it now, or not—for I am not capable to think for my self.

I know your humanity will induce you to a greater care and tenderness of them, if 'tis possible, than ever when you consider them in their present meloncholy circumstances as poor little fatherless children.

I have beged the favour of my friend Mrs. Evance[4] to pay the childrens bills punctually: but my debt of gratitude will always be due. My return to them is at present uncertain, but my heart is with them; and as soon as I can consistent with there interest they may be sure I shall, by the Divine permission, see them.

3. The headmaster of the Camberwell school.

4. Mrs. Evance was the guardian in England to young Charles and Thomas, as Mrs. Boddicott had been to the Lucas children.

I have sent a large barrel of rice which their dear father had ordered to be the best and to be sent to you. The children love it boiled dry to eat with their meat instead of bread. They should have had some potatoes of this country but they are not yet come in.

To George Morly, Esqr.[5]   Augt.

You have known me (My friend Mr. Morly) the happiest woman upon Earth! Can you then possibly guess at the distress I now write to you in when I tell you my dear husband, your friend, my dear dear Mr. Pinckney is no more! The 12th of last month deprived me of the best and most valueable of husbands and of men!

How much happiness did I promise my self, when I found he grew so much better at sea? and was very well for the first month after his arrival here. But my happiness was of short duration. He was soon after taken sick and continued upwards of 3 weeks ill—an example to all about him of the greatest resolution, patience and perfect resignation to the Will of God that ever was known.

He received your kind and friendly letter a few days after he was taken ill, with great pleasure and thankfulness to heaven for hearing his dear children were well. He said it was a cordial to him. He was greatly obliged to you for writing so soon, and with tears of gratitude prayed to God to bless and reward good Mr. Middleton[6] for his kindness to his children. When you see Mr. and Mrs. Middleton, pray thank them, and tell them, their notice of our poor little boys upon our leaving them gave great comfort to the tender heart of their dear affectionate father, the tenderest and best of parents. May theirs never want a tender father and mother to protect their Infant years.

I intended to write to Mrs. Middleton but 'tis too much for me now. I know I need not beg of you good Sir to be kind to my dear fatherless children and to supply Mrs. Evance with what ever mony is wanted for them—which shall be repayd with speed and gratitude. I am not able to write to you now upon business but my nephew[7]

5. George Morly of Somerset House, London, was Mrs. Pinckney's business agent in England.

6. William Middleton (1710–85), the son of Governor Arthur Middleton, was a member of His Majesty's Council. He lived at Crowfield but in 1754 moved to the family estate, Crowfield Hall in Suffolk. Langdon Cheves, "Middleton of South Carolina," *SCHM* 1 (1900): 233.

7. Colonel Charles Pinckney (1731/2–1782), son of William and Ruth Brewton

will do it by this Convoy and send you bills of Exchange[8] (to what amount I cant yet tell) but I shall remitt you for the future all the mony I can as fast as I receive it. And when your debt is payd and the childrens expences repayd be so good to put what remains in the funds.

Pray send the inclosed to Mr. Gerrard by a safe hand.

I can say no more now but return you my grateful thanks for all your friendship and regard to my dear Mr. Pinckney. That God Almighty may reward you for all the good you have ever done or designed him is the sincere prayer of

Your most obliged and obedt. Servt.

E. Pinckney

Since the foregoing I have seen My Nephew and he tells me he has the promise of bills of Exchange for 2 hundred pound sterling, which he will send you by these ships; and the Governor has promised he will write to his Agent to pay you two hundred pound Sterling provided you have not received one hundred from him since we left England.[9] So I hope you will upon the Arrival of these ships receive £400.

My dear Mr. P. had provided some Turtle, etc. for his friends in England, which are now sent, I think, by Ball and Cheeseman; but as I am in the Country am not yet certain. I must beg the favour of you, Sir, to give the person that takes care of them a Crown for every Turtle you receive alive, and what ever you think reasonable for each bird and summer Duck, and send them free of Expence to the persons they are designed for.

Pinckney, had been educated in law by his uncle. He held several public offices in the province and was reelected many times to the Commons House of Assembly. Mabel L. Webber, "Thomas Pinckney Family of South Carolina," *SCHM* 39 (1938): 27–30.

8. Charleston merchants or factors who had established a balance in sterling with an English banker could draw bills of exchange against this balance and sell them to local customers. See Leila Sellers, *Charleston Business on the Eve of the American Revolution* (Chapel Hill, N.C., 1934), pp. 74, 75.

9. William Henry Lyttelton (1724–1808) arrived in Charleston as governor in 1756 and occupied the Pinckney house on East Bay. It had previously been rented to Governor Glen at £100 sterling a year. Edward McCrady, *History of South Carolina Under the Royal Government* (New York, 1901), p. 321; Rent Roll of Estate of Charles Pinckney, Jan. 1753, Rutledge Collection, Pinckney Papers, South Carolina Historical Society, Charleston (hereafter, PP/SCHS). A brief description of the home is found in George C. Rogers, Jr., *Charleston in the Age of the Pinckneys* (Norman, Okla., 1969), p. 68.

soft pipe this spring, he inspired me with the spirit of Rymeing and produced the 3 following lines while I was laceing my stays

Sing on thou charming mimick of the feather'd
and let the rational a reason learn from thee
to Mimick (not defects) but harmony besides your self

If you let any mortal see this exquisite peice of poetry you shall never have a line more than this specimen, and how great will be your loss you who have seen the above may jude as well as

Yr. m. obed. Servt.

Elizn. Lucas

I hope you never forget to pay my Mammas and my best respects to Colo Pinckney and Lady.

To Mrs Cheesman
Madm

The last time I had the pleasure of being with
...... for the Conc.

A page from the letterbook.

The Pinckney coat of arms.

NON · NOBIS · SOLUM

Hampton Plantation, near the South Santee River. This was the home of Daniel Horry, who married Harriott Pinckney in 1768. Eliza Lucas Pinckney spent much time at Hampton during and after the Revolutionary War.
Reproduced from the collections of the Library of Congress.

The handsome house with columned facade that Charles Pinckney built in 1745–47 is shown in this picture of East Bay. Detail from A View of Charles-Town the Capital of South Carolina, *engraved by Samuel Smith in London from a prospect painted at Charles-Town by Thomas Leitch in 1774.*
Engraving in the collection of the Carolina Art Association.

General Thomas Pinckney (1750–
1828), son of Charles and Eliza Lucas Pinckney. Miniature by John
Trumbull.
Courtesy of Mrs. Edward R. Pinckney.

General Charles Cotesworth Pinck-
ney (1746–1825), son of Charles and
Eliza Lucas Pinckney. Miniature by
John Trumbull.
Courtesy of Mrs. Edward R. Pinckney.

Mrs. Daniel Horry (Harriott
Pinckney, 1748–1830), daughter of
Charles and Eliza Lucas Pinckney.
Photograph, made before the acciden-
tal destruction of the miniature, in the
collection of the Carolina Art Association.

Charles Pinckney (c. 1699–1758) married Eliza Lucas May 25, 1744. Artist unknown.

Courtesy of Mrs. Burnet R. Maybank, Jr.

The illustration in the corner of a large prerevolutionary map of "South Carolina and a Part of Georgia" by William De Brahm shows the process of indigo making. The figures under the shed are agitating the liquid in a large wooden vat, and the one in the foreground is engaged in the concluding step, cutting the dried cakes ready for market.

Courtesy of the Charleston Museum.

The silk of this gold damask dress was spun on Eliza Lucas Pinckney's plantation soon after her marriage. The fabrics for this and two other similar
dresses were woven in England.

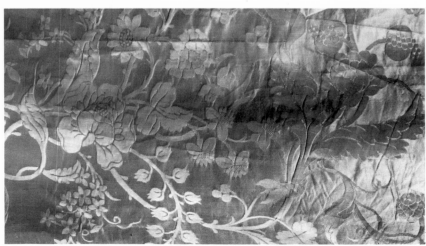

A detail of the fabric.

Silver teapot that belonged to Eliza Lucas Pinckney, made in London in 1752.
Collection of the Charleston Museum.

One of a pair of sauce boats, London, 1744–45, probably by John Pollock.
The escutcheon bears the arms of Pinckney impaled with those of Lucas.
Courtesy of Mrs. Philip St. George Ambler.

A jeweled brooch that belonged to Eliza Lucas Pinckney.
Collection of the Charleston Museum.

THE
SOUTH-CAROLINA GAZETTE,

Containing the freshest Advices, Foreign and Domestick.

MONDAY, April 1st, 1745. [Numb. 575.]

Mr. *Timothy*,

YOU some Time ago favour'd the Publick with a Letter from me, on the Subject of the *NEW* Improvements and Manufactures that were apprehended necessary to be enter'd upon in this Province, in the then declining, and (I think) that new far, unless State of the RICE Planter, particularly That of INDIGO; in Consequence of which Letter, you was kind as to publish here *Labat's* Account of the Culture and Manufacture of that valuable Plant in the *French West Indies*, which gave a full and particular Detail of the Progress in that Affair; for which the Publick is very much obliged to you; and you deserve, no doubt, very particular Thanks, for furnishing us with that Account in so easy a Manner, which it would have been otherwise difficult to have obtain'd, as *Miller's* Dictionary is not in very few Hands.

Since the Publication of that Paper, I have been favour'd by a Friend, with the sight of a very curious Manuscript, on the same Subject, wrote by one Mr *Robert Stevens*, a Gentleman well known in this Province by the Name of ALLEGATOR STEVENS, and which, as it contains (in a very plain and easy Way) the whole Progress of that Work, from the first Planting to the bringing to the Market that valuable Commodity, I shall beg a Place for it in your very next Paper, because the Season for planting the Seed is now at Hand. It is as follows in his very Words,

'INDIGO.

'BY Men of Judgment in the Goodness of INDIGO, it hath been affirm'd, That there has been AS GOOD Indigo made in CAROLINA as in any other Place, but it did thrive only in new Ground, and in that only for One Year, which caused the Planters to desist and neglect Planting of it.

'Mr *Perkinson* in his *Theatre of Plants*, Page 600, describes the Plant truly as he had it from *Vabannes De Laet*, and the Figure he exhibits is a true Figure of the Leaves, but them and the whole Plant is more accurately and livelier printed in —— I have been an Eye-Witness at making of it in *Carolina*, and it was after the following Manner.

'They planted the Herb in Rows, a-bout a Foot distant from each other and

put Ten or Twelve Seeds, and when it is grown and begins to Flower, they cut it with hook'd Knives for that Purpose, and put it into a square wooden Cistern big enough for the Quantity they have, and place it so high, that another wooden Cistern of the same Size being rais'd a little from the Ground, the Top thereof may reach almost as high as the Bottom of the upper Cistern: When the upper is fill'd with the Herbs, there is a Lattis that just goeth into the Top of the Cistern, which keepeth the Herbs close press'd together; then they pump as much fresh Water upon them as will cover them, as high as the Top of the Lattis, and so let it stand in the open Air to ferment; and when it is fermented enough (as they that have Judgment do know) the Liquor is drawn out into the lower Cistern, by pulling out a Plug that is in the Bottom of the upper Cistern, or near it on the one Side, then taking wooden Mashers (of the same Shape with those the Brewers in *London* mash their Grains with in brewing Ale or Beer) they trouble and stir the Liquor violently, insomuch that it will foam and froth ready to run over the Cistern; after that, with a Feather, they throw or sprinkle a little Oyl on the Froth, which allays the extreme Frothing of it; this they leave to the Men to do, while the Master Workman standing by with a Porringer in his Hand takes now and then some Liquor, who, when he finds the Sap or Colour of the Herb to part from the Water in small Particles and settle at the Bottom, he causeth them to cease stirring or disturbing the Liquor, and lets it stand in the Cistern 'till the Sap settles at the Bottom, like Mud, and as soon as they have let the clear Water run out at several Plugs set at several Heights for that Purpose; then they put it into Bags hanging them up to drain the remaining Water away, after which they put it into Boxes about a Yard long, a Foot over, and one Inch deep, where they spread it with Bricklayer's Trowels 'till it is stiff, and then cut it into small Squares as they think fit, and when it is dry they put it into Barrels for a Market or Use.

'Attested for Truth, by me
ROBERT STEVENS.

'9ber. 20th, 1706.

Upon this I would beg Leave to observe, that both *Labat* and Mr. *Stevens*

or thirteen Seeds be put in Holes made at about a Foot distant every Way.' And the last says, 'They planted the Herb in Rows about a Foot Distance from each other, and made Holes in each Row, about Four or Five Inches distant, in which they put Ten or Twelve Seeds, &c.' Now this is much nearer than *Labat* directs, and I think every one must observe, that he has once seen that Plant, that Mr. *Stevens's* Direction is much too close, I shall therefore take Leave (for the Information of your Readers) to tell you, that I have enquir'd of the only Person in this Province that I have heard of, who is a profess'd INDIGO Planter, he having been bred to it from his Childhood, and is now employed by Colonel PINCKNAY, on his Plantation on *Charles-Town* Neck, and he tells me, That he shall begin Planting it the first Week in April, on good Corn Land, which was dug up in the beginning of the Winter. In order to do which, he intends to make Beds of three Foot wide the Length of the Field, leaving Two Feet Distant between each Bed; that in each Bed make three Rows of Holes, with a narrow Hoe, the Hole about Eighteen Inches (length ways) from each other, and in each Hole but only Four or Five Seeds. And this, as the Plant is very large, is certainly near enough; to plant it nearer would soon impoverish the richest Ground, and no doubt was the Reason that gave the *Carolina* Planters occasion to complain it impoverish'd the Ground so much; but I have heard the old Planters say, that That was not the Reason that made them desist from planting INDIGO, but it was the Produce of RICE, which was so beneficial at the first setting out in that Commodity, that made them neglect the other. And as we have now plainly over done the RICE Market, I do not see what we can do better, than to return to the cultivating this valuable Plant, which, as Mr. *Stevens* observ'd Forty Years ago produc'd as good Indigo in *Carolina* as in any other Place: In Support of which Truth, and to encourage the Planter to go chearfully into the Work, I shall give you the Extracts of Two or Three Letters from *London* by the last Ships; by which you will see, that INDIGO made here, in an old Corn Field upon the Hon. Col. *Lucas's* Plantation at *Wappoo*, the last Year, has been prov'd at home to be AS GOOD at least as the *French* INDIGO.

Extract of a Letter from a Gentleman in *London* [...]

The South-Carolina Gazette *reflected the general interest in the province in indigo production by carrying this long article, which included two letters from London regarding the indigo made on the Lucas plantation in 1744. Courtesy of the Charleston Library Society.*

There are 4 large and one smaller Turtle. If they all or any number of them come safe, the largest [is] to be sent to Mr. King in Dover Street or at Ocham Court in Surry and all the Summer Ducks and Drakes and 2 or 3 Non parriels; but if there should be but one Turtle come safe, that to be sent to Mr. King; if more, one to Mr. Edwards in Bedford Row, one to Sir. N. Carew at Beddington, and one to Mrs. Peter Muilman in New Broad Street buildings; and if all the large ones got safe, the small one for Mr. Chatfield; but the 4 first named must be first served. And I beg Mr. Morlys acceptance of all the rest of the birds, how many I cant say. There was a great many when I left town.

N B. Could get only bills for £100 sterling to go by this fleet.

To Mrs. Evance   Augt.
I never wrote to you with reluctance, My dear friend, till now for I surely was the happiest of mortals till the last dismal, fatal month. Oh! dreadful reverse of what I was. Think if you can what is my distress when I tell you the beloved of my soul! all that was value-able and aimable in man! my dear, dear Mr. Pinckney is no more. Great God soport me in this terrible affliction! for tis heavy indeed!

I beg you, my dear Mrs. Evance, to take care of my dear fatherless babes, to comfort their tender hearts; and let them be a little while at home with you upon this meloncholy occasion. Tell them that God Almighty will be their father, their comfort, and their help, and will fulfil the prayers of their pius father upon their heads, and then they must be blessed and happy. Poor dear creatures! What an example, what a Councellour, what a father have they lost!

Adieu, my dear friend. I can say no more. My soul is oppressed with bitter Anguish beyond the power of words to utter. I pray that God Almighty may bless and reward you a hundred fold for all your goodness to my dear, dear fatherless children.

I am yr. obliged and affecte. tho'
truely afflicted friend
Eliza. Pinckney

Mr. Morly will supply you with mony for my poor dear boys and I dont doubt you will let Mr. Gerrard be punctually payd. When I am able I will write to you again. Tis a painful task to have these dismal letters to coppy, but it seems there is a necessity for it—'tis so uncertain whether you will get this.

[To Mrs. Lucas]   So. Ca., Septr. 25th, 1758

With a bleeding heart, Dear Madam, I inform you that since you heard from me the greatest of human Evils has befallen me. Oh, my dear Mother, My dear, dear Mr. Pinckney, the best of men and of husbands is no more! Oh! dreadful reverse of what I was when I last wrote to you.

You were but a short time witness of my happiness. I was for more than 14 year the happiest mortal upon Earth! Heaven had blessed me beyond the lott of mortals and left me nothing to wish for for my self. The Almighty had given every blessing in that dear, that worthy, that valuable man, whose life was one continued course of active Virtue. I had not a desire beyond him, nor had I a petition to make to Heaven but for a continuance of the blessings I injoyed. Think then so truely sensible as I ever was of the happiness I injoyed; for I was truely blessed. Think what I now suffer for my self and for my dear fatherless children! Poor babes. How deplorable is their loss: Their Example, the protector and guide of their youth and the best and tenderest parent that Ever existed is taken from them. God alone, who has promised to be the father of the fatherless, can make up this dreadful loss to them; and I trust he will keep them under his almighty protection and fulfil all their pius fathers prayers upon their heads and will enable the helpless, distressed parent they have left to do them good. Grant, Great God, that I may spend my whole future life in their Service and show my affection and gratitude to their dear father by my care of those precious remains of him, the pledges of the sincerest and tenderest affection that ever was upon Earth.

It was principally for their advantage we returned again to this province, my dear Mr. Pinckney intending as soon as his affairs were disposed of in the manner he approved to return to our Infant Sons. But how much Anguish did the parting with his dear boys give that most affectionate and best of fathers? He parted with life with less pain than with them; for in that awful hour he showed the fruits of a well spent life. His had been the life of a constant steady active Virtue with an habitual trust and confidence in as well as an intire resignation to the Will of the Deity, which made him happy and cheerful through life and made all about him so, for his was true religion free from sourness and superstition; and in his sickness and death the good man and the Christian shined forth in an uncommon resolution and patience, humility, and intire resignation to the Devine Will.—My tears flow too fast. I must have done; 'tis too much, too much to take a review of that distressful hour!

We left England in March (and did not acquaint you with it least you should be uneasey from apprehensions of our being taken) and arrived here the 19th May after being at Sea ten weeks. One of my dear Mr. Pinckneys first inquirys after his arrival here was for a Vessel to Antigua in order to write to you and my brother. We heard of one but she was stoped by an Embargo till after the 12th of July, the fatal day which deprived me of all my soul held dear and left me in a distress that no language can paint. For his Virtues and aimable quallities are deeply imprinted in my heart, his dear image is ever in my Eye, and the remembrance of his affection and tenderness to me must remain to my latest moment—a remembrance mingled with pleasure and Anguish. The remembrance of what he was sooths and comforts me for a time. With what pleasure I reflect on the clearness of his head, the goodness of his heart, the piety of his mind, the sweetness of his temper, the good Sence and vivacity of his conversation, his fine address, the aimableness of his whole deportment, for I did not know a Virtue he did not posess. This pleases while it pains and may be called the Luxury of grief.

This you know is not a picture drawn by flattery or partialty. Many will subscribe to the justice of it; all that really knew him must. But what anguish is in the reflection that these that were my greatest delights and blessings are taken from me for Ever in this world—for in the next I hope there is a Union of Virtuous souls where there is no more death, no more separation, but virtuous love and friendship to endure to Eternity! And this surely must be one of the greatest degrees of bliss a human soul can injoy, except the injoyment of the Deity himself; and this hope is my comfort for every thing below has lost its relish. Earth has no more charms for me.

I indeed have had a large share of Blessings. How undeserving was I, how unexpected was such a treasure, and yet Bounteous Heaven gave him to me! O! Had Heaven but added one blessing more and spared him to see his dear children brought up and let us have gone to the grave hand in hand together, what a heaven had I enjoyed upon Earth! But why these great and uncommon blessings to me? Those already injoyed were beyond desert—vastly beyond desert and expectation.

Great God Almighty, give me thy grace and enable me to drink this bitter cup which Thou hast alloted me, and to submit to Thee however hard the task with that resignation and submission which becomes thy creature and servant, and one that has tasted so largly of thy Bounty as I have done!

How long a letter have I wrote and all on one dismal subject! Forgive me, Oh! my mother, for giving you so much pain while I have indulged my self thus; but my soul is oppressed with bitter anguish and my thoughts intirely taken up with my own meloncholy concerns.

I lately received a letter from good Colo. Talbott to my poor dear Mr. Pinckney with one inclosed from you to me informing us of my brothers being sailed to England. It would have given us great pleasure had it been a year ago. We should then have mett with comfort and pleasure. But my dear boys will rejoyce to see their Uncle, and I hope he will be there before the meloncholy tidings reaches them. My heart is with them and I shall by the Divine permission return as soon as I can consistent with their interest; whether it will be in one, two or three year I cant yet say.

I shall write to you again soon if I am able. I hope you will always command me in every thing wherein I can serve you and be asured it is not more my duty than my inclination to show you in every Instance in my power how much I am

Your Dutiful and affecte. tho'
greatly afflicted daughter
E. Pinckney

To the Honble. Tho. Talbott
Colo. of his Majestys Regiment in Antigua.
Good Sir   Octr. 2nd [1758]
Your letter of the 10th July to my dear Mr. Pinckney found me most miserable for I had then lost the most worthy and valuable of men as well as the most aimable, tender, and affectionate of hus-

bands. My dear, dear Mr. Pinckney is no more!

Your long friendship and goodness to my brother and mother will plead my excuse for troubleing you with the inclosed for my poor mother, who I know will be greatly afflicted at the dismal tidings it brings. I therefore beg the favour of you, Sir, to breake the meloncholy Contents to her before you deliver her my letter; it will be less shocking.

I sincerely pray Heaven may spare you and good Mrs. Talbot many happy years to each other and to see the dear Infant child brought up.

I am with great esteem tho' with distress and sorrow of heart

Sir

Yr. most obliged and obedt. Servt.

Eliza. Pinckney

To Miss Mary Lucas   Octr. 3rd [1758]

It gives me great pain to afflict you, my dear Sister, but 'tis now my unhappy lott—however irksom the Task—by acquainting you with the most distressful Event that ever did or could happen to me in this world. Oh, my Sister, I have lost my dear, dear Mr. Pinckney, the best of men, of husbands, and of fathers, and equally good in every relation and connection in life. Imagine then, if 'tis possible, what is my distress!

If Colo. Talbott is in Antigua, deliver him the inclosed letter. There is one in it for my mother. He will be so good to break the dismal tideings it contains to her; but if he is not in Antigua, the meloncholy Office must be Yours, and in such case you will open Colo. Talbots letter and take that for my mother out and deliver it to her when you think it proper.[10]

I am

Yr. affecte. and greatly afflicted Sister

E. Pinckney

10. This is the last letter in the letterbook to any member of the Lucas family. The register of St. John's Parish, Antigua, records the burial of Eliza's younger brother, Thomas Lucas, on August 11, 1756, of Ann Lucas (probably Eliza's mother) on October 25, 1759, and of her brother Captain George Lucas of Dalzell's Regiment, on January 14, 1760. Vere Langford Oliver, *The History of the Island of Antigua*, 3 vols. (London, 1894–99), 2: 199, 202.

[To Mrs. Evance]

My dear friend

If, as I imagine, you received my letter dated in August last, of which I sent a duplicate by the same Convoy, you have been some months acquainted with my meloncholy situation and heavy affliction for that informed you of the loss of my worthy, my beloved Mr. Pinckney. I was deprived of that greatest of human blessings the 12th of July at Mr. Motts over the water,[11] where my dear creature was removed for the Bennefitt of the air. He was received here with a general satisfaction and every body received and vizeted him with great joy, but in less than two months he bid an everlasting adieu to the people and Country he had loved too well, and but just returned to lay his bones among them in this unworthy land.

The concern for his loss was general and sincere, and even some whom the spirrit of party and opposition had estranged for some time acknowledged with tears they had mett with nothing for many years that had afflicted them so much as the death of that good man. If that be the case with them, what then must be my grief, my friend, that knew him intimately, that knew his inmost thoughts, that knew the goodness of his heart, the piety of his mind, the pleasure he took in relieving and assisting the afflicted by every means in his power, his tender distress and prayers in private when he had not power to relieve the wretched, the sweetness of his temper, the aimableness of his whole deportment; all his Virtues added to his partial fondness and tenderness to me surely makes my grief pardonable if ever womans was.

I would describe to you (for I know serious subjects and solomn scenes are no strangers to your mind) his last sickness and dying scene for there the good man and the Christian were displayed in an intire resignation to the Divine Will and triumphed over the weakness and tenderness of nature as well as the violence of pain, but 'tis too much for me! My Eyes fail and I can write no more.

Tho' I take up my pen again I will not resume the distressful sub-

11. Charles Pinckney died at Jacob Motte's plantation, Mount Pleasant, at the site of the present town of that name across the mouth of the Cooper River from Charleston. The Motte plantation house, later known as the Hibben House, is now 111 Hibben Street. P. R. McIver, *History of Mount Pleasant, South Carolina* (Charleston, S.C., 1960), pp. 11, 17.

ject but turn my thoughts where I trust the Almighty will in pity and mercy give me comfort and where I most desire it. I will talk to you about my dear children. Pray let me know as often as possible how they do, how they look, whether they grow, and say as much as you can about them for the hearing from them and that they are good children and well is the greatest cordial to my distressed mind that can possibly be administered.

Accept your self, dear Madam, and return to all our friends that show any countenance to my dear boys the sincere acknowledgements and thanks of a grateful heart that will ever look upon its self as under the highest obbligations to them for their goodness to my children, especially to good Mr. Middleton, Dr. Kirk-patric[12] and Mr. Morly.

I received your very obliging and friendly letters of the 10th June by Rodgers with those of my boys to my self and their dear father. What joy would those letters have given him had he lived to see them! Though I hope they are now with you in London, they will be at school before this can reach you; I must beg the favour of you therefore to add to the many kindnesses which I know you have indulged them with that of spending a day with them at Camberwell when you receive this to let them know I and their dear little Sister are well. Wont the good Dr. accompany you? I know he takes pleasure in doing friendly and humain [things] and wont think it too trifling to cheer the little hearts of innocent children. Indeed, they have experience[d] much already of his friendly indulgence, for which I most sincerely thank him. I beg leave to insist you will set down the Expences of dinner, coach hire, &c to my account.

I forget whether I mentioned to you before I left England (I know I intended it) that the children should make your Servants some acknowledgement for their trouble at holi-day times—what you think proper. It was what they always did to our own. And at Whitsuntide they used to make Mrs. Greene[13] a present of a guinea for a pound of tea besides the donations at Xmas to Camberwell, so that

12. Identified as the same James Kilpatrick (later Kirkpatrick) who had practiced medicine in Charleston some twenty years before. See Joseph Ioor Waring, "James Killpatrick and Smallpox Inoculation in Charlestown," *Annals of Medical History*, New Series, 10 (July, 1938): 301–8; see also Waring's *History of Medicine in South Carolina, 1670–1825* (Columbia, S.C., 1964), pp. 38–43. Eliza's *Recipe Book* contains two prescriptions from the English doctor "For a Dia Drink."
13. The housekeeper at school.

if Mrs. G had it not last W [hitsuntide] they must carry two next W.

As soon as I get to town I shall communicate such parts of your letter (to my dear Mr. Pinckney) as is necessary to Mrs. Cooper. Had I not had so much to lament for my self and for my children in the loss of that valueable dear man, I should have been much concerned for many, particulary for you; for you have lost a faithful friend who would have made your interest his own. He was much concerned least Mr. Raven should be disapointed in his remittances, and while he lay sick abed settled some matters with Mr. Gibbs, his agent, for him, and sent several pressing messages to Colo. Gibbs to remit him mony by the first ships—and he would settle all the affairs with him as soon as he was able. Indeed I believe he told him before he imagined Mr. Raven must be distressed for mony, but Col. G. was desireous to give up every thing at once; but as he was never able to finish that matter, I dont know whether he has been supplyed.[14]

Now I am upon this subject I must do my Nephew C. P. justice with regard to Mrs. Gibb's Will. He did not draw it, but Colo. Gibbs himself. I have not been in town since my great misfortune, but at my friend Mrs. Golightlys in the Country[15]—from whom I have experienced the greatest tenderness—but I shall return in a fortnight or three weeks to my own solitary habitation in Charles Town, where 'tis necessary I should be on account of business.

I hope you and Master Evance have got perfectly well. I was greatly concerned to hear you had been ill.

To Vigerous Edwards, Esqr.
in Bedford Row, London
Dear Sir   [February 1759]
Though my Eyes at this time [are] so weak I am very little able to write I should reproach my self if I did not send you a line by this Convoy to thank you and Miss Varier for your friendly Notice of my poor dear children—who I find with good Mr. and Mrs. Bromfield made them very happy soon after we left England. Your affectionate and truely pius letter of the 12th of May to my dear Mr.

14. See Henry S. Holmes, "Robert Gibbes, Governor of South Carolina, and Some of His Descendants," *SCHM* 12 (1911): 81–83; also "Wills and Miscellaneous Records, Charleston County," 100 vols. (typescript of manuscript), Charleston, S.C., County Library, 13: 886.

15. Mary Butler Golightly, the widow of Culcheth Golightly, lived in St. Andrew's Parish. Mabel L. Webber, "Hyrne Family," *SCHM* 22 (1921): 111–12.

Pinckney which informed him of our childrens health and that of your own and familys would have been a Cordial to the best and tenderest of all fathers as well as the most affectionate and sincere of friends had he lived to receive it. But, my good Sir, your friend, my dear Mr. Pinckney, one of the most valuable of men and best of husbands is no more! Thus am I from being the happiest of mortals become most wretched and afflicted by the loss of this worthy man! I dont know a Virtue he did not posess, nor one qualification he wanted to communicate comfort and happiness to all about him. He had a clear head and sound judgment, an honest heart and a pius mind added to a most aimable and sweet natural disposition that made every thing happy that was connected with him. That surely if extream sorrow for any thing that happens to us in this life is excuseable, mine may be pardoned for this dreadful loss for he was an Instrument chosen by Providence to convey every blessing to me, and I experienced for more than 14 year as [much as] a state of mortality is capable off. May that Divine Being—whose works are all done in Wisdome and who gave him to me and has taken him from me—enable me to submit to his Will and to drink this bitter cup, however grievous and afflicting which he has alloted me.

Give me leave, good Sir, to thank you with the most unfeigned gratitude for your affection and friendship to my dear dear Mr. Pinckney. May the Almighty restore you a hundred fold for all your friendship to him. I can never make you amends, but my prayers shall be constant for your happiness for 'tis impossible you could any other way have laid me under such obligations to you as by your affection for him.

We arrived in this province after a tedious passage of ten weeks in pretty good health and great spirrits to see our friends who received us with great joy. But how short was the injoyment, for in less than two months he was taken ill and lay 3 weeks sick, in all which time the good man and the Xtian appeared in his whole deportment in the most unexampled patience and intire resignation to the Divine Will that ever was known.

I cant be more particular for a review of that dismal scene is too much for me; 'tis more than I can bear. Tho' I flatter my self your regard for him was such that it would not be tiresome to you to hear any particulars that might give you a true Idea of the man that loved and valued you so much as my beloved Mr. Pinckney did; nor need

I, I hope, apologize for having said so much on my own meloncholy concerns to one of your Humanity and indulgence.

I shall be greatly obliged to you and Dear Miss Varier for your countenance and friendly advice to my dear fatherless children. They have mett with the greatest of losses in their dear father, whose example and advice under the Divine blessing would have made them happy. As to fortune, he has left them enough (if 'tis pleas[ing] God to prosper it and keep this province out of the hands of the French) to make them happy and useful men if they are wise and good ones; if otherwise (which God Almighty forbid) the greatest fortunes will not be sufficient. My heart is with them, and by the Almighty's permission I will return to them as soon as [I] can consistent with their interest, but am determined to punish my self however painful the separation till then, and how long that will be I cant say.

I have been with a tender friend in the Country ever since my great misfortune so that I know not how things passes abroad, or indeed any News of any sort.

I wrote to Miss Varier the 6th June and inclosed it to Mr. Morly which I hope she received from

Dr. Sir

Yr. most obliged and affecte
humble Servt.
E. Pinckney

By the Febr. fleet.

To George Morly, Esqr., London
Dr. Sir   [February 1759]
I perceive by yours of the 16th Nov. to my Nephew you had received our letters acquainting you with my great misfortune, an Event ever to be lamented by me and my children with the deepest sorrow to our latest moment; but as I know your regard for that valuable man and worthy friend that subject may give you pain. I will not therefore indulge my own meloncholy at the risk of increasing it in you.

The above mentioned letter to my Nephew gave me great comfort. You were very good to let me know how my dear boys did as well as to insert the paragraph of Mr. Gerrards letter relating to them. And [I] make no doubt, Sir, you will continue your friendly

Offices to the dear remains of your deceased friend and all the Comfort I have upon Earth.

As you say nothing to the Contrary I hope you have injoyed your health since we left England—an account of which will always give me pleasure.

I am much concerned for the distress of our August fleet. Indeed, I have reason on my own and your account as by the destroying of the letters you did not receive the 200 £ of Gov. Littletons Agent; for I cannot be easey till your debt is payed least any accident should happen to this province in these precarious times, but bills [of exchange] are extreamly dificult to be got. However, I have the promise of one hundred pound sterling which I hope to inclose you in this letter and shall lose no time to remit you more as soon as possible, and hope you will be so good to supply Mrs. Evance and Mr. Gerrard (to whom I am greatly obliged for their tenderness to them) with what mony is wanted for my dear children.

As I have the greatest reason imaginable to think you interest your self in our welfair, I shall in my next send you an account of our affairs here. The fleet sails shortly and as I have been but a month in town have much business on my hands and cant do it now.

Your letters to my dear Mr. Pinckney of the 2nd and 27th May, the 14th June, the 11th July, 31st July and 21st Septr. I duely received and sent those directed to Mr. Gerrard to him. The Prussian mantle which was Mrs. Bulls came safe. It is very hansome and I am much obliged to you for the trouble you took in it.

Be so good to make my grateful acknowledgements and Compliments to good Mr. and Mrs. Middleton and their family, and to Dr. Kirk-patrick, to Mr. and Mrs. Freeman; and inform Mr. Freeman, who I intended to write too by this fleet, but shall not now have time, I received his friendly letter to my dear Mr. Pinckney of the 28th June.

I hope I shall be able to write to Doctor Kirk-patrick now to thank him for his care of my dear boys. If I should not, be so good to excuse me to him and let him know my gratitude is not the less sincere because I do not immediately tell him how much I think my self obliged to him. I am very sorry for the loss of his valuable the Duke of Grisors in France. I received his very friendly and obliging letter of the 26th July joyntly to my beloved husband and my self inclosing one of an older date.

[109]

Colo. B ['s] mony is ready as soon as he sends to receive it.

My kindest Compliments to Mr. and Mrs. Corbett and believe me to be with great truth

Yr. m: o: and obedt Servt.

E. Pinckney

I now inclose you a 100 £ sterling [note] drawn by Messrs. Oglivy and Wand on Francis Mannock, Esqr., London. I am this moment informed I cant have a small bill of Exchange which I thought my self sure of and intended to send to Mrs. Evance. I must therefore beg the favour of you to present her with 20 £ Sterling out of the hundred I now inclose as a small acknowledgement for her care of my children.

Original By Capt. Man. ⎫
in Febr. ⎬
Coppy by Mrs. Wright ⎭

NB   Notwithstanding the above got the 20 £ bill for Mrs. Evance.

My dr. Children   [February 1759]

I had the comfort to hear from Mr. Morly that you were both well the 16th Novr. He inserted a paragraph of Mr. Gerrards letter to him giving you both a character which I hope you will endeavour to deserve and which will make me happier than any thing else upon Earth.

Your Uncle Lucas arrived here last month and informed me you were both well; that he was hurried down to Hamshire and thereby prevented taking his leave of you and bringing your letters. I beg, my dear boys, you will write me a letter every month if 'tis but two lines and whether you know of ships coming or not, and send them to good Mr. Morly in Sommersett house, and he will take care to forward them properly.

Remember me in the best manner to Mr. G [errard] and Mrs. Greene and thank them most heartily for their care of you both. I should have wrote to Mr. Gerrard now, but I have been at a friends house in the Country ever since our great misfortune and am but lately come to town, which occations me much business just now and the fleet sails to-morrow. I cant possibly do it at this time. I hope he received my letter by Mrs. Murphy inclosing one to you both, and that the almighty has soported you under the meloncholy contents of it. It gave you an account of an Event that must be remembered by you and me, my dear children, with the deepest sorrow to our latest moment. But be comforted, my dearest boys, and thank God you had one of the best of men and tenderest of parents for your Father, and consider you have a heavenly Father infinite in power and goodness who I doubt not will take you under his almighty protection and make you wise and good men—and then you cant fail to be happy ones. Pray to him to give you his grace to guide and direct you in all your ways; and I trust he will enable me to exert all my little abilities for your Service in every way in my power. And be asured you are as dear to me as tis possible for children to be to a parent, and all the happiness of my life is centered in you and your dear Sister.

I thank God my dear Tommy has got well through the measels. I hear he had them at school. Asure Mr. Gerrard of my utmost gratitude for his care and tenderness of you of which I have not the least doubt. I shall write to him very soon. In the mean time [I] hope to hear from him and you; for to hear you are well and good boys is the greatest joy I can possibly receive.

Remember me kindly to all our friends, particuary those that are so good to take notice of you. Pay my affectionate Compliments and tell Mrs. Chatfield when you see her I am greatly obliged to her and Mr. Chatfield. 'Tis not in my power to write to them at this time, but will make it up very soon. I am also indebted to Mr. and Mrs. Watson for their goodness to you. Remember me kindly to them. Mrs. Wright who brings this has been so good to take charge of 3 guineas; one for each of you and one for Master Tomm Evance.

Your Sister desires her tenderest affections to you both, and be asured of mine in the highest degree as I am

My beloved children
Your most affectionate Mother
E. Pinckney

My love to Master Draytons;[16] I shall
write to them soon.
By Mrs. Wright in Febr.

16. William Henry and Charles Drayton, the sons of John and Charlotte Bull Drayton, were at school in England. William Henry (1742–79), the future Revolutionary patriot, had accompanied the Pinckneys to England in 1753, where he completed his education at Westminster and Oxford. Charles took his degree in

[To Charles and Thomas Pinckney]   May 11th

I wrote to my darling boys by Mrs. Wright but cant omit any good opportunity to inform them we are, I thank God, very well. Pay my Compliments and grateful thanks to Mr. G[errard] and assure him that nothing in my power shall be left undone to serve him at all times and upon all occations, tho' I think nothing that I can say can possibly be so effectual a recommendation as what speaks for its self—that the most remarkably tender and affectionate of Parrents, which was your dear father, after a five years tryal should continue you under his care. This must be as of great weight with all reasonable people for actions speak more than words.

I cant think of answering Mr. G's truely kind and friendly letters of the 15 and 25 Novr. in a cursory manner and therefore hope he will excuse my not doing it now as I really have not time, having lately much writing to do.

Pray remember me in the kindest manner to Mr. and Mrs. Walton and Mrs. Evance. Excuse me to the latter; I cant possible write to her, I did very fully by Mrs. W[right] since which I received her favour of the 29th Nov., which was extreamly friendly and acceptable.

Your sister desires her most affectionate regards. Our Compliments and thanks to Mrs. Greene, and love to Master Draytons. My blessings and prayers continually attend you both. Be good children, love one another, take care of your selves. And may the almighty God bless and preserve you and your dear Sister, guide and direct you, and make you his own children for time and for Eternity, is the first and most devout petition that is made to Heaven by, My Dear Children

Yr. truly affectionate mother
E. Pinckney

By Capt. Rains

[To Mr. Morly]   [c. May 1759]

A Thousand Thanks to you, My Dear Sir, for all Your goodness to my poor dear boys and for your favours to me of the 25th Novr.

medicine at the University of Edinburgh in 1770. Taylor, "The Draytons of South Carolina," pp. 13–18; John Drayton, *Memoirs of the American Revolution* (Charleston, S.C., 1821), p. xiii; also William M. Dabney and Marion Dargan, *William Henry Drayton and the American Revolution* (Albuquerque, N.M., 1962).

and 1st December, which it would be an indulgence to me to answer more fully than I am able to do at this time, for my Eyes are but weak and I have lately wrote a good deal as you will perceive by the inclosed packett, which I beg the favour you will forward and excuse me to Mrs. Evance for not writing to her.

The condolence and consolations of such a friend as you are softenes and aleviates—though Nothing but the Divine Hand which gave the blow can heal the wound that is made in my afflicted heart —but the attempts of friendship are extreamly kind. With gratitude I acknowledge them and subscribe to the strength and truth of your reasonings. They are just and unanswerable, and be asured I pay the greatest regard to your advice. Your tender simpathy soothes and comforts me for I well know your affection for my beloved Mr. Pinckney and the pleasure you take in doing justice to his worth, which must ever be the most grateful sound to my Ear while I have either life or Virtue left.

I have made another attempt to fulfill my promise to good Mrs. King and Mrs. Chatfield; and Capt. Ourry in his Majestys ship Success has been so obliging to take charge of 2 Turtle for me. If they go to Portsmouth, I have saved you the trouble of them; but if to London, I must again trespass on your friendly indulgence and beg you will send the largest of the 2 (tho' there is but little difference) to Mrs. King in Dover Street or to Ocham, and the other to Mrs. Chatfield. But if but one lives Mrs. King must have that, and I must beg Mrs. Cs patience a little longer.

If the bottle you mention is Cayan, it was designed for Mrs. Peter Muilman with one of the Turtle. Be so good, when you send it, to let her know a Turtle accompany'd it but died in the passage. If 'tis possible I will send some birds by this fleet, which if they come safe beg you will accept off.

I wrote to you by Capt. Man in Febr. inclosing bills of Exchange for a hundred and twenty pound sterling. Coppyd that letter by Mrs. Wright. Wrote to you by the Britannia and inclosed Coppys of the aforesaid bills, and again by what ship I know not (my Nephew forwarded and inclosed besides the two before mentioned one for 30 £ sterling drawn by my brother. I now inclose a 3rd [copy] of the same.[17]

17. Sending duplicates of important letters and bills of exchange was common practice. The ordinary number of copies was three. Henry Laurens about this time

To Mrs. Pocklington

Dear Madm.   [c. May 1759]

I have been wholly taken up with my own moloncholy concerns that I have not been able to perform my promise in informing you of those particulars in which you are so greatly interested and will doubtless be impatient to know.

It would have been cruelty to have delayed it, and in any other case great ingratitude not to thank you for the many friendly offices and polite treatment we received from you and good Mr. Pocklington during our residence in England; but, My dear Madam, the greatest of human Evils has since befallen me. My dear, dear Mr. Pinckney is no more! In him I have lost one of the best and worthiest of men, the tenderest and most affectionate of all husbands, and best of Fathers to my children. He was indeed equally good in every Connection in life—my amiable companion under the influence of whose virtue and sweet disposition I was for more than 14 years the happiest of mortals. I was truely sensible of it and therefore as truely feel the sad reverse!

But I will quit the painful subject to asure you I, upon my first arrival here, took all the pains it was possible and that the nature of the inquiry would admit to find out the truth of the storys you heard before we left England and cant find the least foundation in the world for any such suspicion. And in a Country like this it would be impossible to conceal any thing of the sort; besides you know our two friends are both above mean artifice, and such harmony as is between them could never subsist where mutual faith and confidence were wanting, and I really believe that Gentleman as little deserves any aspersion of that sort as any man in the world.

Miss W[ragg] is a fine blooming girl, a most delicate complexion, but is not tall. Miss Judith is grown the last year surprizingly and improves much in her person. My much loved friends Mr. and Mrs. Wragg are both well.[18] Mr. W. has had some little Complaints pro-

was sending five copies of some letters. David D. Wallace, *Life of Henry Laurens* (New York, 1915), p. 49.

18. William Wragg, onetime appointed chief justice of the province (he declined) and member of the Royal Council, died in a shipwreck in 1777. Wragg Barony, which William inherited from his father Samuel, lay along the west bank of the Ashley River above Middleton Place. Henry A. M. Smith, "Wragg of South Carolina," *SCHM* 19 (1918): 122–23 and chart, and "The Baronies of South Carolina: Ashley," *SCHM* 11 (1910): 86ff. and map.

ceeding, I believe, from something of a scorbutick habit of body. They went to the Barronny last week where they intend staying two months to my great motification, for as I see but little company and can relish none but a very few particular friends 'tis to me a great loss; and I have too much tenderness for Mrs. Wragg to trust my self in the Country with her alone.

It would give me great pleasure to receive a line from you tho my Corrispondance can promise nothing lively or entertaining, and letters dictated amidst gloom and sorrow must partake of it in spite of every endeavour to the contrary, and the contagion will reach the tender and humain mind tho' not designed to be affected by it.

My affectionate Compliments pray present to Mrs. etc.

I am

y. m. af. humble St.

E. Pinckney

By Mr. Parnham in the May fleet.

To My Lady Carew of Beddington   May 1759

Your pius and friendly letter, My dear Madm. reached me in March. The consolations of such a friend soften and aleviate, tho' nothing less than the Devine Hand that gave the blow can heal so deep a one as is made in my afflicted heart. Could you not guess, my much loved friend, when I neglected you that the greatest of humain Evils had befallen me, that I had lost the most valuable of men and best of husbands. Oh, my dear Lady C., what have I suffered or rather what have I not suffered since I last saw you by this cruel separation from the beloved of my soul! Tis not in the power of words to paint my distress. My Nights have passed in tears and my days in sighs without a single exception since the fatal 12th of July when I was deprived of what my soul held most dear upon Earth. And tho' you had some knowledge of the worthy and amiable man I lament and exteemed him much you knew him not half enough to conceive how uncommon a loss I have mett with.

His closing scene was of a peice with his life, all patient, pius and resigned so that those about him could not help useing the expression of Beallam, Let me die the death of the righteous and let my latter end be like his! I will not be more particular in pity to you or tress-pass longer on your friendly indulgence by dwelling longer on this meloncholy scene. Indeed my tears flow too fast and I must have done.

Thus you see, my friend, how your partialliaty has misrepresented me to you, how little time, fortitude and Xtian resolution I have had, nay even the consideration of the hurt the impairing my health must be to my Infant, my fatherless children! and which you kindly and justly use as an argument why I should exert my utmost ability to soport this heavy stroke have not been able to help me! How stupid must I be when I neglect any thing that may tend to the advantage of those dear pledges of the sincerest affection that ever was upon Earth; yet this creature am I. But Heaven, I trust, will still aid me and enable me to exert more resolution than I have done the last ten months especially for their sakes—poor dear creatures, the most tender and valuable of all parents is taken from them, whose example as well as council was a constant and living leason to them.

Thanks, a thousand thanks, my dear madam, for your goodness to my dear boys. Your Ladyship and good Mrs. King with my other friends were extreamly kind in leting me know they were well. Those accounts from diferent hands confirmed they were so; or I should have sunk under the apprehension of any additional misfortune befallen them as I had not a line from them and began to suspect the accounts of my friends who had immediate care of them in pity to my suffering concealed any ill now for a time from me. But you kindly set my mind at ease with regard to them. I have since heard the poor little creatures were so much affected with their great misfortune they were not able to write.

I am not so wholy ingrossed by my own meloncholy concerns but I can still feel for you. Poor Miss Carew! How I pity you, but you, my friend, have learned wisdom in the school of affliction. God almighty grant I may make as great a proficiency in that school of wisdome, and that the consideration of the necessity as well as Wisdome of an humble resignation to his will may reconcile me to those cruel vicisitudes that are annext to human life. I have long and so still see how closely connected piety and happiness are together and so far as we transgress the one we lose the other. But [I] hope I can still joyn with my friend in saying tho' we cannot now we shall in time or Eternity be convinced of the expediency of these things which now appear so grevious, and that the alwise and gracious Being will make all these Evils work together for good and enable me

[116]

to pass through life with less misery than I have done the last 10 months.

What, Dear Madam, is this new affliction which you dont explain? By the friendship that commenced so early and has subsisted so long between us, I have a right to share it with you. Pray Heaven deliver you out of it.

Eliza. Pinckney

Memdm. Have not time to coppy any more of this letter at large, but acknowledged the receipt of her Ladyships letter of the 21st April. Wrote upon the subject of Miss Martins Marriage. About the Turtle lost in the August fleet, etc. Sent in May by Mr. Parnham under cover to Mr. Morly.

To The Honble. Mrs. King
Dear Madm.   May [1759]
Grief has not so far dejected me as to make me wholly indeferent to the oppinion of the virtuous and the good especially those I so justly love and esteem as I do you, or I should spare you reading a letter dictated amidst gloom and sorrow for you must think me most insensible and ungratful should I delay answering your favours of the 25th Oct. and 25th Nov., letters that could only be wrote by the most sensible and benevolent as well as by the most simpathizing and pius mind, and for which you will, I hope, accept the sincere thanks of a grateful heart. Indeed the hearing that those I love and esteem are well and happy is the only pleasure I can now injoy, when the whole world unconnected with those seem to me a perfect blank.

Your arguments, my dear Madam, why I should submit to the afflictive stroke and moderate my grief, are unanswerable and friendly. I subscribe to the truth and justness of them; but you are too partial to me when you think I have done my duty in this great tryal. I had little fortitude, and truely Xtian resolution, and my loss was great and uncommon. I had lived for more than 14 year in the most uninterrupted felicity with one of the most worthy and best of men that ever woman was blessed with; his mind and temper were the most unexceptionable I ever mett with or heard of in a human being, and to me the most tender, partial and affectionate of husbands; nor had I ever an angry moment in that time, He was every thing that was aimable to me, nor had I—so uncommonly blessed was I in the 14 year I was his wife—an hours anxiety for my self in any shape. What affected him and his Children indeed was sensibly felt by me, but for my self I had not a petition to make to Heaven but for a continuance of the blessings I injoy.

All that were well acquainted with him know in some measure his worth, but as none was so intimately acquainted with his more private and retired life, none can be equally sensible of the Virtues of the aimable, good man I lament. The greatness of my loss will I hope in some degree, tho' I know not greatly, extenuate my fault in not exerting more resolution; for the stroke is from Infinite Wisdome! and though 'tis a bitter cup indeed! I ought to drink it. And who is it has lived and not known sorrow? Heaven grant I may be the better for it; it has sett heavy indeed on me, for I have not know[n] one day or Night since the fatal 12th of July free from tears and sighs. That both my sight and health have been much impaired, the latter is, I thank God, much mended, and I will still hope that time, tho' a tedious Phisician, aided with the comfortable prospects that life beyond the grave will assist me in pasing through life with less misery than I have done the last ten months.

Poor Miss Upton! How I pity her! I could ever feel for others; but now I really share in the distresses of every body whose trouble is in any thing similiar to my own.

I am at a loss how to express my self in terms suitable to the grateful sence I have of my good Lord and Lady Kings as well as yours and Mr. K's for your notice of my poor little boys. I was surprized when you told me my dear Charles had wrote to his Lordship, as he has an uncommon share of modesty, but I hear from his master it was a letter of thanks for his Lordships notice of him at Ripley last summer. My most grateful respects and acknowledgements are due to my Lord and Ladyship.

You enquire, Dear Madm. the time of my return to England? My heart is there tho' all Countrys are now to me alike, nor do I prefer any one to another, and could I transport all those that I love hither I would not Cross that frightful Ocean for all the wealth your rich Island affords. But as my dear boys are fixt there, I am impatient to return, and I need not tell you who are your self so tender a parent what I feel at this cruele separation from my beloved children, but am determined what ever anguish I suffer to submit to it for their advantage. And 'tis very clear to me and my friends here that my stay a year or two longer must be greatly so with regard to their fortune. The Case then stands thus: they must suffer in their interests, or I in my mind. Cruel alternative! But I do not hesitate. I commit them to the Divine protection and submit.

Pardon me, dear Madam, for having tresspassed so much on your friendly indulgence. 'Tis weak to complain, but some relief to an oppressed heart, over burthened with a sence of its own sufferings and unhappy situation, deprived of the best of husbands, and separated at such a painful distance from his dear remains, my darling children.

I always wish to be remembered in the most affectionate manner to Miss Kings. If Miss Mina had sent H.[arriott] P.[inckney] a present of 10000 pound it would not have made her half so happy as her very pretty and kind Epistle. She is excessive proud of it and now answering it. [She] is grown a good deal taler and is, I thank God, a very good child.

I think we were very unluckey not to get one Turtle safe out of 6 fine ones all in good order, and that had been kept above a month in Tubbs before they went on board. I hope for better success in what I now send, and beg the favour You will accept of the largest that comes alive. I send it to the care of Mr. Morly. 'Tis the finest season of the year to send them to England that I have great hopes this will come safe. There is no such thing at this time as a wild Turkey to be got alive. I have laid out for some young one[s] and hope to send them still before the summer is out.

If, as I hope, you have received the Summer Ducks I sent by the Penguin, Capt. Mann,—NB. no Turtle to be got at that time—you will wonder I should send such a scrip as I gave him near 4 thousand mile, but my Eyes were bad and I had not resolution to attempt a letter at that time.

I wrote to our good friend Mr. Edwards and beg now to be remembered in the best manner to him and Miss V.

I thought the plants you received would be a pretty ornament in my Lords Green-house and therefore took the liberty to send them. I never saw any of them in any of our Rambles in England. 'Tis the Pennento Royal;[19] it bears the most noble bunch of flowers I ever

19. Pelatiah Webster, in his *Journal of a Voyage to Charlestown, in So. Carolina, 1765*, describes "the piemento tree which has a leaf like a flag and stalk like a large

saw. The main stem of the bunch is a foot and half or two foot long with some hundreds of white flowers hanging pendant upon it. 'Tis a Native of this Country, but I doubt if they will do out of doors in England.

I am much obliged for the trouble you took to send my letter to Mrs. Onslow. Poor Lady. I am quite concerned she is such a prisoner. Will you be so good when you see her to excuse me for not answering hers of the [*blank*] of Aug. Tis much my inclination, but I am not able. Indeed, my friends have no reason to regret the want of my letters especially at this time.

We very sincerely simpathized with poor Mrs. Brodrick and family on the unhappy accident to the Admiral. I hope they have quite got over it. Pray remember me to them and all our good Neighbours.

Adieu, dear Madam, and believe me with the warmest heart and most unfeigned Esteem

Your most obliged and obedt. Servt.
Eliza. Pinckney

By Mr. Parnham inclosed to Mr. Morly.

[To Mrs. Chatfield]

I have thanked you, Dear Madam, a thousand times with the warmest gratitude for your friendly notice of my poor dear boys; and if my prayers are pius enough to reach heaven, yours will never stand in need of the Countenance of strangers but be under the immediate inspection of affectionate parents, or if they should, may Heaven restore them a hundred fold for your kindness to my now fatherless children.

My dear Mrs. C, what have I suffered since I last saw you, or rather what anguish have I not suffered. 'Tis not in the power of words to convey the Idea, and tho' you had some knowledge of the worthy and aimable man I lament, you knew him not half enough to conceive [how uncommon a life I have mett with.][20]

cabbage stalk and bears large tostling white flowers." *Southern Historical Association Publications* 2 (1898): 144.

20. The end of this sentence, included here in brackets, appears in Eliza's copybook (1759–60) in the Pinckney Family Papers, Manuscripts Division, Library of Congress, but not in the letterbook in the possession of the South Carolina Historical Society. The completed letter to Mrs. Chatfield is the only item in the

[To Mrs. Evance]   July 16th, 1759

You never were more happy, My dear Mrs. Evance, in your con-
jectures than when you imagined me ever impatient to hear from
my dear babes. What comfort then must your favour from Bath give
me when it informed me they were both well. And how many
thank[s] are due to you for your tenderness of them—more than I
shall ever be able to pay; all that I am you have a just right too.

It was very good of you to take my dear little creature [Thomas]
to Bath. He gives a proof how well he knows his Mama when he
says she will not be angry with you for giving him pleasure. The
greatest I could injoy is to know it was principally in order to [do]
that and not want of health in any great degree. But tell the dear
Saucy boy one scrip of a penn from his hand would have given his
mama more joy than all the pleasures of Bath could him—great as
they were. 'Tis impossible to tell you how much I long to see them,
fully satisfied as I am of the care and tenderness they injoy.

I believe indeed 'tis better for them I am at this distance, painful
as it is to me; for I find such an over-flowing of tenderness for them
that might degenerate into weakness had I an opportunity for such
indulgence.

I am sorry you should stay for an Answer from me as you and our
other friends think fenceing would be of Service to Charles, as you
may be asured I shall always chearfully acquiesce in every thing
that may tend to the good of either their bodys or mind. If Mr.
M.[orly] aproves of it I should think the 12 Guineas down would
be best, but that as you and he think proper. Am greatly obliged
to the Doctor for his attention to them.

My affectionat Compliments attend good Mr. Morly, and my love
your dear little folks who have a right to it. I am glad the salt water
has been of Service to Miss Evance. I hope it will quite restore her.
Pray pay my best Compliments and thanks to all my friends, particuarly for their goodness to my children. Asure Mr. Keat[21] and

Library of Congress copybook that is not included in the letterbook. Since the
copybook is very neat, containing no inserted words, the assumption is that Eliza
used the letterbook to draft her letters, and in the other book made an exact copy
of what she had written to send.

21. A friend of the Pinckneys in Surrey, George Keate was a poet, naturalist,
antiquary, and artist. For some years he lived at Geneva, where he was an intimate
of Voltaire. His best-known work was the *Account of the Pelew Islands*, printed
in 1788. See William P. Courtney, "Keate, George (1729–1797)," *DNB*; Ravenel,
Eliza Pinckney, p. 222.

Mr. Bridgen, when you see them, of the grateful Sence I have of their friendly Notice of my dear boys, and would have answered their letters now but chuse rather to do it by a more certain opportunity. The books and breef from Mr. Bridgen came in very good order. H. P. joyns in thanks for them, and will answer his obliging letter in a short time.

The Childrens bills I think unexceptionable. My little fellows Bath Expences I expect in the next. I in my last desired you would allow them to give somthing to your Servants at holiday time. I am sorry they did not the last year.

My Compliments to Mr. R.[22] and tell him his little Daughter grows a fine girl and is taken much care off.

Adieu, dear Madm. Asure my dear Children of my blessing and believe me

Yr. truely affectionate as well as obliged friend
and humble Servt.
E. Pinckney

[To Mr. Morly]
Dr. Sir   Crs. Town, July 16th, 1759
I cant help sending you a line by Ball tho' I have wrote you so often lately, which letters I hope you have received, particularly those by Mrs. W[right], Capt. Man, and Mr. Parnham with the bills. I most heartily thank you for yours by Ball and particularly for your note on the outside of my dear Charles' of the 7th April informing me my dear little Tomm was returned well from Bath. I know you can feel for others and must know what a mother in my situation feels at such a distance from her beloved children, therefore am persuaded you will give me the Comfort of a line if tis but a single one as often as possible to inform me how they and their worthy friend Mr. M. does.

I have heard, tho' you dont mention it, of Mr. M. death whereby you have lost your Post here. I am greatly concerned at it; but this is a life [of] tryal and disapointment. Please God there is no extraordinary disapointment.

I shall remit you some more mony the beginning of the Winter. Pray pay my best respects to Mr. and Mrs. W. and family and

22. Probably Mr. Raven.

asure them Mr. D. has had great injustice done him; for he is ex-treamly fond and tender of his Lady and has ever been so. She is now pretty near lying inn.

Compliments to all our friends and blessing to my dear boys. H. P. begs to be remembered to you and them, and I am

Dr. Sir

Yr. most obliged and obedt.

Servt.

E. Pinckney

Be so [good] to tell Mr. Shubrick I
received his letter by Ball and shall
answer it by the next opportunity.

[To Charles Cotesworth Pinckney]

My dr. Crs.   Crs. Town, July 16th, 1759

You can as little conceive as I express the comfort it gave me to receive your letter of the 22nd March accompanyed by one from Mr. G[errard] of the 7th April wherein he informs me of your dear little brothers return from Bath well. Pray God Almighty preserve both your healths and make you good children; to be informed of which is the greatest Comfort I can injoy on this side Eternity.

Your sister received your very sensible and affectionate letter which she will answer very soon but postpones it for the same reason I shorten mine—the uncertainty of its reaching you as it goes by a single ship. This I give you as a reason for my writing a short letter, but I shall not accept it as a good excuse from you for not writing at all by single ships, for I am ever impatient to hear from you. I hope you have begun to learn to fence as your friends think 'twill be of Service to you. For you may be asured there is nothing in my power that can contribute to your and your dear brothers advantage in any shape but will chearfully be complyed with by your truely affec-tionate mother

E. Pinckney

My blessing attend my dear little fellow and your Sisters love, which accept your self; and tell him how much pleasure it gives his Mama to see his little scral if 'tis but in writing his name. I find Mr. Gerrard never received the Rice that was ordered him. I look upon my self in his debt for it and shall desire Mr. Morly in the next remittance

I make him to pay Mr. Gerrard the value of it. Pray my compliments to him and all our friends.

[To Mr. Morly]   Sept. 19th, 1759

How, Dr. Sir, shall I thank you sufficiently for leting me hear so often from my dear boys. 'Twas with the utmost gratitude and thankfulness I received your 4 letters by Capt Webb a few days since by way of Bristol. Could you guess the Comfort they give me and with what eager impatience I opened them, you would, I am sure, not repent the trouble you have in doing so charritable a work.

The first letter is the 29th May. I am greatly at a loss to understand a paragraph in the letter as I am quite a stranger to any thing between the Doctor and Col. B. The paragraph is as follows: "Doctor Kirk-patrick is very much obliged to you for mentioning that Col. Barnwels mony is ready for him."[23] My accidentally mentioning Col. B's mony being ready for him (Col. B) immediately after my message to the Doctor must have led to the mistake. I mentioned it for your satisfaction imagining you must know what I meant; but find I was too short. The affair was this: My dear Mr. P. received a sume of mony for Col. B. but as he was to leave England it was necessary he should give security for it. You were that Security. And I must now let you know how the matter stands; I had occation to apply that mony to other uses and the Col. was so good to give me time to pay it inn, but shall hope to pay the whole off this Winter.

I shall be very glad to have it in my power to serve Dr. Kirk-patrick in his affair with Col. B. If it is it will give me pleasure if he will command me. I beg my Compliments and best thanks to him on my dear Childrens account.

I received Mr. Davidsons note inclosed in yours of the 5th June. I my self forwarded a letter of Advice from my brother to him, but by what ship I have intirely forgot.

I thought my Nephew had acquainted you of the Receipt of the Coppy of my dear Mr. Pinckneys Will. I did not know there was any thing necessary to be returned to you as I have not yet looked into those papers, but shall now do it as soon as possible and send you what is Necessary by the first good opportunity.

23. Nathaniel Barnwell (1705–75), aide to General Oglethorpe in the Florida expedition of 1740. A. S. Salley, "Barnwell of South Carolina," *SCHM* 2 (1901): 51.

I am much obliged for the trouble you took with the Turtle, letters, &c., as well as for the letters I received from my good friends Mr. Edwards, Mr. Keate, Mrs. Onslow and Mrs. King—all which I shall answer by the first convoy from hence.

H P Joyns in Compliments to all friends.

Our last accounts from the Cherokees are more agreeable than any we have had [in] a great while.

I am hurryed for my letter and must conclude. And that Heaven may bless, preserve and reward you is the sincere prayer of

Dr. Sir

Yr. M. O[bliged] and O[bedient] St.

E. Pinckney

To Mr. Morly

Dr. Sir   Nov. 3rd, 1759

As I wrote to you the 19th of Septr. 'tis not necessary to trouble you again so soon, but I cant resist the temptation of writing to you by a Man of Warr which is to sail imediately unless there are Merchants enough that will be ready soon to go under her Convoy, and then she will make a longer stay.

The papers will inform you of our publick transactions and that The Governor with a body of men set out on Fryday, the 16th Octr. for the Cherokee Nation in order to obtain satisfaction for the murders commited by them and make a good peace at the head of an army, or take satisfaction by carrying the warr into their own Country. They have been very insolent and 'tis high time they were chastised.[24] Be so good to asure my dear boys we think our selves very safe in Crs. Town, or they may be frightened on the rumour of an Indian Warr.

My blessing attend them. They are continually in my thoughts

24. In 1759, after two years of Cherokee raids on the frontier, Governor William Henry Lyttelton planned a punitive expedition against the tribe and mustered fifteen hundred men. Hearing of these preparations, a large delegation of the tribe came to Charleston hoping to treat peaceably with the governor. He offered to let them return to their lands in safety escorted by his army, but when they reached the Congarees the Indians were arrested and imprisoned at Fort Prince George, a post on the upper banks of the Savannah near the Indian town of Keowee. David Ramsey, *History of South Carolina from Its First Settlement in 1670, to the Year 1808*, 2 vols. (Charleston, S.C., 1809), 1: 7, 95–96; Hayes Baker-Crothers, "Lyttelton, William Henry (Dec. 24, 1724–Sept. 14, 1808)," *DAB*; M. Eugene Sirmans, *Colonial South Carolina* (Chapel Hill, N.C., 1966), pp. 329–33.

and the constant subject of my prayers. I can't give them a greater proof of my affection than suffering this painful separation from them. My continuing here some time longer must be (with the Divine blessing on my Endeavours) so much for their interest that I am determined to be regardless of suffering in my own person to serve them in the best way I can; and while they have such tender friends as have hitherto taken care of them, I hope it will not be necessary for me to be with them imediately. I cant thank you too often, dear Sir, with good Mrs. Evance and Dr. Kirkpatric and my other friends for your goodness to my Children. It would give me great pleasure could I [in] any manner of way show you the sence I have of my obligation to you.

Be so good to forward the inclosed letters to Sir Richard Littleton and Miss Mackeartney as directed in the safest manner and place any Expence attending it to my account.[25]

I congratulate you on the taking of Quebec,[26] but shall my self more on hearing you and my dear boys are well by the fleet (which heaven grant I may); for there all my little remains of Earthly happiness is fixt, when my dear girl is joyned, who is, I thank God, a good child and well. She says she cant send her compliments to such an old Gentleman and good friend as Mr. Morly, and therefore begs I would give her duty to you.

My compliments to all friends and believe me

Dr. Sir

Yr. truly obliged and obedt. Servt.

E. Pinckney

Since the foregoing I inclose another
letter which I beg the favour you will
forward to Mrs. Onslow.
To Mr. Morly, inclosing one to Sir Richard Lyttleton, one to Miss Mackeartney, and one to Mrs. Onslow. Sent by the Trent man of Warr, Capt. Lindsay; but had them returned again—he not sailing

25. Sir Richard was Governor Lyttelton's brother, and Miss Mary Macartney of County Longford was the young lady the governor was to marry June 2, 1761. Apparently Mrs. Pinckney acted as intermediary for letters they did not wish sent through the Colonial Office. Ravenel, *Eliza Pinckney*, p. 195.

26. The capture of Quebec on September 13 was a signal triumph for the English and a decisive step in wresting Canada from the French. See Lawrence Henry Gipson, *The Great War for the Empire: The Victorious Years, 1758–1760* (New York, 1949).

to England imediately, and sent them to Messrs. Smith and Nutt to forward by the Brigantine Spy, William Lyford. Novr. 24th, 1759.

[To Mrs. Onslow]
Dr. Madm.   Crs. Town. Novr. 4th, 1759

Nothing but the heaviest affliction could have made me thus long neglect improving a corrispondance which I so much desired and had so industriously sought as yours. But as Heaven had blessed me so much beyond the common lot in one of the best and most valuable of men as well as the most partially tender and affectionate of husbands with whom I had passed more than 14 year in such harmony as nothing but the strongest reciprocal affection and friendship could produce, so my distress must naturally bear some proportion to the greatness of my former happiness when that Union was disolved by death; in spite of my utmost indeavours to sopport so severe a tryal with that resignation to the Will of the All Wise disposer of Events, which was my indispensible duty as a Christian and His creature, who had partaken so largely of his bounty as not for many years to have a petition to put up to The Divine Majesty (for my self) but for a continuance of the blessings I injoyed.

I received a most affectionate letter from my dear Mrs. Onslow dated June 22nd, 1758, which I never answered, yet she was kind enough to repeat the same Instance of her goodness to me the 30th April, 1759, for both which I thank you most sincerely. 'Tis an additional proof of your great good nature in doing so soon as well as your good sence in doing it at all. I say your good Sence for you must have wanted that penetration which I know you Mistress off could you have imputed my Silence to an indiference at hearing from you or to any thing but the real cause—not want of Inclination.

Be asured then, dear Madam, I share much in your happiness, and every addition to it will be an increase to my felicity as I am satisfied from your merrit as well as the constancy of my own disposition you must ever hold a considerable place in my esteem and affection. Therefore it will be great charity in you to send me a line as often as your leasure will permit.

I congratulate you most cordially on the Collonels promotion and on the arrival, health, and pleasing expectations you have of the dear little babe. May Heaven spare you both to see it brought up, and

[127]

grant you as much happiness as this uncertain state will admit off.

Poor Mrs. Tury! I am very sorry for her. The loss of her child, her husband absent and exposed to great danger, and her own bad health makes her case really pitiable. I truely simpathize with her. Pray tell her so. My particular Compliments and good wishes attend her and Colo. Onslow.

You oblige me much in giving me so particular an account of my Surry Neighbors. My Compliments to them all and particularly to those you know I most esteem.

We have just heard of the taking of Quebec on which I congratulate you. The news of it must reach you before this letter, as perhaps the news of our being ingaged here in an Indian Warr, which from the goodness of your heart must be some allay to the former good news. As to my own part, unconnected with those that are very dear to me, I have nither hopes nor fears, so perfectly stupid with regard to any thing that may happen to my self am I, that I am more like a thing petrified past feeling than one in fear of losing their scalp. However, 'tis a very serious affair and I hope for the sake of my own children and friends in particular as well as the people in general that the Almighty will protect us in safety and give success to our Gov's Endeavours to attain a firm and lasting peace. He is thought to have both courage and conduct, and both are very necessary in a Commander, expecially against these savage Enemys. He set out last week for the Cherokee nation to demand satisfaction at the head of an army for the Cruel murders they have commited on our back settlers. What the Event will be Heaven only knows. We hope a good and lasting peace.

Adieu, Dr. Madm. Believe me to be with great truth

Yr. most afte. and o. h. St.

E. Pinckney

Sent by the Brigantine Spy, Capt. Lyfor, by way of Bristol.

[To Mr. Keate]

Pardon, Good Sir, the seeming ingratitude of my long silence, occationed by the heaviest stroak of affliction that could be sopported by a poor mortal with life.

You, Sir, knew, esteemed, and loved, the valuable man I mourn!

You will then surely forgive my having thus long neglected to thank you for your many friendly offices to my dear children, nor take less notice of the innocent boys for their mothers fault, especially when you remember their fathers virtues and consider that such a union as ours could not be dissolved with a less shock than I sustained, and such a one as disabled me from doing any thing as I ought. If you upon a 5 years acquaintance loved and lament him, what must I do that knew him long and intimately! How high must he rise in my estimation, that knew his secret and retired as well as his more public virtues: His piety to his God, and numberless acts of benevolence and tenderness to his fellow creatures that no other less intimately connected with him could know.

I ever thought him the best of men, as such he had my highest regard; but how greatly he merrited that highth of affection I ever had for him is more than I can express, for 'tis impossible to say enough of the sweetness of his temper as well as the aimableness of his whole deportment. And this sweetness of temper and his good Sence added to his partiality and uncommon tenderness and affection for me produced a harmony between us which never was interrupted by the least domestick Jarr, or one word in anger the whole time (for more than 14 year) I was his happy wife.

What shall I say to you to give you a true Idea of your worthy departed friend? I cant find words to convey the aimable light I ever did, now do, and would have all the world see him inn. Truth obliges [me] to say, when I devest my self of all partiallity, that he was the tenderest, most affectionate, and best of husbands, fathers and friends, and equally good in every connection of life. Justice demands thus farr and leaves nothing for love and gratitude, those magnifiers of the beloved object, to heighten.

With great gratitude and pleasure I received your most humain and friendly letters of the 27th of Febr. and 20th July. They confirmed me in what I before experienced—that the tenderness and condolence of friendship soften and aleviate, tho' nothing but the Divine Hand that gave the blow can heal the wound that is made in my afflicted heart.

Tho I have not before told you so, I have thanked you a thousand times and prayed to Heaven to bless and reward you for your goodness to my children. My worthy friends Mr. Morly and Mrs. Evance have given me the comfort to inform me of the many repeated kind notices you have taken of my poor dear boys—as well as the dear little creatures themselves. 'Tis Generous and kind in you, Sir, to countenance those dear remains of your deceased friend, young, in-experience[d], fatherless, and in a strange Country as they are. They stand in great need of the friendship they receive from you and a few more such valuable friends, which Heaven has blessed them with. I hope they will always act in such a manner to deserve your esteem, as far as such tender years is capable. I make no doubt you will be so good to add to all your other kindness that of your councel and advice, and may the Almighty in whose Hand is every blessing restore you a hundred fold in such blessings as you stand most in need off for all your goodness to my dear children, and for the comfort you thereby give to an afflicted parent separated at such a painful distance from those darlings of her heart.

I received yours of the 11th June, 1758, to My beloved Mr. Pinckney. It soon grew wet with tears and brought to my remembrance the happy hours when we used to read together entertaining letters in your own agreeable manner from deferent parts of Europe to your friends at Riply, and made me then make, as I often do, the meloncholy applica[tion] of those lines in Dr. Young to my self. He says, speaking of thoughts:

> Strays Wretched Rover! o're the pleasing past
> In quest of wretchedness preversly strays;
> And finds all desart now; and meets the Ghost
> Of my departed joys, a Numerous train!
> I rue the riches of my former fate;
> Sweet comfort's blasted clusters make me sigh.
> I tremble at the blessings once so dear
> And every pleasure pains me to the heart.[27]

I am surprized when I look back at the length of my letter and all on my own meloncholy concerns.

H P. is a little piqued at your soposing she has almost forgot you. She desires me to ask you

Memdm. Not time to Coppy it fully.

---

27. From "The Complaint: Night the First," by the contemporary poet Edward Young (1683–1765). Here again the author quotes from memory, changing one of the lines from "Sweet comfort's blasted clusters I lament."

Memdm. Decr. 1759. Wrote to his Excellency Gov. Lyttleton to the Cheerookees, and informed him I had forwarded 2 of his letters to England by the Brigantine Spy, Capt. Lyford, to Bristol.

1760

[To Dr. Kirk Patrick]
Sir   Febr. 1760

Nothing less than the meloncholy excuse I have to plead can intitle me to your pardon for having thus long neglected to write to you and thank you as I have done in my own mind a thousand and a thousand times for your care off and kindness to my poor dear boys in whom with their dear Sister is centered all the happiness I have or desire upon Earth.

Your favour of the 11th Septr. I duely received and am gratly obliged to you for that Instance of your good nature and regard for me and mine, particularly for your friendly and pius advice in my present distressful situation. Heaven only knows how much I have endeavoured to take it: To drink the bitter cup and resign my self to the Divine Will. But I know how ill I have acquited my self in the great tryal and how little I deserve the Compliments you are pleased to make me, tho' consious of the duty I owe to the almighty Sovereign, as the Supream and all Wise disposer of Events as well as the gratitude I owe Him for those blessings that remain, and especially for having injoyed the greatest so long—for none of his creatures have tasted more largly of his bounty than I. I now find to my Sorrow how little truely Christian fortitude I have possessed. All I can say in excuse for my self—if it is not rather an agravition of the guilt than an excuse—is that the Almighty had blessed me beyond the common lott! Had blessed me with one of the best and most aimable of men.

I knew the sincerity of his heart, his private and retired as well as his more public virtues. Therefore, tho' many knew him well, none knew him so intimately as my self; so none can so fully know the valuable man I lament, and consiquently how great the resolution required to soport his removal. Besides his other aimable qualities, the sweetness of his natural disposition (was as I never knew in any other) and his partial affection and tenderness to me was so great

[131]

that I must be the most ungratful of wretches or the best of Christians to feel less than I do. I had as great an affection for him as ever filled the human heart; that, with his virtues and partiallity to me, produced a union as great as ever existed between mortels, nor could it be disolved with a less shock than I sustained, great as it was and greater than I thought I could have lived under! The pity and tenderness of friends and Phisicians on one hand, self flattered on the other, make the stroak sudden and unexpected to me, not to him. His Conduct upon his arrival here was truely great and Christian, and Heaven seemed to have fitted him for the world he was soon to be removed too. He continued well above a month after his arrival, was then seized with Rhumatic pains and upon being first taken told me he did not expect to live, but blessed his God for giving him such a composed mind and said he was intirely resigned to his Will; that upon mine and his childrens account he wished to live, otherwise he would prefer puting off that frail body of pain and trusted in his Saviour for a better life; but from hence forth desired to have no Will of his own but to be intirely resigned to the Divine Will. He continued ill 3 weeks, and I have reason to think suffered more anguish at parting with his unhappy wife than at the separation of soul and body; for that God whom he loved and served with sincerity soported him wonderfully in this trying hour, strengthened his faith, composed his mind; and in spite of pain and weakness he was during his whole sickness the most patient, thankful and resigned soul and great example of Xtian fortitude that could possibly be. I cant be more particular or proceed on this too tender subject. Pardon, Good Sir, thus far; 'tis weak, tho' some relief to indulge a mind oppressed with sorrow by giving it utterance. And 'tis unkind to make our friends suffer with us, but your own humanity and good nature has drawn it upon you. You must thank that and excuse me.

You give me great comfort by teling me you saw my dear boys so lately well, and that my dear little Tommys health is so perfectly restored. The apprehension of the contrary has given me many anxious hours. You that are your self a father can feel for me. I love them tenderly as they are my own children, but much more as they are the remains of my beloved husband. I therefore intreat you, Good Sir, to continue your friendship to them, councel and advise them, when you have opportunity, how they ought to conduct themselves. 'Tis a charitable work indeed to lead children, especially fatherless ones, in the paths of Virtue and religion. As a Phisician, I depend on your care, and though my gratitude must be for ever due for your attention to either their bodys or minds—as I can never sufficiently repay the obligation to them that are kind to my children—yet you may be asured I shall not be unmindful of what is in my power, but cheerfully and thankfully pay by the hand of my friend Mr. Morly (what ever you think reasonable) to whom I now write and beg the favour of him to present you with 6 Guineas; not that I think that sufficient for the trouble you have had tho' you modestly charge but 2, but to show you I have not quite forgot it. My dear Mr. P. did not intend what you received from him and which you now mention to be accoun[t]ed for, but as a retainer on the childrens account, used in the phisical way, nor was it so much as he intended had he not met with some disapointments before he left London.

Harriott is greatly obliged for your kind remembrance of her. She is, I thank God, a good child, has had hitherto a fine state of health and grows tall.

You obligingly enquire when we return to England. I wish I could with any certainty fix a time for, though all countrys are now to me alike nor would I take the pains to cross again the Ocean for the best fortune in England. I have such inducements for coming that when I can prudently leave this Country and have fixt a sume in England to soport my self and children in a retired, comfortable, and decent way—not in a ostentatious or vain one, for I have no ambitious views of any sort—nither fatigue, or suffering any thing in my own person, shall detain me longer from them for my heart bleeds at our separation. 'Tis no paradox to say nothing but the greatness of my affection keeps me from them, as it appears to me and my friends here that it will (with the Divine blessing) be much to their advantage for me to continue here a couple of year longer; and when the question is whether I shall please my self or do them real service I should be inexcuseable to hesitate a moment.

Long before now Mr. Morly must have set you right about the blunder of Colo. B.'s mony.

It can never be out of date to acknowledge obligations tho' it may be long before one can have an opportunity of doing so. I therefore most gratfully acknowledge the receipt of your Joynt letter to my dear Mr. Pinckney and my self of the 26th of July, 1758. I very sincerely congratulate you on the great success you have lately had in the inocculation, and Mr. Corbet on his recovery of Le herps Fine.[28] You oblige me much by informing me of any feliciety that happens to my friends and acquaintance; indeed it is the only pleasure I now have any relish for, and I am not so wholly ingrossed by my own meloncholy concerns to be quite insensible of the pleasure that results from hearing of the happiness of others.

I have endeavoured dureing my writing this to forget I am writing to a man of witt and learning and consider my self only as conversing with the Compasionate friend, or should be ashamed to send you this tedious incorrect Scrale. I wish to be intelligible (you and Mr. Morly know I am not always so). 'Tis all I aim at or can pretend too at any time, and I have now a more confused head than ever. Notwithstanding which, it must be sufficiently clear to you as well as me that I am
Sir
Your most obliged and most obedt. Servant
E. Pinckney

[To Mr. Gerrard]   [c. February, 1760]
I am greatly obliged to you, Good Sir, for your favour of the 15th and 25th of Novr. 1758. The justice you do to my dear Mr. Pinckneys memory in applying those beautiful passages of Job to him, and the friendly and respectful tenderness with which you speak of him gives me sincere pleasure and satisfaction and convinces me that you really knew him. You have given him a great and good character, and give me leave to asure you tis a just one without exaggeration or mistake. Sacred be his ashes and his memory, beloved by every good man. My affection and gratitude can never cease unless I cease to be.

I cant be sufficiently thankful to you for your care and tenderness of my dear boys, particularly for the tender regard you shewed them when the afflicting news of their irreparable loss arrived. I should be very miserable could I have any doubt of your care either of their bodys or minds but which I do asure you, Sir, I have not the least apprehension off. I have indeed many heart akes for my dear little Tomm from the tenderness of his constitution (not from any want of care tho' I know a great deal is required to so tender a child),

28. Herpes is an acute skin disease. *Fine* could have the meaning of an extreme case.

but I hope my compassionate creator will pity my sufferings and restore and establish him in perfect health and preserve him and those other valuable remains of my beloved husband to my latest hour and many comfortable years beyond it.

I duly received your favours of the 7th of Septr. and 7th of April, 1759. The account you give me of my dear boys gives me the greatest comfort. There is no pleasure I can injoy upon Earth like hearing that they are well and good children except being near them, a happy witness of all those virtues which you are so good to ascribe to them.

I am very much concerned for the treatment you have mett with from some whom we recommended, and far from thinking you are at all obliged to me for taking all the pains in my power to do you justice, you certainly have a right to it, which makes it no merit in me. Could I do you any real service it would give me more pleasure than you could possibly receive from any such service. And I hope to live to convince you by every way in my power how much you have obliged me by your care and tenderness to my children.

You have been too modest never to mention you did not receive the Rice designed you in August 1748 [sic]. I now write to my good friend Mr. Morly and beg the favour of him to pay you the full value in mony.

I am very glad Charles wrote to good Mrs. Figg. I received all her letters, but my mind has been in such a strange situation, some times overwhelmed with meloncholy on my unspeakable loss, at other times much ingaged and hurried with puting things here in order and I hope on a better footing than when we were in England, that I have not been able to write to her, tho' I love and value her for her own merit as well as for her great affection to my beloved Mr. Pinckney.

I hope this will also serve as an apoligy for my so long omitting to answer the above mentioned obliging letters of yours.

I should have wrote to Mr. Baron imediately upon the receipt of yours but he was then dangerously ill, I heard.[29] If he recovered he would be in town as soon as he was able to come so far when I intended to have expostulated with him on the ungrateful usage you have received from him but as I have waited long in vain I shall now send to him and indeavour to conclude the affair I hope amicably but if it cant be done in that way it must in the other.

29. This paragraph and the following one are crossed through in the manuscript, apparently deleted at the time the postscript was added.

I shall write to you again by the fleet when I hope to give you a satisfactory account.ˣ

Pray pay my best respects and thanks to Mr. and Mrs. Watson for their kindness to my children and to all our other friends that are so. My love and Compliments to Master Draytons and Mrs. Greene. I received Master Draytons kind and pretty letters which I shall answer by this fleet. They may always be assured of my affectionate regard.

My blessing and prayers ever attend my dear Children. I am much pleased with their letters. Charles has long wrote well, but no body but my self will believe that Tomm wrote one of those signed with his name. The writing is so much beyond what they think a child of his age capable [of], but I know his brother wrote as well at that age. And tell my dear little man I dont imagine he will come short of his brother or any body else in any thing that is good or laudable.

Pray Heaven preserve them and reward you for all your goodness to them, which is the sincere prayer of

Sir

Your most obliged and obedt. Servt.

E. Pinckney

I return your letter to Mr. Barron.

ˣ When I received your Power of Attorney poor Mr. B[aron] was dangerously ill, of which illness he soon after died. I am told his circumstances were bad, [so] that I doubt whether you would have been better off had you been earlier. I have put the affair in my Nephews hands, and if there is anything to be got he will do his utmost to secure your debt.

[To Miss Varier]   Febr. 1760

The great distance between us, My Dear Madam, and the few good opportunities of sending letters to England has been an interruption to a more frequent Corrispondance with my best beloved and most valued friends in England (among the first of which I shall ever with justice place your family.) 'Tis the greater mortification to me as the hearing that my friends are well and happy is all that now gives me real pleasure in this world. Your favour of the 15th Feb, 1759, I duely received. It was as kind as it was sensible. The friendly consolations of a simpathizing friend is balm to a wounded

[136]

mind, and the humain attempts to comfort the afflicted a work of true Christian charity, and most grateful to those that receive it. I must with gratitude acknowledge I have experienced the greatest tenderness from all my friends, and as many aleviating circumstances attended my great tryal as I could have had.

I beg that you, dear Madam, and My worthy friend Mr. Edwards will accept my most grateful acknowledgment for the kind part you have acted by me and mine; and may He who alone is able to reward you as such actions deserve repay it with every blessing both spiritual and temporal.

My dear children as well as their Master have informed me of Several instances of your goodness to them since we left England. I hope you will add one more to the many they have received, which is to reprove them if ever you know them to do any thing wrong—for heedlessness and inadvertence is almost inseperable from youth.

Lady Mary Drayton, who you have some knowledge off, has lately laid inn of a fine boy.[30] Her Sister Lady Ann Mackenzie,[31] a pius sensible young woman, has been so good to stay chiefly with me ever since I came home.

NB. not time to finish the Coppy.

The Honble. Mrs. King

My dear Madm.   Febr. 1760

The ill state of yours and Mr. Kings health which I learned by your favour of the 31st May by way of Bristol was an alay to the pleasure I always injoy at receiving a letter from you; but I was happily relieved from the pain which I felt for some months on your account by your very obliging letter of the 25th July by which I perceived you were able to go abroad. How very kind you are, dear madam, in mentioning my dear boys so particularly and how flattering to a parents' partiallity.

Your writing me a second letter, the first unanswered is really like your self, above every thing that is little and trifleing. I hope you

30. Thomas Drayton (1759–1801) was born October 17. Taylor, "The Draytons of South Carolina," p. 8.

31. She married in turn Edmond Atkin, superintendent of Indian Affairs, and Dr. John Murray, who owned property on the upper Ashley. A. S. Salley, ed., *Marriage Notices in the South Carolina Gazette and Its Successors (1732–1801)* (Albany, N.Y., 1902), p. 26; Henry A. M. Smith, "The Upper Ashley; and the Mutations of Families," *SCHM* 20 (1919): 172–73.

know me well enough to be asured I can never be wanting in respect or affection to a Lady I have and always had so high an oppinion off and so many obligations to as to you.

I lament good Mr. Weston. He was indeed in years, but every year of a good mans life (especially when the sand is almost run and we know we cant long injoy them) is precious to their friends and acquaintance.

You repeatedly desire I would mention what you could send me from your part of the world that would be agreeable; in anwser to which give me leave to asure you there is nothing you could send me from England that would be half so agreeable as a letter now and then. Besides our Climate is such and the Masters of ships so careless it would be to little purpose to give our friends trouble.

I am as much obliged to Mr. King for the beer as if I had received it. It would have stood no chance had it come last year. Our Summer was excissive hott and they generally are, so that unless there should be a good opportunity with Convoy after Sept., there is no probability of our geting it safe; if there should be such, I beg Mr. King will not be too liberal. A small quantity will be sufficient.

My affectionate Compliments attend both Miss Kings, and my particular thanks to Miss King for the trouble she took about the Riply house. Be so good to remember me to Miss Brodricks when you see them. Poor young ladies! I pity them very much. They have lost a tender, good parent; but submission is our indispensible duty.

There is so little chance of letters by single ships geting safe, I am obliged to trouble one friend to tell another I have wrote to them, which is the case at present. I must beg the favour of you when you see Mrs. Onslow to make my best Compliments to her and inform her I wrote to her in Nov. last by the Spy, Capt Lyford, to Bristol, inclosed to Mr. Morly. If it has miscarried she must think me most ungrateful and I have too much regard for her to suffer in her oppinion without being uneasey.

Gov. Lyttelton with our army are safely returned from their Cherokee Expedition, where they went to demand satisfaction for the murders commited on our people—the first Army that ever attempted to go into that wild Country. They had been very insolent and commited several Murders and Outrages in our back settlements, nor ever expected white men would have resolution enough to march up their Mountains. Mr. Lyttelton has acted with great spirit and conduct and gained much honour in the affair, and obtained from them what Indians never before granted: such of the murderers as they could then take and Hostages for the rest till they could be taken.[32] If you have any curiosity to know more particulars Mr. Morly to whom I inclose it can furnish you with the Carolina Gazett.

I beg you will accept and try a few of our Myrtle Seed. Our Winters are sometimes very cold. They grow in the woods and are never hurt.

Memorandum. Have not time to Coppy the whole letter. Informed Mrs. King how to get the wax from the berrys and that I chuse to send a few seed at a time fresh, rather than wait to get a compleat collection as there might not then be an opportunity till they were too old.

Memdum. Wrote to Mr. Morly in Feb., 1760, by Capt. Cramp, and Lambert Tree, inclosing Several letters, Viz.: one to Mrs. King, one to Miss Lyttelton, three to Miss Mackeartney, one to Mr. Keat, one to Miss Varier, one to Dr. Kirk-patrick, one to Mr. Gerrard.

Crs. Town, So. Carolina, March 12th, 1760

[To Vigorous Edwards]

Many, Many Thanks, my Dear and Worthy friend, for your letter of the 29th May, 1759, the piety and friendliness of which was a comfort and pleasure to me.

May the Almighty long continue that health to you [which you] inform me you have injoyed since we left England, and be assured I account it among the first of temporal blessings to know that the much valued friends of my beloved Mr. Pinckney are well and happy; I mean as much so as this uncertain state will admit—a very

---

32. Lyttelton decided to hold twenty-four Indians hostage at Fort Prince George until an equal number of trouble-making Indians were surrendered to him, an action D. D. Wallace has called "immoral and stupid." Twenty-three Indian murderers were handed over to Lyttelton. Lyttelton left twenty-one hostages at the Fort until even more Indians were surrendered. When enraged Indians retaliated by raiding settlements along the South Carolina frontier and even attacked Fort Prince George on February 14, the garrison murdered the hostages. Historians have criticized Lyttelton for his handling of the Cherokee situation, but he received a royal welcome when he returned to Charleston on January 8, 1760. David D. Wallace, *South Carolina: A Short History, 1520–1944* (Columbia, S.C., 1961), pp. 177–79; Sirmans, *Colonial South Carolina*, pp. 333–34.

mixt one at best, and not designed for our home. That we are not to stay here always is indeed one of the happiest considerations for life drags on but heavily when those dearest to us on Earth are removed. I have found it so and experienced the deferent Vicisitudes; for I have shared largly of the Divine Bounty and suffered most exquisitely under His Correcting Hand by the removal of my [husband]. The Goodness was His, the suffering in a great measure of my own making; for happiness is so closely connected with religion and Virtue that so far as we deviate from one we lose the other. We are not to fix our happiness on any thing beneath the supream Good nor Idolize the best man on Earth, or pay dearly for it. Nor must we express real and lasting comfort to the torn heart till it returns to its duty by patience and submission to The Infinitely good as well as Wise disposer of all Events. To Him I desire to be resigned in all things, and To Him I recommend my dear children and trust he will preserve them from all evil, natural and moral. I know 'tis only in His protection they can be safe whether they are with me or from me—and in that they are, be they where they will. Yet so weak am I, that my heart bleeds at our separation and I long more than I can express to be with them.

Accept Good Sir, my grateful acknowledgments for your friendship and notice of them and for mentioning them so particularly to me in your letter.

Be so good to pay my most respectful Compliments to good Lady King, Lord King, and all the family; and inform Mrs. King I did my self the honour to write to her by the last ships, inclosed to Mr. Morly, and at the same time wrote to Miss Varier to whom pray pay my affectionate Compliments.

The Cheerokee Indians have been very insolent the last year and commited many murders on our back Settlements; and in all probability we should by this time have been engaged in an Indian War, the most dreadful of all war, had our Gov. acted with less judgment and resolution. He marched an army up into their Country and demanded satisfaction at the head of it for the Murders they had commited or would then take it. They were much alarmed, pretended it was only some of their hot headed young men, and not aproved by the whole; would have excused giving the Criminals up by saying they could not be found, but after some time brought some of them in and gave Hostages for the rest. A treaty of peace and friendship was concluded upon it, and I hope and we have great reason to think, we are upon a better footing with those people than we have been many years.[33]

Pray remember me to Mr. and Mrs. Bonny and all our good Neighbors. I am very sorry the number of them is reduced by the loss of good Mr. Weston and Mrs. Brodrick.

Harriott desires her duty to you and love to Miss Varier. She is, I thank God, a very promising good Child, injoys a fine state of health and grows tall.

Adieu, dear Sir, I wish much to converse with you verbally. Till I am able to do that, give me the satisfaction of hearing from you. 'Tis a very great one, for I am, very sincerely

Yr. affecte. as well as most
obliged and obedt. Servt.
E. Pinckney

To Vigorous Edwards, Esqr., aged 88
Sent by Mr. T. Smith

[To Master MacKenzie]
Sir

Your very obliging and polite letter of the 10th o' April deserved a speedier acknowledgment than I have been able to pay, accationed by a succession of circumstances to tedious to trouble you with—the principal ones bad health and spirrits since my great misfortune. But as I am now in better health than I have been a great while I endeavour to pay my debts of gratitude as far as is in my power. Accept then, Sir, my best thanks for your notice of my dear boys. It was extreamly obliging to go to see them. I know it must cheer their little hearts and make them very happy.

You are not at all indebted for any civilities received from us here. You know the melloncholy situation we were in by my dear Mr. Pinckneys declining health before we could get into a house of our own, which prevented those civilities we should certainly have payd.

---

33. Actually the rejoicing over Lyttelton's seeming triumph was scarcely ended before news came that hostilities had been renewed by the Cherokees. Sirmans, *Colonial South Carolina*, p. 334. The Cherokee viewpoint is nicely developed in David H. Corkran, *The Cherokee Frontier: Conflict and Survival, 1740–1762* (Norman, Okla., 1962).

Your Little fellow traveller, who is very much obliged to you for your kind remembrance of her, is, I thank God, perfectly well, has her usual spirrits, and grows tall. She will write to you her self and return you thanks for the books you were so good to send her.[x]

I am much obliged to you for the fine beef. It was extreamly good and admired by every body that see it.

[x] She is fond of learning, and I indulge her in it. It shall not be my fault if she roams abroad for amusement, as I believe 'tis want of knowing how to imploy themselves agreeably that make many women too fond of going abroad.

My dear Children   March [1760]

The fleet being just upon sailing (and I lately so hurry'd about other matters that I began late to write to England) will prevent my writing to you so fully as my inclination leads me to do and as your pretty letters of the [blank] demand. Be asured I shall answer them more particularly very soon. In the meantime I hope my dear Charles will readily acquiesce in changing his school as the air of Camberwell does not agree with his dear little brother. I know your grateful and affectionate temper and know it will give you a good deal of pain to leave Mr. Gerrard, but your affection to your brother and the defference you will, I know, always pay to the judgment of our friends in England who advise it and can more properly judge of matters than I can at this distance. Rely intirely on their friendship and judgement in the case—which I hope will make you the more readily give up your own judgment and inclination to theirs.

I dont yet know where you are fixt or would write to your Master to whom pray pay my Compliments and inform him so. My Lady Carew was so good to inform me you wrote to me the day before she did in Dec. last, but your letters are not yet come to hand. I impatiently expect them. You know, my dearest boys, how near my heart you lie, and that all the happiness I have upon Earth is centered in you and your dear Sister. Let me then hear from you as often as possible if 'tis but 2 lines to say you are both well.

And now, my dear little Tomm, your Mama has one petition to make to you. 'Tis to think of her frequently when you are tempted to eat unripe or too much fruit. If you knew how much anguish I suffer upon every apprehension of your want of health I am sure you would punish your self to give me this consolation. You and your dear brother are the dayly—almost hourly—subject of my prayer and thoughts. Do not therefore forget to take care of your selves and joyn with me in imploring the Divine blessing upon you.

Your Sister is, I thank God, well and will write to you if the ships stay a day or two longer. Be good children, mind your learning, and love one another; and that the Almighty will bless you both with your dear Sister, protect and guide you and make you his children is the most devout petition that is put up to Heaven by, my dear boys,

Your ever affectionate Mother
Eliza. Pinckney

By Mr. T. Smith

[To Mr. Morly]
Dear Sir   March 14th, 1760
Since mine of the 3rd o' Nov. by the Brig Spy, Capt. Lyford, to Bristol inclosing 3 letters, one to Sir Richard Lyttleton, one to Miss McCartney, and one to Mr. Onslow, I received your favour of the 31st of Aug. inclosing Coppys of 3 I had before received dated the 29th May, 5th June and 17th July, for all which pray accept my most grateful thanks.

I was in hopes to have inclosed you a bill for a hundred pound sterling by the last ships but could not prevail on the person I was to have them from to draw before the fleet sailed. I now inclose them and beg the favour as soon as you receive it to present Doctor K with 6 Guineas for his attendance on my children, and Mr. Gerrard with the value in lieu of a barrel of Rice which he ought to have had long ago, and Miss Bartlett the ramainder of the Legacy of ten pound.[34] I am very much obliged to you for what you advanced her of it before. It was very kind and you may be sure what I must approve.

The beginning of this Year there was such a fine prospect on our plantations of a great Crop that I was hopeful of clearing all the mony that was due upon the Estate, but the great drought in most parts of the Country, such as I never remember here, disapointed

---

34. Charles Pinckney's will provided for ten pounds per annum to his first wife's sister, Mrs. Sarah Bartlett of London, and "ten guineas for mourning" to Miss Mary Bartlett. Webber, "Pinckney Family of South Carolina," p. 19.

those expectations so much that all that we make from the planting interest will hardly defray the charges of the plantations. And upon our arrival here we found they wanted but every thing and [were] every way in bad order, with ignorant or dishonest Over Seers.

My Nephew had no management of the planting interest, and my brother who had, by a stroak of the palsey, had been long incapable of all business.[35] I thank God there is now a good prospect of things being deferently conducted. I have prevailed upon a conscientious good man (who by his industry and honesty has raised a fine fortune for 2 orphan children my dear Mr. Pinckney was guardian too) to undertake the direction and inspection of the overseers. He is an excellent planter, a Dutchman, originally Servant and Overseer to Mr. Golightly, who has been much solicited to undertake for many Gentlemen; but as he has no family but a wife and is comfortable enough in his circumstances, refuses to do it for any but women and children that are not able to do it for themselves. So that if it please God to prosper us and grant good Seasons, I hope to clear all next year.

I find it requires great care, attention and activity to attend properly to a Carolina Estate, tho' but a moderate one, to do ones duty and make it turn to account, that I find I have as much business as I can go through of one sort or other. Perhaps 'tis better for me, and I believe it is. Had there not been a necessity for it, I might have sunk to the grave by this time in that Lethargy of stupidity which had seized me after my mind had been violently agitated by the greatest shock it ever felt. But a variety of imployment gives my thoughts a relief from melloncholy subjects, tho' 'tis but a temporary one, and gives me air and excercise, which I believe I should not have had resolution enough to take if I had not been roused to it by motives of duty and parental affection.

I have not yet proved the Will and am advised not to do it as it would be attended with much trouble in taking particular Inventery of every thing, the most minute, which must be returned upon oath; and the proving of it 'tis said is unnecessary as there is but little due from the Estate and no body to call me to account. And the Will it self must remain good and in force as it is a record. However if you think it best, I shall not mind the trouble but will still do it, as

35. William Pinckney was incapacitated by a paralytic stroke in 1758 but lived until 1766. Webber, "Pinckney Family of South Carolina," p. 17.

I would perform the Sacred trust to the utmost of my ability in every Tittle in the best manner I can.

I hope you received mine of the 19th Septr., acknowledging the receipt of yours that inclosed several from my other friends, the answers to some of which and some former ones I have last month and now trouble you with.

The long experience I have—and still daily have—of the friendly part you take in our concerns has occationed you the trouble of so long a letter. Be so good to pay my Compliments and thanks to Mr. Chatfield for his management of our little affairs at Riply and for the trouble he and Mrs. Chatfield[36] are so good to give themselves to indulge my dear boys. I am really ashamed to give Mr. Chatfield so much trouble about the house. I should be much obliged to you to do for me what you think I should do in the case either to make him, as he is a man of business, an acknowledgment for the trouble by way of commissions or in what way you think best.

I wrote you a short letter in Febr. last in such a hurry that I kept no coppy by Capt. Cramp, and Coppy by Lambert Tree, inclosing several letters in each packet, Viz: one to Miss Lyttelton, 3 in two packets to Miss Mackartney, one to Mrs. King, one to Miss Varier, one to Mr. Keat, one to Dr. Kirkpatrick, and one to Mr. Gerrard.

Your favour of the 19 Novr. by way of Bristol gave me great pleasure as it informed me of my dear boys health. Indeed, Sir, 'tis not only friendly but really charitable to let me hear as often as you can from them. My heart bleeds at our separation but it must be so for a time.

The day after I wrote the foregoing I received your favour of the 31st of Decr. by Capt. Rains and another from my friend Mrs. Evance by the same opportunity; but none from Dr. Kirk-patrick or my children as you imagined I should. You may be sure, My good Sir, that I acquiesce in every thing you and my other friends do with regard to my children. You are upon the spot and must be better judges of their care than I possibly can be at this distance. The prospect of the change of air's establishing my dear little babes health is of it self a sufficient reason for removing him and I should not chuse to have the brothers separated if I could help it. I have always heard

36. Several recipes from Mrs. Chatfield are given in the *Eliza Lucas Pinckney Recipe Book, 1756*. Other English acquaintances supplied entries: Mrs. Blakeney, Mrs. King, and Miss Broderick.

a great character of Harrow school, but if that at Kensington is equally good as there is fewer scholars and tis nearer London and the air aproved for tender constitutions I should think that would be to be prefered.[37]

You are very good to have given your self so much trouble about the 30 £ bill on Mr. Davison. My poor brother[38] has been very ill many months, so that matter must rest for the present.

My best Compliments to the D. and Mrs. E.

I am

I received Lady C. letter
Sent this letter by Mr. T. Smith, inclosing bills for a hundred pound, and the Coppy by the Trent with a 2nd Set of bills.

[To Mrs. Evance]   March 15th, [17]60

With how much pleasure I receive your letters, My Dear friend, I wont attempt to say, and the comfort I have at hearing my dear children are well your own maternal heart can better conceive than I express. So far I can with great truth affirm that 'tis the greatest felicity I have upon Earth. In consiquence of this tender attachment I am under very frequent apprehensions for my dear, dear little Tomm from the tenderness of his constitution. Pray God Almighty bless and restore him. Mrs. King, Mr. Morly, etc., all inform me of your great care of and tenderness for him. You have obliged me, my dear friend, beyound all acknowledgement by your goodness to them. May the Almighty bless and reward you in sending every blessing both spiritual and temporal on you and yours, and enable me to convince you you have not bestowed the most acceptable of all services on an ungrateful heart. You make me very happy by the account you give me of my dear Charles.

I saw Mr. Raven the day he arrived.[39] I went every where in pursuit of him till I found him and had the satisfaction to hear from

37. Her sons moved to school at Kensington, a western borough of London which had a reputation for healthiness because of its gravel soil and pure atmosphere. William III, in fact, had resided there to ease his asthmatic symptoms. The school was located in the section of the village known as the Gravel Pits. See "Kensington," *Encyclopedia Britannica*, s.v.

38. William Pinckney, Eliza's brother-in-law.

39. John Raven was Mrs. Evance's brother.

him that you and all yours as well as my own children were well. He called once afterwards; I happened to be out. I imagine he has been in the Country and very busey or he would have let me seen him, since in all this time I had a hundred little Chit chat questions to ask him about you all.

How could that strange woman treat you so! You desire me not to be concerned at it; I really cant help being so and beg of you, my dear Madam, not to lay your self open to her ill usage to save me a little mony. I would much rather pay it than have my friend treated in an ungentile way.

I joyn very cordially with you in the great opinion you have of Mr. Gerrard. I am much concerned on his account and believe he has had great injustice done him. I know my self to be under great obbligations to him. He is, I verily believe, a good man, very capable of all he undertakes, and will do his utmost for my children. To his knowledge I am sure there will be no neglect, but if there should be any thing material with regard to their health, &c which he cant know I rely on your friendship in a thing of so much consiquence to me as to inform him of it; and if my dear little Creatures state of health should be too tender for a boarding school, will you, my dear Madam, extend your charity so far to take him home and let him go to an academy in London in the day and be with you at Nights till his health is mended. What ever you think proper to charge for his board I will with the greatest cheerfulness and thankfulness repay. If I can procure a bill of twenty pound to send you by this fleet I will do it; but if not now, as soon as I can.

A great cloud seems at present to hang over this province. We are continually insulted by the Indians on our back settlements, and a violent kind of small pox rages in Charles Town that almost puts a stop to all business.[40] Several of those I have to transact business

40. This epidemic, said to have been brought back by Governor Lyttelton's troops from the Indian country, was possibly the worst in Charleston's history, in spite of thousands of inoculations by physicians. On April 19, 1760, the SCG reported: "The Small-Pox may be now said to be pretty well over. . . . 'Tis computed that the Number of Persons who took the Disease by Inoculation and in the natural Way, in this Town, since the beginning of February last can fall little short of 6000; and that about 380 Whites (including a very considerable Number of Acadians and Soldiers) and 350 Negroes have died during the Progress of it." See also R. C. Aldredge, "Weather Observers and Observations at Charleston, South Carolina, 1670–1871," Year Book, City of Charleston, 1940 (Charleston, S.C., 1941), p. 200. Acadians men-

with are fled into the Country, but by the Divine blessing I hope a month or two will change the prospect. We expect shortly troops from Gen. Amherst,[41] which I trust will be able to manage these savage Enemies. And the small pox, as it does not spread in the Country, must be soon over for want of subjects.

I am now at Belmont to keep my people out of the way of the violent distemper for the poor blacks have died very fast even by inocculation. But the people in Charles Town were inocculation mad, I think I may call it, and rushed into it with such presipitation that I think it impossible they could have had either a proper preparation or attendance had there been 10 Doctors in town to one. The Doctors could not help it—the people would not be said nay.

We lose with this fleet our good Gov. Lyttelton. He goes home in the Trent man of warr before he goes to his Government at Jamaica.[42]

My sincere thanks to Mr. and Mrs. Watson.

Poor John Mott who was inocculated in England is now very bad with the small pox; it could never have taken then to be sure.[43]

I had but just finished the above when I received your favour of the 3rd Decr. by Capt. Rains, and beg leave to asure you, however great my oppinion of and partiallity to Mr. Gerrard, I absolutely aprove what you and my other friends have done in removing my children, if there were no other reason in the world for it but the air's not agreeing with Tommy. I always thought my self very much obliged to Mr. G for his care and tenderness to them and really think him too reasonable a man to wish them to continue when the circum-

tioned by the *Gazette* were part of the former French colonists scattered throughout the British Empire after 1755. See Ruth A. Hudnut and Hayes Baker-Crothers, "Acadian Transients in South Carolina," *American Historical Review* 43 (1938): 500–513.

41. Jeffrey Amherst in 1758 was given command of an expedition to attack the French in North America. After his direction of the capture of Louisbourg (July 16, 1758) and other successes, he was given chief command of all the forces in the war theater. In 1759 he played a major role in the capture of Crown Point and Ticonderoga, and in the march on Montreal in 1760. Shortly thereafter he was named governor general of British North America. See Henry M. Stephen, "Amherst, Jeffrey (1717–1797)," *DNB*. A more complete account of his career is J. C. Long, *Lord Jeffrey Amherst* (New York, 1933).

42. Lyttelton sailed for his new position on April 4, and went on to have a distinguished career as minister to Portugal and as an Irish peer. Baker-Crothers, "Lyttelton, William Henry," *DAB*.

43. Mr. Motte did recover from the smallpox according to Ravenel, *Eliza Pinckney*, p. 198.

stance of health is in the case. I would inlarge but the ships are so near sailing, and I must write a line to my dear boys, that I can only say I am

Your truely obliged and affecte.

E. Pinckney

My Compliments to the Lady at Kingston
March 18th, 1760
Memorandum. Had not time to Coppy fully this letter.
Inclosed it to Mr. Morly by Mr. T. Smith.

To George Morly, Esqr.
Dr. Sir   April [1760]
I wrote you so fully by Mr. Thos. Smith the 14th March and inclosed you a bill of Exchange for a hundred pound sterling drawn by Messrs. Smith and Nutt on William and Richard Baker, Esqs., with Several letters inclosed, and Coppy by the Trent man of warr with the 2nd bill that I shall not trouble you further at present, only to inclose you a 3rd of the same set of Bills by the Vernon to Poole and a letter to Miss Mackartney in Hanover square, which I doubt not you will forward in the best and speediest manner.

The small pox is, I thank God, much abated. Those that now have it have it most favourably; indeed few have it now but by innoculation.

Our Indian affairs are much in the same situation as 4th Apr. when the Trent sailed.

Be so good to pay my Compliments to all friends. My blessing to my dear boys. I long for [Capt.] Balls arrival to hear how they do and where they are placed.

Accept the most grateful thanks your self of
Dear Sir

Your most obliged and obedt. Servant

E. Pinckney

Coppy by Mr. Raven in Capt. Rains, June 4th.
PS. I inclose you a bill of Exchange for 30 £
sterling drawn by Messrs. DaCosta and Farr on
Mrs. Nicholson and Company. The first of the same
tennour and date is now aboard Capt. Barnes and sails this day.

[149]

[To Mr. Morly]   June 4th, 1760
Memdum. The following letter coppyed and sent by the St. Andrew, Capt. Moat, by whom I sent a trunk and inclose in this letter (to which I wrote a postscript longer than I have room to insert in this place) a 3rd bill of Exchange drawn by Messrs Da Costa and Farr on Mrs. Nicholson and Company for 30 £ Sterling, and a 2nd by Mr. Shirly drawn on John Biggin and Anthony Bacon, Esq., for Eighty six pound, 6 shillings and 8 d.

Dear Sir

I wrote you lately by the Vernon to Pool, inclosing another of the same sett of bills for 100 sterling sent by Mr. T. Smith and a letter to Miss Mackeartney in Hannover Square, since which time Capt. Ball is arrived by whom I received a Coppy of your favour of Dec. 31st, inclosing the account Current, the original received by Rains and acknowledged by the fleet in April. I am greatly obliged to you for the trouble you take with my dear children and hope Kensington will answer all our expectations. I have before wrote you fully on that subject. 'Tis impossible for me to write to Mr. Longmore now; I am so much hurry'd for my letter, but shall in a few days by Rains.

Be so good when you see Dr. Kirk patrick to deliver him the inclosed packet. I inclose a bill of Exchange for 30 £ St[erlin]g drawn by Messrs. Da Costa and Farr on Mrs. Nicholson and Company, 20 £ of which I beg when received you will present with my Compliments to Mrs. Evance; and I beg your acceptance of the other 10 to buy a ring in memory of your deceased friend, my dear and ever to be lamented Mr. Pinckney.

Charles's letters are full of gratitude to you. He tells me that your life may be spared to them is part of his dayly prayers. H. P. joyns in affectionate Compliments to you, with
Dr. Sir
Your affecte and obliged Servt.
E. Pinckney

I have beg'd the favour of Mr. Stone
to deliver you this at the Caroline
C[offee] House him self.

Dr. Sir   June 19th

I two days ago received your favours of the 31st March and 1st of April for which pray receive my most unfeigned thanks. Every letter of yours lays me under fresh obligations when the debt before was greater than I shall be ever able to pay. You make me happier than I have been [in] a great while by the account you give me of my dear childrens improved health by the change of air; tho' the Dr. writes me poor Charley had a little disorder upon him when he wrote but thought it would be of no great consiquence.

I most sincerely congratulate my self as well as you on your recovery. I was so happy not to hear of your illness till you were well again, which saved me much pain. May Heaven long preserve you to your friends.

Pray return my most grateful Compliments and thanks to good Mr. and Mrs. Middleton and Mr. Keat for their kind remembrance and countenance to my children. My Compliments also to Mrs. Brailsford.

[To Mrs. Evance]   June

My dear little Tomm very justly observes his Mama loves long letters. Yours, My dear Madam, are always the more agreeable for being so, and I am very much obliged to you for yours of the 2nd Jan. But was it so long that you could not say a word of your own little ones or do you think it intirely indefferent to me whether they are in the land of the living or not. Miss E. was in an indeferent state of health when we left England. I do not from you hear a word about her, nor how Mr. Evance goes on with his mercantile affairs. This is really unkind, therefore pray make it up to me in your next.

I send a small bill of Exchange by this opportunity to my good friend Mr. Morly and when received beg the favour of him to present you 20 £ with my best thanks. I wont attempt it because 'tis impossible for me to say how much I think my self obliged to you for your goodness to my children. Heaven only can reward you, and I doubt not will.

Your brother, Mr. J. Raven, who comes to England for his health will deliver you this. Poor Gentleman! I heartily wish he may recover and that he may not have delayed his voyage too long. He will give you a more particular account of our melloncholy affair here than I can by letter. Therefore I refer you to him.

The Almighty has delivered us from as great dangers, and I trust will still. His power and mercy are the same.

Pray pay my Compliments to Mr. and Mrs. Wright and thanks to Lord and Lady C[arew], Mr. and Mrs. Baker and all our friends who are so good to take notice of my poor dear children. I should be glad [if] they would go next time they are in London to pay their respects to Lord and Lady C.

Mr. Raven has been so good to take charge of my dear Mr. Pinckneys picture which I send to his children that the Idea of his person may not wear out of their Infant minds. I make no doubt they will venerate even his shadow and I dare say you will be so good to give it a place in your parlour for the present if 'tis not very inconvenient. I hope to send Mr. Morly another bill this summer, and when that is received I beg the favour of you to get a decent plain frame for it. When I am able I shall get it coppy'd by a better hand than could be got here.

By Mr. Raven.

[To Mrs. Evance]   June 19th, 1760
I received, My Dear Mrs. Evance's favour of the 29th Febr. and 3rd April with the seal open. Whether accationed by accident or curiosity I cant say, but as I love to think the best I can of people I will sopose the former; however 'tis of no great consiquence if 'tis the other. It may teach them the art of writing prettily and obligingly and show how capable women are both of friendship and business, and I am sure to find my account in what ever raises the reputation of my particular friends or my sex in general by the pleasure it gives me; thus I make my self amends for the impertinance of the over curious.

'Tis with the greatest pleasure I obey any of your Commands. I shall as soon as I return to town beg the favour of Mr. Cooper to let me see in order to chuse which of the houshould goods to send you, and I expect that will be before this ship sails. I write so early least I should by any accident be prevented, and leave my letter in town with a Trunk of my dear Mr. Pinckneys cloaths which I must trouble you with to have altered when you think proper for the dear

[152]

boys. They will not fitt his relations here that I should chuse to give them too.

Be so good to put Charles in mind of writing to his Uncle. I know it will give him pleasure. Poor man, he is in very much altered [condition] ever since he was so violently struck with the palsey.

I hope Mr. Keat has long ago received a letter from me dated last Jan. or Feb. I should have wrote to him long before but wanted spirrits not inclination. If my friends at a distance know how desireous I am of conversing with them, they would not give too great an incouragment to such an imp least I become troublesom. Indeed I should imploy most of the little time I have to spair that way did not my thoughts generally take so gloomy a turn as must give my friends pain rather than pleasure.

I am just going out of town for a little air and Excercise, having, I thank God, finished my superintendentcy over a little small pox Hospital, a very small one indeed as it did not consist of more than 15 patients, not as the Doctor was informed 200, which is more than our whole number. I lost one only—a valuable Carpenter who took it the natural way. Many poor wretches in the beginning I believe died for want of proper nursing.[44]

You rejoyce me much by the account you give me of the air agreeing so well with my dear boys, which happiness Mr. M[orley] and the Doctor have also communicated to me. I received both their letters as well as the childrens by Muir and Smith, which I have to answer by this ship, if not, as soon as possible.

I am much obliged for the present of China which Mrs. Cooper lately sent me. More fully I shall write you again soon. In the mean time Harriott joyns with me in grateful acknowledgements to you for your goodness to our darlings, in Compliments to Mr. E, and in love to all the dear little ones. And believe [me] to be what I truely am

Dr. Madm.
Yr. Affectionat and most obliged
and obedt. Servt.
E. Pinckney

I have directed the Trunk to the care of Mr. Shubrick, but as I am upwards of a hundred pound in his

44. This sentence is crossed out.

[153]

debt I must have recourse to my friend Mr. Morly
if [he] does not chuse to pay the freight.
By the St. Andrew, Capt. Moat. To be delivered
him by Mr. Neuville withe the trunk of cloths.

[To Mr. Morly]
Dear Sir   Belmont. July 19th, 1760
Having been some time in the Country I but just heard of these
ships sailing to-morrow to London, so that I shall not now be able
to write to my dear children or any of my friends but your self and
to Mrs. King to acknowledge the receipt of the very gentile present
she sent to Harriott by Capt. Muir, which box you were so good to
forward and he took great care off. I think my self obliged to him
tho' I have not had an opportunity to thank him.
    I now inclose you a 3rd bill drawn by Mr. Shirly on John Biggin
and Anthony Bacon, Esqs., in London. The two first of the same
tenor I hope you will have received before this can reach you.
    Be so good to forward the inclosed to Mrs. King.
    Our Indian affairs are in a poor way. Col. Mongomerie at the head
of 16 hundred men including rangers marched into the middle
Cherokee Towns and destroyed 5 towns, which raised the spirrits of
people much. But while we imagined he was proceeding to Fort
Loudon he began his march towards Charles Town in order to return to Genl. Amherst, in consiquence of whose orders 'tis said he
returns.[45] The Gov. by the desire of the assembly has sent to desire
his continuing in the nation. We impatiently wait his answer, as we
also do one to an express sent from hence to Genl. Amherst. We have
no doubt but the Creeks will soon joyn the Cherookees.

45. Lieutenant Colonel Archibald Montgomery's forces, the Highlanders and
Royal Scots, had arrived in Charleston on April 1, 1760. Joined by 350 provincial
troops, they destroyed the lower Cherokee towns in the present counties of Ander-
son, Pickens, and Oconee. Montgomery's brief campaign was annoying rather than
decisive. But the colonel's orders had been to strike a quick blow and then return to
Jeffrey Amherst and the Canadian campaign. He left four companies to protect the
frontier, but Montgomery's hasty retreat sealed the doom of Fort Loudoun, a post
of 200 men in the Upper Cherokees at the junction of the Little Tennessee and
Tellico rivers. Alexander Hewat, *Historical Account of South Carolina and Georgia*,
2 vols. (London, 1779), 1: 205; Wallace, *South Carolina: A Short History*, pp.
179–80; Sirmans, *Colonial South Carolina*, pp. 336–37; John R. Alden, *John Stuart
and the Southern Colonial Frontier . . . 1754–1775* (Ann Arbor, Mich., 1944), pp.
106–7.

We have an all powerfull and merciful Protector who governs all Events and that is the greatest of Comforts.

I am, with my blessing to my dear boys and Compliments where due,

Dr. Sir

[To Mrs. King]

Dr. Madm. Belmont. July 19th, 1760

I had the honour of yours of the 16th Febr. last with yours and the young ladies very gentile present to Harriott. Indeed, Madam, you are too good to us. Either of the three would have showed us the honour you do us in remembering us, expecially as there is such a risk of things being taken at this time. 'Tis a most compleat suit and universally admired. The fann I think a curiosity and the pompon the prettiest we ever saw. The little girl is quite happy, and the more so as they are the first that have reached this part of the world, so she has an opportunity of seting the fashion. I doubt whether she would part with them to purchase a peace with the Cherookees who are become extreamly troublesome to us. Nor have the highland troops under Col. Mongomery, sent by Genl. Amherst, done much more than exasperated the Indians to more cruel revenge. And they are now about to leave us to the mercy of these Barbarians.

I hope the good people of England wont give all their superfluous mony away to French prisoners and to build foreign churches, but reserve some for their poor fellow subjects in America. For if they go on to make new conquests in America and neglect the protection of their old Colonys, you may soon have importations of distressed people from the southwardmost part of North America to exercise their charity upon.

My most respectful Compliments wait on Mr. King. He obliges me very much in imploying me to get him some seeds of any kind we have here. [If] there is any in particular that may Escape me I hope he will be so good to mention them. Our talest trees are Oaks, which we have of Various sorts; fine Magnolia which in low moist land such as Ocham Court grow to a very great height and is a most Beautiful tree; as well as the Tall Bay which grow to a prodigious heighth. Nither the Acorns or cones are got ripe enough to gather or I would send them in this ship, but will certainly do it by the first good opportunity after they are ripe.

Harriott joyns in affectionate Compliments and thanks to Miss Kings.

We have had so short warning of this ships sailing to-morrow she will not be able to make her acknowledgment [to] Miss Wilhelmine for her very obliging favour of the 11th March at this time.

My most Respectful Compliments wait on My Lord and Lady King, and I am

Dr. Madm.

with great gratitude

Yr. most obliged and most obedt.

Servt.

Eliza. Pinckney

My best wishes attend all my good Neighbours.

To Mr. Longmore at Kensington Gravil Pitts

Sir   Augt. 31st, 1760

My friends have informed me they found it necessary to remove my two sons from Mr. Gerrards Academy at C[amberwell] and have placed them with you at Kensington. The intire confidence I have in their judgment and friendship leaves me no room to doubt of the goodness of the Choice they have made and increases my desire of being better acquainted with a Gentleman to whom I am likely to owe so much as to you. I therefore take this opportunity of commencing a Corrispondance with you to whose care is intrusted the greatest treasure I have upon Earth.

They are, Sir, with one little girl all the remains of a worthy good man, whose great Virtues and aimable qualities are well known and must be remembered with veneration and affection by all that knew him. They are all the remains of the best and most valuable of husbands to whose memmory I owe all the gratitude, duty and affection that can be due to Virtue, the most steady, uniform and unshaken that could possess the heart of man; to whose most examplary Conjugal tenderness, partiallity and affection I owe all that can be due to man from a grateful woman.

[156]

From hence, Sir, arises a stronger call than even that which nature makes upon me to desire the happiness of my children; and as that, I am convinced, in a great measure depends on a right Education, I must intreat you, Sir, to consider them as children deprived of their best friend and example and as such make more particularly demand upon your humanity to give them the utmost attention than those that have parental instruction added to your care of them. The care of their morals and forming their tender minds to early habits of Virtue and piety was the principal reason that their father prefered a private to a Public school for them.

Pray give my blessing to my dear boys and excuse me to them if I dont write to them now as I write this in great haste, having been a good while in the Country. Have but just heard of this ship and am told she is ready to sail. I am, Sir

Yr. most obedt. Servt.
E. Pinckney

My friend Mr. Morly to whom I inclose this
will forward any letters to me.
So. Carolina. Belmont.
By the Buely, Capt. Gibbons.

[To Mr. Morly]
Dr. Sir   Augt. 31st, 1760

I hope before this comes to hand you will have received my Several letters by Messrs. Smith, Stone and Raven to your self and other friends with the bills of Exchange inclosed. I now trouble you with a letter to Mr. Longmore, my little boys master, and the 4th bill of Exchange on Messrs. Biggen and Bacon. I have been a good while out of town and did not expect this ship, the Buely, Capt. Gibbons, to sail this ten days; and now find she only waits for a wind [so] that I shall not have time to write to any other friend at this time. I beg my Compliments to them and blessing to my beloved children. I send them a box of Pomgranates directed to Mrs. Evance to the care of Mr. Richard Shubrick, put on board by Mr. Logan or Mr. Farr. And will you, good Sir, take the trouble to inquire about it for the poor little fellows.

As Charles grows a great boy, if you think it proper I think he should have an addition of 6d a week to his pocket mony, which will make it a shilling a week. And let my dear little Tomm know his shall be augmented when he grows a little older.

I am with the utmost gratitude for your many repeated favours you are constantly bestoeing on me and mine—Dr. Sir

Your most obliged and affecte. Servt.

E. Pinckney

Pray let me know by the first opportunity
the price of rice and what 'tis like to sell
for the ensueing [year].
Memdm. The same time wrote a few lines to my dear boys.

1761

[To Charles]   Crs. Town, Febr. 7, 1761

'Tis with the greatest pleasure, My Dear Crs., I acknowledge the receipt of your Letter by Mr. Smith. You have my best thanks, my dear boy, for the comfort and satisfaction that Letter gave me, which I do asure you was not a little.

I and some friends here that I have consulted think it high time you were fited for the University. Of all the Publick schools Westminster I think is to be prefered and therefore would chuse you should go to that school. Master Tommy Evance's going to Warrington would be a great inducement to your going there also, but I think the distance you must then be from your dear brother will be too great. Besides I am informed the business of that school is to fitt young Gentlemen for the ministry; and as you are not to be brought up to the Church, it will not do so well for you. Harrow, I think, can hardly be called a public school, and as Dr. Thackery is dead I dont think of that. Others advise rather to a private Tutor than any public school.

There is indeed an objection to all public schools and a very great one if true that the morals of Youth are taken little care off. But I have so good an oppinion of your sobriety and modesty and flatter my self you have rather a serious than Wild turn of mind that I hope I may venture to trust you to Westminster without running any risk of what must be fatal to me as well as to your self; Vizt: corrupt principles.[46] For be asured, my dear child, I would not hesitate a moment were it in my choice whether I would have you a learned man with every accomplishment or a good man without any. But as I hope you will be both, I commit you to the Divine Protection and guidance and recommend to you to be very careful of what acquaintances you make and what friendships you contract, for much depends on the example and advice of those we are fond off, and deviations from Virtue even small ones are extreamly hard to recover.

Consider, my dear Child, you will be in a City surrounded with temptations with every youthful passion about you. It will therefore require your utmost vigilance to watch over your passions as well as your constant attendance at the Throne of Grace. Be particularly watchful against heat of temper; it makes constant work for repentance and chagrine and is often productive of the greatest mischiefts and misfortunes.

I send this open to Mr. Morly and beg you will show it to Mrs. Evance to prevent my writing the same thing often over and hope they will joyn with me in oppinion, which if they do, I think you should be fixt as soon as a decent notice has been given to Mr. Longmore.

'Tis with the utmost pain I think of separating you from your dear brother tho' the distance is so small I doubt not you will often see him.

You tell me You and your brother are treated in all respects by Mrs. Evance as her own children. I dont doubt it; I think I know Mrs. Evance. I wish I knew as well how to express my gratitude and the sence I have of my obligation to her.

I shall write to my precious Tommy if I can by this ship. My blessings attend you both.

My affectionate Compliments to Mrs. Evance and all her family; and let her know I am told a glass of good red wine once a day will be of Service to your brother and beg the favour she will order some to Mr. Longmores for him.

---

46. Charles Cotesworth Pinckney did attend Westminster, whose headmaster was the formidable Dr. William Markham. Marvin R. Zahniser, *Charles Cotesworth Pinckney: Founding Father* (Chapel Hill, N.C., 1967), pp. 12–14.

May every blessing both temporal and spiritual attend you and your dear Brother is the constant prayer of

My dearest Charles
Your truly affectionate Mother
Eliza. Pinckney

P. S. My greatfull Compts. attend
all that are kind to you.

[To Mr. Morly]
Dear Sir   Charles Town, Febr. 8, 1761

That you have heard from me but once for the last 5 months was oweing intirely to want of ability; for after being weakened for a year before with a preying grief which I had not strength of mind enough to get the better off and which occationed a complaint in my stomach that reduced me so low I could but just walk without sopport, I was attacked the last day of Sept. with a violent fever which lasted 7 days without intermission and seized my spirrits in such a manner that was you to be told the musk and other high Cordials [that] were given me in 30 hours to keep life in me you woud not Credite it. Three times in two months I was brought to the Verge of the grave and have kept my Chamber over 4 months. I thank God I am now well and recover my strength apace—with great pleasure make use of it to thank you for your favours by Mr. Smith and Mr. Rutledge,[47] both [of] whom I found had been so good to see my dear boys.

To prevent my writing a long letter at this time, I must beg the favour you will peruse the inclosed to my dear Charles as 'tis upon the subject of his going to Westminster school. And if you aprove it, I think the sooner he goes the better, as he will be 15 before you receive this. Be pleased to keep the letter till you see him in London that he may at the same time have an opportunity to show it to Mrs. Evance.

My Compliments to Mrs. Evance and our other friends. I received an obliging letter from Mr. Keat in the summer and one by Mr. Rutledge from Dr. Kirkpatrick. Pray thank them for me.

47. John Rutledge (1739–1800), later governor of South Carolina, was called to the English bar in February, 1760, and returned later that year to Carolina. Mabel L. Webber, "Dr. John Rutledge and His Descendants," *SCHM* 31 (1930): 14, 15. A good brief life is Robert L. Meriwether, "Rutledge, John," *DAB*.

I should not remain long a letter in either of their debts by choice, but necessity has no Law. Be so good to inform the Doctor I have procured him better intelligence with regard to the small pox here than *I* could possibly have given him myself. Dr. Chalmers has promised me to send him a letter on the subject which I hope he will receive at the same time that this comes to hand.[48]

I am with great Esteem

Dear Sir

Your affectionate and obedient Servant

E. Pinckney

[To Thomas]   Bellmont, Febr. 8, 1761

You cant conceive, my precious Boy, the Joy your letter by Mr. Smith gave me as well as his having seen you and your dear brother well.

Pray pay my Compliments and thanks to Mr. and Mrs. Longmore. I hope Mr. Longmore received my letter of the 31st of August by Capt. Gibbon, by whom I sent you some Pomgranates.

Make my affectionate Compliments to Mrs. Evance and tell her I hardly know how to write her a short letter or I would write to her now. I have two of her most friendly letters by me unanswered, not by choice. I hope to be able very soon to indulge my self in a letter to her.

My Compliments also to Mr. Raven. I am extreamly glad to hear he is so much mended in his health.

Take care, my much beloved child, of your health. Be a good child, mind your learning; and May The Almighty God pour every blessing both spiritual and temporal upon you and your dear brother and sister is the Constant prayer of, my Dearest Tommy,

Your truely affectionate Mother

Eliza. Pinckney

Your Sisters love and best wishes attend both
her dear brothers. She intends to write to
you both by this opportunity.

48. For the smallpox epidemic in Charleston, see Waring, *Medicine in South Carolina*, pp. 74–86.

[To Mrs. King]

Dear Madam

'Tis with great regret I send Mr. King so small a collection of seeds, especially as I have an opportunity to send them by a private hand; but I was taken in Sept. with a most severe fever which held me many days without intermission and seized my spirrits in such a manner as brought me to the Verge of the grave 3 times in 2 months, and several relapses afterwards has confined me to my chamber 4 months.

As soon as I was able I inquired how my directions were observed concerning the Seeds, and tho' I had sent posi[ti]ve orders to 3 places for diferent sorts of seeds, they were observed but at one. Poor Mr. Drayton had also promised me a large quantity of Magnolia and Bay seed, but he was taken ill about the same time I was, and died.[49] I am a good deal mortified at the disapointment as there will be a year lost by it, but please God I live this year, I will endeavour to make amends and not only send the Seeds but plant a nursery here to be sent you in plants at 2 year old. And I think I know a method that will preserve the trees very well, by which means I imagine you will save 2 if not 3 years growth in you[r] trees, for I believe a tree will grow as much in 2 years here as in 4 or 5 in England.

Harriott writes to Miss Whilhelmina by this opportunity and I am greatly obliged to that young Lady for the pretty manner in which she conveys advice to her, which (especially to one of Harriotts lively disposition) will be more serviceable than graver lectures might be from older people, besides her great fondness (in which she is very constant) to Miss W K.

I am really sorry for Miss B's for giving up through their own fault a valuable acquaintance which might have been a great advantage to them.

For the future I shall not be surprized at anything I see in your news papers; Oh, modesty, where is thy Blush! Left surely in the Cherokee nation. If I can recolect some lines upon the subject by a Gentleman here I will insert them at bottom.

Be so good, Madam, to pay my particular thanks to Mr. King for

---

49. Thomas Drayton (*c.* 1700–1760) lived at Magnolia plantation on the Ashley River. He was buried November 13, 1760. Mabel L. Webber, ed., "Register of St. Andrew's Parish," *SCHM* 14 (1913): 216; Taylor, "The Draytons of South Carolina and Philadelphia," pp. 5–6.

the beer he intended me by the last ships. I imagine it will come by the next; by some accident which I dont yet know, it was not sent at the time you intended.

Sure nob[od]y but your self would have thought so well of everything and have sent what you very rightly judged we could not get here, Viz., a straining Cock for the Hops.

To George Morly, Esqr.   Crs. Town, April 11th, 1761

Since mine to you by Mr. Simpson in the Febr. Fleet, I received your favour by Ball of the 4th Nov., and the hogshead of beer in very good order except the straining cock which I sopose was lost on board—also Mrs. Kings letter by Mr. Rutledge, but he forgot your verbal message about the beer, so that I gave it over for lost till Ball arrived. I hope the box of seeds for Mr. King sent by Mr. Simpson in the man of war in Feb. is safe arrived. Mr. Longmores and my dear childrens letters by B[all] also arrived safe. My thanks and best wishes are continually due to you. My dear Harriott joyns with me in affectionate Compliments.

Our Army is marched for the Cheerokees. We are also in expectation of Major Rodgers and 50 Mohocks to joyn them. The Mohocks are the best people that could possibly be sent there.

I with many others that hire boats have for want of that conveniency (as there is a large crop of Rice made here this year) not been able to get it to market to go by this fleet, for which reason I am uncertain whether I shall be able to send you a bill now. How ever I will do my endeavour, and if not now, as soon as possibly.

My blessing to my children and Compliments to all our friends.
I am with the greatest regard and gratitude
Dear Sir

I hope you have received mine concerning Charles going to a publick school and that he may be fixt at Westminster this summer.

I take the liberty to put you in mind that the 3 years Insurance of Riply house is near if not quite expired. I beg the favour you will insure it for 3 year more.

The Insurance was had at the Sun Fire office.

I inclose many letters. My packet is very large. I shall therefore send it to Capt Ball if he does not sail this 10 days and beg the favour he will keep it till he comes to the Carolina Coffee house.

N. B. imperfectly Coppyed.

[To Mr. Longmore]
Sir   Crs. Town. April 11th, 1761
   Your favour of the 30th of Octr. (lately receive[d]) gave me a most sensible pleasure and for which I beg you will accept my best acknowledgments. The character you give me of my dear boys produces a satisfaction not to be equaled but by being my self a happy witness of their growing virtues—a happiness which for their sakes I must not yet injoy.
   As you dont mention receiving any letter from me I imagine mine to you dated the 31st of August by Capt Gibbons in the Buely must have miscarried. I therefore take the liberty to send you now a Coppy of it lest you think me such a parent as I wish not to be esteemed by any good man.
   Pray pay my Compliments to Mrs. Longmore. By the Character I have heard of her, I dont doubt I am much indebted to her for her care and kindness to my poor little boys.
   My friends tell me it is time Charles should be removed to a publick school to fitt him for the University and that tis necessary they go first to a public school which is the only reason I desire him to be put to Wistminster. My dear little Tomm will continue with you.
   My blessing attend my children, and love to Master Evance.
                                          I am
                                             Sir
                                             Yr. most obedt. Servt.
                                                E. Pinckney

The following is a Coppy of the above mentioned
letter by Buely, Capt. Gibbons.

To the Honble. Mrs. King
Dr. Madm.   April 13th, 1761
   I cant resist the temptation of paying you my respects when a fleet sails though I did my self the honor To write you by the Man of

War in Feb.—which letter with the Seeds for Mr. King I hope are safe arrived by this time.

Our hopes and Expectations are a good deal raised by the great fleet we are told that is bound from England for America this spring. We flatter our selves they will take The Mississippi in their way, which if they succeed inn must put an end to all our Indian Warrs, as they could never molest us if the French from thence did not supply them with arms and Ammunition. Our army has marched for the Cheerokee nation.[50] They consist of regular troops and provincials. 'Tis a disagreeable Service but they have this to comfort them, that whether they are successful or other ways they may be pretty sure of gathering Laurels from the bounty of the English news writers; for after the incomiums opon the last Cheerokee expedition, there surely can nothing be done there that dont merit praise.

If the 50 Mohocks arrive safe that we expect from Genl. Amherst, I hope we shall be able to quel those Barbarians; for the Mohocks are very fine men—five of them are now here—and they are looked upon by the rest of the Indians with both dread and respect for they think them the greatest warriors in the world.

Many thanks to good Mr. King for my beer, which came in very good order and is extreamly good, though it had a long voyage and went first to Lisbon.

My most respectful Compliments wait on My Lady and Lord King and the young Ladies. Harriott is out of Town with Lady Mary Drayton and dont know when the fleet sails or would do her self the honour to write to Miss Whilhelmine by it.

I am with great gratitude and affection.

Dr. Madm.

Your most obliged and most obedt.

Servant

E. Pinckney

I hope Mrs. Roberts, Mr. Weston and the two little Westons are well. Be so good to present my Compliments to them when you see them.

Memdum. The same month wrote Mrs. Evance a very long letter.

50. Early in January, 1761, Lieutenant Colonel James Grant arrived with 1,200 regulars. Together with the troops left by Montgomery to guard the frontier and the South Carolina militia, Grant commanded 2,250 effectives. In June and July Grant's army burned fifteen towns and all crops in the Tuckaseegee and Little

To Mrs. Evance
My dear Madam   April 13th, 1761
If you have received my tedious letter consisting of more than a
sheet of the largest post paper you will readily excuse, I doubt not,
any more from me by this fleet, but I cant so readily excuse my self
for not saying a word about what you desire me to do with regard
to your part of Mrs. Gibb's goods. It was impossible for me to do it
imediately upon the receipt of your letter for reasons too tedious
now to mention and afterwards Mrs. Cooper told me you had
altered your mind.

Your last letters are at Belmont, and I in town. You will therefore excuse me if I forget to answer any thing particularly mentioned in them. If you received the above mentioned long letter do
not blame Charles by imagining he acquainted me. What an Enemy
I had in Mrs. Watson to whom I thought my self greatly obliged for
her civilities to my children (while a[t] Camberwell) since we left
England. For I asure you I had only a hint from him about it, tho'
the poor child seemed greatly affected by it; but I had it more particularly from another hand, which shall be nameless. I know I need
not desire you, if you can possibly avoid it, to let my childrens vizets
to that house be no longer troublesom. Young and innocent as they
are, misrepresentations may be made of them; and with regard to her,
they cannot be more innocent of offence than their mother has ever
been.

Pray pay my Compliments to Mr. Raven. I hope I may now congratulate him on his perfect recovery, and that he will never forget
the tender offices of his good Sister.

I find, my friend, you are still very ungentile and old fashioned in
your notions tho' I am told you are hansomer than ever and have so
many Lovers you dont know which way to turn your self. But how
comes it into your head that all the wives in the world should be as
simple as your self or your humble servant that they should be Idle
enough to run about the world with a husband purely out of affection to him, or from as weak a notion of it being a point of duty to

Tennessee valleys. Those Indians not killed were driven into the mountains to starve.
A peace treaty was finally signed with the Cherokees on December 18. Wallace,
South Carolina: A Short History, pp. 180–81; Sirmans, *Colonial South Carolina*, pp.
337–41.

attend a sick husband across the Ocean When 'tis there duty to stay at home and mind the affairs there. This, you know, is having great command of the passion; and it is certainly a mark of great wisdom to restrain those sentiments of tenderness and affection which good husbands are apt to inspire into minds that are not greatly raised above the common level. But the best of all is they are happy while their husbands live and still happier when he is at rest, can injoy themselves uninterupted by days of sighs and Nights of tears. Nor can the foolish notion of constancy to the memory of one, when he cannot be injured by taken [taking] another husband, take posession of such Heroic souls.

But to have done with Irony and be serious, I really think that Ladys conduct unkind and unaccountable; and how she can answer it to her self I cant conceive. I make no doubt she is by this time sorry for it.

My dear Crs.   Crs. Town. April 15th, 1761
I wrote to you the 7th Feb. last by the fleet that sailed from hence in that month, which letter I hope you have received. It was upon the subject of your going to a publick school; but least that should Miscarry I will repeat my desire that you go to Wistminsters if Mr. Morly and Mrs. Evance aprove it.

Since that, I received your dutiful and affectionat letter by Ball, who also brought me a very pretty one from my dear little Tomm, for which I thank you both most heartily. In your letter you mention going to the Charter House. I own I prefer (and most people I know do prefer) Wistminster. In answer to what you say of being more under Mrs. Evances care at the Charter house, I think if a youth for his own sake will not be careful of his conduct 2 or 3 mile distant from his Gaurdians, I fear all the pains thay can take a little nearer will be ineffectual. From you, my dear Child, I hope better things, for though you are very young, you must know the welfair of a whole family depends in a great measure on the progress you make in moral Virtue, Religion, and learning, and I dont doubt but the Almighty will give you grace and enable you to answer all our hopes, if you do your part. In order to which, indeavour to fortifie your self against those Errors to which you are most easily led by natural propencity. What I fear most for you is warmth of temper. Learn, my dear Charles, To subdue the first emotions of Anger.

I received a letter from you last year wherein you seemed much affected with some ill Usage I had received from a person you thought I looked upon as my friend. You only hinted at the ill Usage, and you acted very Judiciously in not being more particular, however I had the affair more particularly stated to me by another hand, which I have answered. I was much affected with it, and I dont wonder you were. But consider how much more Laudable it is to bear patiently ill usage as well as how much more comfortable to our selves. Nay, as Xtians 'tis an indispensible duty. Besides, were it not, their is a greatness of mind in being above revenge, which little minds are incap[ab]le off. When we or any belonging to us are Injured, let us Justifie our selves as farr as truth will bear us out and prove to them the falsity of their assertions, but put it not in their power if you can help it (without great inconveniencey to your self) to make unkind observation upon you, or by any connection whatever to Injure you. But let me urge you not to return it in kind, and whatever you do, avoid revenge; for remember Who it is that has said, Vengence is Mine. I will repay saith The Lord. Power and Wisdome are in his hand and leave all your concerns with him. To be patient, humble, and resigned is to be happy. It is also to have a noble soul, a mind out of the reach of Enve, malice and every Calamity. And the earlier, my dear boy, you learn this leason, the longer will you be wise and happy.

I never know when to have done when I am writing to my dear Children, but I have several other letters to write and must not now indulge my self further than to send my blessing and tenderest affections to your dear brother, to whom I wrote in Feb., and fear I shall not have time now to write to him again. Your dear Sister is out of town with Lady Mary Drayton. If she comes down before the fleet sails will write to you both.

I sent by Capt. Gibbons in August 70 fine Pomgranates for Mrs. Evance, you and your brother.

Our army is on their March to the Cheerokees. They consist of regular troops and provincials, and we expect soon to joyn them 50 Mohock Indians. They are very fine brave fellows and the rest of the Indians both dread and respect them. They think them the great-

est Warriours in the world. So I hope they will do us some good.
Adieu, my dr. Child. I am ever

Yr. most affectionate Mother
E. Pinckney

I send you the inclosed for Mr. Gerrard because I am loath he should pay postage; therefore beg you will take a Coach and carry it or send a poster with it. Pay the poster and note upon the Packet postage payd and let it be charged in my bill! There is a letter inclosed for Master Drayton.

[To William Henry Drayton]
Dear Billy   April 16th, 1761
As I remained long in your debt for several very affectionate and obliging letters, I ought not to stand so strictly with you for an answer to my last before I write to you again expecially when I imagine that I may by a hint to you put you upon rectifying some little mistakes which I think you have lately been guilty off. To keep you no longer in suspence, I must inform you that your Papa showed me a letter he received from you by Mr. Wright which was not wrote in the manner you are generally used to write. There was too much warmth from you to your parent and something like abraiding. Consider, my dear child, how much duty, defference and affectionate respect is due to a parent, and I am sure one moments reflection will be enough to make you very sorry for displeasing your father in ever so small a matter. I said as much as I could in excuse for you and was much mortified I could not insist upon your being in the right.

I am sure if you do me justice you must know on which side my partiallity rests and that I would much rather throw blame on your father than you. I should have wrote you on this subject long ago but a severe and long Illness prevented me till now. Pray give my love to Charles. I also see his letter to his Mama is a very different stile from yours.

Mr. Wright joyned me in petitioning for 50 Sterling [in] addition to what your papa intended to allow you. How we have succeeded you best know.

I have been so long confined to my Chamber that I have not seen him these 6 months. He has also been a good deal out of order tho' now very well.

I have wrote Mr. Guerrard by this Conveyance that I have nothing to add but my Compliments to him and Mrs. Greene. And I am with great truth both your brothers and

Your sincere and affectionate friend
E. Pinckney

[To Charles]   Belmont, June the 9th, 1761

I wrote so fully to my dear Child the 15th of April by Capt. Ball that I have little now to add, but as Mr. Martin was so good to tell me he would see you and your brother, if it would be a satisfaction to you, I with great pleasure accepted the offer. And as he intends to return in a years time I hope for the satisfaction of hearing good accounts of your health as well as your further progress in Learning by him. He is a very worthy man and a Gentleman of great politeness as well as learning. He and his lady comes to England for their health. I dont doubt you will follow any advice he is so good to give you.[51]

I received 2 letters from you, one from Mr. Longmore and one from my dear little boy since mine to you in April. The dates I cant recollect and the letters are in town. Pray pay my Compliments and thanks to Mr. and Mrs. Longmore. I wrote to Mr. Longmore by Ball and shall answer his last favour very soon.

Pay my affectionate compliments and let Mrs. E[vance] know I have done what she desired me with regard to her share of Mrs. Gibbs goods. I have wrote her two such long letters lately I will not interrupt her again so soon as this. I hope Mr. Gerrard and Master Drayton will have received the letters I inclosed you for them before this can reach you! though the above mentioned letters of the 15th April to you inclosing them did not leave this place till the last day of May.

51. The Reverend Charles Martyn was sent as a missionary to South Carolina in 1752 by the Society for the Propagation of the Gospel in Foreign Parts. Martyn served St. Andrews Parish until 1770. He was known as a man of the strictest integrity and as a firm believer in observing the Sabbath in a sober way. Frederick Dalcho, *An Historical Account of the Protestant Episcopal Church in South-Carolina* ... (Charleston, S.C., 1820), pp. 340–42.

Adieu my much loved Child. Take care of your self and your dear brother. And that The Almighty may bless you both with your dear Sister with every blessing both spiritual and temporal is the Constant and most devout prayer that is put up to Heaven by

My dear Crs.

Yr. most affectionate Mother

Eliza. Pinckney

[To Mr. Morly]

Dr. Sir   Belmont. June the 11th

I received your favours of the 27th Jan. and 17th Feb. with the greatest pleasure imaginable for tho' many have reason none can have more to rejoice at your perfect recovery than my self, and I pray that the Almighty may long continue you in perfect health a blessing to me and mine and the rest of your friends. I find we were both extreamly ill at the same time and both have reason to adore and thank that Merciful hand that has raised us.

I thank you for the friendly hint you gave me. Mrs. Evance's advice is very good. I will indeavour to follow it to the utmost of my power.

I am much obliged to you for your favour in March with the Feb. magazines. I had before received the Jan. M. If you knew the pleasure the sight of your hand writing gives to my whole family, I am sure you will never regrett the trouble you are at—great as it is—in writing frequently to me. Some of the very slaves know your hand and rejoyce at a letter directed by you. They are sure it will put their Mistress in great good humour and consiquently make everything about her as happy as she can. I hope before this reaches you, you will have received the packet by Ball which he has promised to deliver you him self.

I have now Cash by me to purchase a bill of exchange and have my self as well as our Factor taken all the pains we possibly could to procure a bill of Exchange to go by this Man of Warr, but hither too in vain. I shall how ever leave my Letter unsealed as long as I can.

If you receive a turtle from me by this fleet, be so good to send it to my Lady Carew with my Respects (I shall not be able to write to her Ladyship at this time) unless you would oblige any friend of your own with it in such case 'tis intirely at your service.

I hope Charles is by this time at Westminster. If not, I beg he may go as soon as possible. The Rev. Mr. Martin, a very worthy Gentleman who is the bearer of this has been so good to say he will see them. I must therefore beg the favour you will direct him where to find Charles whether at Westminster or Kinsington.

Many thanks to good Mr. Middleton for his remembrance of my poor boys. My affectionate Compliments attend Mrs. Middleton and all her family. I am sincerely glad to hear of her perfect recovery. Pray pay my grateful acknowledgments and Compliments to my good friends Mr. Keat and the Doctor, and accept of mine and Harriots best wishes, as I am
        Sir
        Your affectionate and obliged humble Servant
        E.P.

Wrote by the fire side in So. Carolina

[To Thomas]   So. Caroa. Belmont, June 11th, 1761
I wrote to my dearest Tommy the 8th of Febr. and find I was in his thoughts much about the same time I wrote by his pretty of the 11th of the same month, wherein you desire me to write you a little letter—a pleasing request, my dear boy, to one that loves you so well as I do. And If you are a good boy and mind your learning as I dont doubt you are, I shall grant all your petitions with equal pleasure as far as my power extends.

The Rev. Mr. Martin, a very worthy Gentleman, an Inhabitant here, is the bearer of this, who I hope will bring me the greatest comfort I can injoy which is good accounts from you and your dear brother.

You are both much obliged to Mrs. Longmore for her favourable Sentiments of you, as I learn from Mrs. Wragg, My amiable friend.

Pray pay my Compliments and thanks to Mr. and Mrs. Longmore and Mrs. Evance.

Your dear Harriott sends you her love. She writes to both her brothers now. My blessing attend you both, and that the Almighty may bless and make you both happy in time and in Eternity is the Sincere and ardent prayer of, My Dear Child,
        Your truely affectionate mother
        E. Pinckney

To Mr. Morly

Dr. Sir

I have at length (as a great favour) obtained a Bill for £50 Sterling from Messrs. Smith and Nutt[52] on Sir James Coolbrooke, Bart., Arnold Nisbet, George Colebrook and Moses Franks, Esqs. The first Bill I now inclose you. I have already wrote to you and my dear Children by this ship, the Dolphin Man of Warr. The ships are now going down and I must conclude, after sending them my blessing and beging the favour of you to present my Compliments to Mrs. Evance with £10 from me. Could I have got a larger bill it should have been twenty, but the other ten shall come as soon as I can procure a bill of Exchange.

I am

Dr. Sir
Yr. o. h. St.
E. Pinckney

Coppyed by The Friendship,
Capt. Ball in Febr. 27th, 1762.[53]

[To Mr. Morly]

Dr. Sir

I this minuet heard of this opportunity to England and imbrace it to send you the 3rd bill of Exchange drawn by Messrs. Smith and Nutt on Sir James Colebrook, &c. The 2 first of the same date went by our last fleet, one in the Dolphin, and the other by a merchantman.

I know not what to tell you of our affairs in the Indian Country on which to found any real satisfaction. Our army are still there. We have destroyed Several of their Towns, but when you consider what Indian Towns are, and how soon rebuilt, you will think we need not be too much elated with the success we have had hithertoo unless we had killed more Indians. This is certain, we know but of two that have been yet killed though they tell us several are missing.

52. Probably John Nutt, a prominent merchant who had close financial ties with the Benjamin Smith family of South Carolina. George C. Rogers, Jr., *Evolution of a Federalist* (Columbia, S.C., 1962), pp. 10, 21, 60. See also Rogers's references to the Nutt family's commercial connections in *Charleston in the Age of the Pinckneys*, pp. 13–14, 37, 51.

53. This postscript appears to be a later entry referring to a second copy of the letter.

Our Crops, I believe, will turn out much better than we expected in the beginning of the year.

Pray give my blessing to my dear children and Compliments to all friends in which number none are more deservedly included than your self.

The Turtle mentioned in my last were left behind and dyed. I am mortified that I cant show my friends in England that I think of them but I cant help it.

1762

[To Mrs. King]   Crs. Town, Febr. 27th, 1762

How very kind and acceptable, my Dear Madam, was your favour of the 5th of Octr. I had just before received a letter from my friend Morly informing me you had been so good to send me two letters which he had inclosed and forwarded to me by the Britania, a ship that I knew had been taken some months. I was lamenting heavily to Harriott that I should not have a line from you this fleet, for though I have so largely experienced your goodness to me I thought it was too much to expect at such a time, especially as you could not know I had lost the above mentioned letters.

How, dear Madam, could you think of this remote spott in the midsts of the splendour of Royal Weddings, Coronations, Gay Courts[54] and the attendant cheerfulness that must follow in their train long after. But though I have long had a high oppinion of Mrs. Kings Virtues, [I] thought she acted in a way almost peculiar to her self. I now begin to rob you of all merrit and think every thing that is humain, polite, generous and good is so much a part of your constitution that you cant help making every thing happy within your reach, and that 'tis as much impossible for you not only to improve but make opportunities to exercise those aimable Tallents Heaven has blessed you with as tis for a nice peace of machinery to resist the Laws impeled upon it by the artist. Thus have I gratefully returned all your friendship and favours by depriving you of that good sence

54. Mrs. Pinckney refers here to the wedding of George III and Charlotte Sophia of Mecklenburg on September 8, 1761, and their coronation two weeks later, occasions of great celebration in London. For a description, see Paget Toynbee, ed., *Letters of Horace Walpole*, 16 vols. (Oxford, Eng., 1940), 5: 107–10.

and judgment which every lady allowed you and reduced you to a peace of mere Clock work.

You cant think how many people you have gratified by your obliging me with so particular a discription of the Queen. We had no picture of her Majesty nor discription that could be depended upon till I received your favour. And what was excisively provoking, the few friends that wrote to me did not doubt but I had a description of the Queen and coronation from others and therefore was most mortifyingly silent. If, Madam, you have ever been witness to the impatience of the people of England about a hundred mile from London to be made acquainted with what passes there, you may guess a little at what our impatience is here when I inform you that the curiosity increases with the distance from the Center of affairs; and our impatience is not to be equaled with any peoples within four thousand mile.

Lady Ann Atkin happened to be with me when I received your favour. I told her as she was a woman of Quality, she should be first treated with a discription of her Majesty and accordingly had that honour, but not a Plebean out of my own family should hear a word of the matter that day. In half an hour after I was favoured with a vizet from our new Gov., Mr. B[oone],[55] lately arrived here from his former Government in the Jerseys, who I found (tho' he has an extensive good acquaintance in England) knew as little of the New Queen as we did here. I had the pleasure to read him also the discription. And the next day numbers received the same sort of pleasure. All smiled at least at the new fashoned name for the coulour of her hair, which indeed I should not have guessed at had you not been so obliging to tell me what it was. On the whole I am a very Loyal Subject and had my share of Joy in the agreeable account of my Sovereign and his Consort.

I rejoyce to hear you, Mr. King, the Young ladies and all the worthy family at Ocham are well. I beg to pay my most respectful Compliments to them.

I hope the seeds I now send Mr. King will arrive safe and in good

55. Thomas Boone, transferred from the governorship of New Jersey, arrived in Charleston December 22, 1761, and served as governor until 1764. Boone's governorship is discussed in Sirmans, *Colonial South Carolina*, *passim*, but see especially pp. 349–57.

order, especially the Magnolia, which I think the most beautiful of all trees. I have seen them here in level moist Land grow to a prodigious height though they do very well also in high land. The seed of the flowering shrub I send Miss Kings I found wild in the woods and have named it the Royal purple. Its coulours are gold and purple, but if they chuse to alter it in honour of the Queen or any thing else I have no objection.

I cant conceive how such an improbable peice of news as my going to be married could be invented here and mologated to such a distance as Riply, though very small appearances give rise to those things in this part of the world. And upon recollection, I sopose it must arise from an offer I had about that time which in point of fortune must have been to my advantage, but as entering into a second marriage never once entered into my head and as little into my inclination—and I am persuaded never will—the affair took not a moments hesitation to determine; and indeed I did not think it could have got air enough to have wafted it to England.

The obliging manner in which you mention my dear Charley is very pleasing and flattering to me. He must disapoint my hopes of his judgment greatly if he does not make use of every opportunity you are so good to allow him of improving so valuable an acquaintance.

When, my Dear Madam, shall we have peace? Till then I have little prospect of seeing my Children and friends in England; and a Spanish warr we are told is unavoidable. We are pretty quiet here just now, but 'tis much feared it will continue no longer than the winter. We never was so taxed in our lives, but what is our taxes to yours. However, we are a young Colony and our Seas does not throw up sands of gold, as surely the British does to enable you to bear such prodigious Expences.

Harriott says she Envys no body so much as Miss Upton.

Medm. Had not time to coppy this fully.

To Mr. Morly
Dr. Sir   Febr. 27th, 1762
I had the very great pleasure of receiving your favour of the 1st July though at the same time was much mortified to find I had lost a letter from you inclosing several from my friends and children by

Currys' being taken. I doubt not you have received mine by the Rev. Mr. Martin who went to England in the Dolphin man of war, and another letter by the same ship inclosing a bill of Exchange for £50 Sterling. A second and 3rd bill of the same date I have also sent you and now inclose a bill for a hundred pound, 2 shillings and 6 sterling drawn by Major Rodgers on John Calcroft, Esq. in Channel Row, Indorsed by Messrs. Ogilvie and Forbes.

You will probably hear of all our publick Transactions at the Coffee house,[56] therefore I will not trouble you with them here.

I only write a short letter to my dear children as this comes by a single ship, which I look upon as a very uncertain conveyance. I defer writing to my other friends till the Convoy goes.

When you have received the Cash for this bill, be so good to present Mrs. Evance with 10 £ and my best Compliments and thanks.

I impatiently wait the arrival of the fleet which we expect every day, and hope to hear you are all well. I thank God I am now in better health than I have been this 4 year and am grown fatt.

As I shall write you again soon will only add that I am what I always have been and ever shall be

Dr. Sir

Your most affectionate and most obliged

and obedient Servant

E. Pinckney

Coppy'd and Sent by the Friendship,
Capt Ball.

[To Lady Carew]   July, 1760
    Friendship, Thou soft propitious Power!
    Sweet Regent of the social Hour!
    Sublime thy Joys nor understood,
    But by the virtuous and the Good!

56. The first London coffeehouse was founded about 1650. Coffeehouses soon became centers of political, social, and literary influence; philosophers, politicians, writers, and a public eager for the latest news frequented them. Certain coffeehouses became identified with political factions that met in them to discuss issues of the day. See Bryant Lillywhite, *London Coffee Houses: A Reference Book of Coffee Houses of the Seventeenth, Eighteenth, and Nineteenth Centuries* (London, 1963), pp. 17–28. A brief description of the Carolina coffeehouse is found on pp. 147–49.

This beautiful quotation so applicable to your Ladyship came into my head as soon as I took up my penn to write to you; for you, My Beloved friend, well understand it in all its aimable appearances. You can share and by shareing lighten the load of woe that oppresses the afflicted heart by the tender simpathy you afford it. How soothing and acceptable was your Ladyships favour of the 30th Nov. to me! Tho' pleasure and pain alternately succeeded each other while I read the most sensible, tender and polite letter that could well be penned.

I have so little curiosity that I often think I carry it to a degree of stupidity and yet your letter, my dear Madam, awakened every spark within me and taught me my mistake by my inquisitiveness to know what relates to those I love. I tryed (but in vain) to find out what new trouble had happened to my friend which had so wou[n]ded and distressed her mind, a mind which for some years past had been used to heavy tryals and had been as used to bear them with a courage superior to her sex. Sopport still, my dear Lady Carew, be the tryal of what nature it will, the same masculine Virtue and pius resignation and it must bring peace and comfort at last here and happiness for Ever.

How much I feel for you is easier to imagine than to Express. I began to think just before I received yours that the external appearance of sorrow was with me almost at an End, that the very springs were dryed and I could shed no more tears; but I soon found I had enough in store for you and wanted only to know that you were unhappy to make them flow.

I know you would be better pleased if I told you I had acquired strength of mind enough to feel less both for my self and you, though I know none has a more tender sensibility for their friends than you have. But to bear so much and so many sorrows—so much your own too—with the patience and resignation you have done I admire and wish but cannot imitate, and find I must come behind you in every thing. And I am not only content but pleased to do so except in Virtue and personal merit (such a Virtue and aimableness as first and very early attracted, and afterwards fixt an affection which nothing but death can obliterate in me). In this I wish to overtake you, not to bring you down to me, but this is in vain; for I find my self sinking under the weight that has so long laid upon my spirrits and I look more like a walking Ghost than any thing else.

And now my dear little girl is taken very Ill, and I have so little strength left that Heaven only can soport me under it. I must finish another time.

[February 1762]

After 18 months, Dear Madam, I resume my penn, I thank God, in good health and better spirrits than I have known for the last 4 year.

As soon as Harriott had recovered from a severe fever, I my self was seized with one which held me several days without intermission and in the weak state I was, it seized my spirrits in a very violent manner. This added to a complaint I had some time before in my stomack, confined me to my room 7 months; in which time I received a very obliging letter from Mr. Saunders from Jaimaica giving me an account in what manner I lost the letter your Ladyship honoured me with by him. The loss I regreted very much, but should have certainly answered Mr. Saunders' letter imediately had I had the ability, but my long Illness was succeeded by almost as long and tedious a weakness. And I am afraid as he did not know the cause of my silence he must think me a very rude Creature.

My most respectful compliments and best wishes attend Sir. N. and dear Miss C.

Why, my dear Madam, would you give your self so much trouble with my little rough school boys? They are indeed with their Sister the darlings of my heart, the subjects of my waking thoughts and nightly dreams, but a how doo now and then would give them and me sufficient honour and give us much pleasure. But I cant think without blushing of your Ladyships troubleing your self with them at home for we all know what children are—expecially school boys. The best of them must be troublesome. I shall, however, leave saying any more on the subject; for I really want words to express the sence I have of your goodness to me and mine. But I hope you will be able to read my thoughts, and there you will perceive more plainly the returns of Gratitude and affection than by my saying that I am
      Dr. Madam
            Your Ladyships most obliged and affectionat
                  humble Servant
                  E. Pinckney

This letter was begun in July 1760
and sent in Feb. 1762.
My affectionate Compliments to Miss Saunders. I
hope she injoys that inestimable blessing, health.

[To Mr. Keate]   Febr. 1762

A Tedious Illness of seven months succeeded by a long and more
tedious weakness prevented me taking the earliest opportunity of
acknowledging My Worthy and much esteemed friend Mr. Keats
favour of the 3rd of July, a letter that deserved my warmest gratitude and for which you have my sincerest thanks. As it would be no
small mortification to me to lose the place in your remembrance I
flatter my self to have, you cant imagine what an increase it would
be to that mortification was I conscious of being my self the cause of
it; and therefore was very desireous you should be made acquainted
by my friend Morly (to whom I wrote with many pauses and much
difficulty) with my Inability to indulge my self in an Epistolary
intercourse with my friends. But as, I thank God, I am much better
than I have been for the last 4 year, I please my self with the revival
of an imployment which was always agreeable to me, for when I
am volontaryly silent 'tis to indulge my friends, not my self. Indeed
when I reflect on what a distance from all thats gay or new and can
find nothing from within or without to entertain them agreeably,
I am ready in pure charity to them to bid adieu to scribling and am
only prevented by this one consideration: that I must then bid adieu
to hearing of' there welfare, a pleasure I am very loath to part with
as long as I live.

Mr. Morly informed me you were so good to give him a letter for
me which he inclosed with some others from my friends and forwarded by the Britania, but unluckily for me she was taken by the
French and I lost my packet. I regret the loss so much that I look
upon my self as one of the greatest sufferers by the Capture, for
those that had their wealth on board were insured, and I lie intirely
at your mercy to make me amends.

What great doings you have had in England since I left it. You
people that live in the great world in the midst of Scenes of' entertainment and pleasure abroad, of improving studies and polite amuse-

ment at home, must be very good to think of' your friends in this remote Corner of the Globe. I really think it a great virtue in you; and if I could conceal the selfish principle by which I am actuated I could with a better grace attempt to persuade you that there is so much merrit in seting down at home and writing now and then to an old woman in the Wilds of America that I believe I should take you off an hour some times from attending Matine[e] and the other gay scenes you frequent.

How different is the life we live here; vizeting is the great and almost only amusement of' late years. However, as to my own particular, I live agreeable enough to my own taste, as much so as I can separated from my dear boys.

I love a Garden and a book; and they are all my amusement except I include one of the greatest Businesses of my life (my attention to my dear little girl) under that article. For a pleasure it certainly is to cultivate the tender mind, to teach the young Idea how to shoot, &c., especially to a mind so tractable and a temper so sweet as hers. For, I thank God, I have an excellent soil to work upon, and by the Divine Grace hope the fruit will be answerable to my indeavours in the cultivation.

I know not how to thank you sufficiently for your Notice and kindness to my poor boys, but if my prayers are pius enough to reach Heaven, you and yours are secure of every blessing; for I make none with more sincerity and devotion than those that are offered for them and their friends.

How does good Mr. Hungerford, [illegible] Lutral and their families do?

If you wont think me Romantick I will communicate a scheme I have if I live a few years longer (not purely for the pleasure of scribling a long letter) but because I really want your opinion and advice in it, as your residence at Geneva must make you more capable of judging of the matter than those that never were there. Upon a Peace (I cant think of crossing the Atlantic before) I intend to See England and after Charles has been two years at Oxford to go with my two boys to finish their studies at Geneva. I must determine upon my plan before I leave this [country]. Be so good, therefore, at your leasure to tell me what you think of it.

Harriott pays her Compliments. She is much ingaged just now

with Geography and musick. And 'tis high time to disengage your attention from this tedious Epistle by asureing you that I am, with great truth,

> Sir
>
> Your most obliged friend and most obedt.
>
> Servant
>
> E. Pinckney

To Mrs. Onslow   Febr. 27th, 1762

Instead of apologizing, My dear Madam, for not writing to you before, I ought to ask your excuse for writing now, destitute as I am of agreeable subjects both from within and without to support an Epistolary intercourse agreeably. Tho' more than a year has Elapsed since I received your most friendly and entertaining as well as most sensible letter of the 21st July, 1760, the remote corner of the globe in which I am situated so distant from every thing that is new and entertaining makes me almost resolve to give up scribling in pure charity to my friends. But the modest fitt is soon suppressed by the consideration of what I my self must suffer from their silence in return; for 'tis with great truth and sincerity I say that one of the greatest pleasures I have in this life is to know that my friends are well and happy. And as I have few Intimacys and no friendships but with those whose real Virtue and Internal merrit (abstracted from every external advantage and consideration) attracted and fixt my Esteem, it would be the greatest mortification imaginable to me never to hear of them. And this must plead my excuse with those I love for engageing their attention without being able to pay for the trouble with improvement or pleasure.

I very sincerely congratulate Col. Onslow (tho' so long after) on being chosen for Guilford, and I hope I shall soon have an opportunity to do so on his receiving a Generals Staff;[57] but it is with still

57. George Onslow served in Parliament, 1760–84, from Guildford, a parliamentary division in Surrey. Onslow was described by Horace Walpole as "one of those burlesque orators who are favored in all public assemblies, and to whom one or two happy sallies of impudence secure a constant attention, though their voice and manner are often their only patents, and who, being laughed at for absurdity as frequently as for humour, obtain a license for what they please." During his parliamentary career Onslow was a onetime defender of John Wilkes. Later, during the American Revolutionary War, he opposed the peace effort of 1777 and became a supporter of Lord North. Horatio Walpole, *Memoirs of the Reign of George the*

greater pleasure I congratulate him on what is of ten times more consiquence to him, your better health, and which I hope to hear soon is quite established. A repetition of the Bristol waters, as you have already found benefitt by them, I think would tend greatly towards that desireable end.

Be so good the next time you favour me with a line to give me a description of the dear little girl. What is the coulour of her Eyes, her hair; what her complexion. Who is she like? Is she like the Queen? I have a notion she is much hansomer (tho' by discription I think the Queen must be very agreeable). All these particulars Harriott is very impatient as well as my self to be made acquainted with and longs as impatiently to see the sweet child. But that pleasureable Event is still at a distance from us, for here I believe I am immovably fixt till a peace—and am just now told a Warr with Spain is inevitable.[58] Thus the distance between me, my dear boys and my friends in England whom I languish to see seems to increase rather than grow less. However 'tis some relief in the painful interval to hear from and of them.

Though I seemed in the beginning to make a merrit of the Chasm in our corrispondance I have not hypocrisy enough to bear me out to the end, but must honestly own it was inability that prevented me answering your favour by the next fleet after I received it. When it arrived I was very ill in bed and had been so for 2 months before. It was carefully locked up, but as it came from England and was sealed with black wax I was not permitted to see it for some months after.[59] This was unluckey, for I am persuaded had they showed me the letter as soon as I could read it it would have amused and done me more good than their musk Cordials &c., which they fed me upon.

Believe me, Dear Madam, your letters would always give me great pleasure were they to relate nothing but that you and those most dear to you were well and happy. But you have the pleasing talent of treating every subject so Judiciously and agreeably that

Third, ed. George F. Russell Barker, 4 vols. (London, 1894), 2: 286–87; George F. Russell Barker, "Onslow, George (1731–1792)," *DNB*.

58. Coming late into the Seven Years' War (1756–63), Spain joined with France against England and Prussia. England was regarded as Spain's great enemy because of their competition over America, Gibraltar, and Minorca. Shortly after conclusion of the third "family compact," England declared war on Spain (January 4, 1762). Watson, *Reign of George III* (New York, 1960), p. 75.

59. Black wax was a symbol of mourning.

you cant hit upon one that would not entertain. And as I cant help interesting my self in those I have been acquainted with, you cant think what an entertainment it was to me at this distance to have so particular an account of my old Neighbours—tho' the account of poor Mr. Edwards really Chagrined me. 'Tis hard the memory of a good man should not be treated with the respect I am pursuaded his deserved. I subscribe without a moments hesitation to the justness of your sentiments of him: people must allow some thing if they would be just to the infirmities of so advanced an age. As to my own particular, he must ever live in my memory with that regard and esteem which he so justly merrited, expecially from me; for he exhibited every hospitable and social virtue almost to excess with regard to us.

I did not know whether to laugh or sigh at those odd girls you mett with at B[ristol] which you so justly and humourously describe, but to be sure to be right I did both. I never knew so great a contraste in the same persons for they have each of them Sence, good nature and obligingness; simplicity, crossness and hardly common decency of behaviour; Generosity and meanness—all this blended and Tumbled together and governed by a Capriciousness hardly to be equaled. Wealth is the object of their adoration, and I am much mistaken if the Idol makes them one whit happier than they were before. Is not the brothers going into the Army quite in character? I wish them health and happiness, in order to which I wish that they could find a mineral any where that could cure them of whim and inconstancy of temper, a worse disease than any other they are affected with. And then they would stand a chance of being as happy as the rest of their fellow mortals.

You obliged me much, My dear Madam, in mentioning Mrs. King's being in better health than she had been and very much in the Justice you do her great and good qualities. She is certainly a worthy and most aimable woman. Her real and unaffected piety and goodness of heart is a noble foundation for all her other virtues, of which I think she has as many as can come to one womans share, besides being clever in every thing; for that she is one of the most ingenius ladies I ever knew. Thus farr justice demands from me, without considering my own particular obligations to her, which are many. I never receive a letter from her, but I admire the constancy, the condesention and the goodness of her disposition, one proof of which is her so frequently remembering at this distance a person she had once honoured with her acquaintance from the vicinity of situation, without one inducement for the continuance of it but the exerciseing of her own Benevolent temper in giving comfort and pleasure to others. Her daughters (who the more they are known, the more they must be beloved) will I doubt not follow close so good an example. And may she long be continued to them, for I really think, to speak my sentiments in the Eastern stile: happy is the man that has made her his wife, Blessed is the Child that calls her mother.

I write to my good friend Mrs. Chatfield by this fleet, to whose friendly offices and Mr. Chatfields I am much indebted. I hear I have lost my good Tenant Mr. Waple, and Admiral Brodrick has Sold his house at Riply, but Mrs. King does not say who bought it.

I am glad Col. Onslow takes pleasure in his Garden. Tis natural to be please[d] at others take[ing] pleasure in the same things we do. I think it an Innocent and delightful amusement. I have a little hovel[60] about 5 mile from town, quite in a forrest where I find much amusement 4 or 5 months in the year, and where I have room enough to exercise my Genius that way, If I had any. However, I please my self and a few that are partial to me. I am my self head gardener, and I believe work much harder than most principal ones do. We found it in [such] ruins when we arrived from England that I have had a wood to clear; and indeed it was laid out in the old taste so that I have been modernizing it, which has afforded me much imployment.

Being a sort of anthusiaste in my Veneration for fine trees, I look upon the destroyers of Pyrford Avenue as sacrilidgious Enemies to posterity, and upon an old oak with the reverencial Esteem of a Druid. It staggered my philosophy to bear with patience the Cuting down one remarkable tree which was directed by an old man by mistake, and I could not help being very angry with the old fellow tho' he had never offended me before in his life. Indeed it was planted by my dear Mr. Pinckneys own hand, which made it doubly mortifying to me. What must Col. Onslows vexation or Philosophy be if he loves trees but half as well as I do to see so many fallen—and probably planted by some of his ancestors.

I will now conclude. Surely 'tis time when I can find nothing more

60. Belmont.

animated to entertain you with than stocks and stones, or you will
think me as senceless as they which I must be to be any other than
what I am

My dr madam

Your most affectionate

Most obliged and obedient Servt.

E. Pinckney

You may depend upon it. Every
thing in a free Corrispondance
is sacred with me.
Be so good to pay my best Compliments to
Mrs. Furer. I hope she and the Colo. with
their little family injoy their health.
Pray is poor old Mrs. Sayer in the land of
the living?

Index

Denain, 65
DeRenne, George Wymberley Jones, ix
Desbrisay, Captain Albert, 16
Deveaux, Andrew, 10, 24; making indigo, xix
Dictionary of American Biography, ix
Dieskau, Baron, 86n
Dobrusee. *See* Desbrisay, Captain Albert
Dogood, Silence, ix
Dolemott. *See* De la Motte
Dolphin, 173, 177
Drayton, Charles, 112, 136; identified, 111n
Drayton, Charlotte Bull (Mrs. John), 25, 111n
Drayton, John, 25n, 111n
Drayton, Lady Mary, 137, 165, 168; letters to, 93–94; identified, 93n
Drayton, Thomas (d. 1760), 93, 162
Drayton, Thomas (1759–1801): birth, 137n
Drayton, William Henry (Billy), 112, 136, 170; letter to, 169–70; identified, 111n
Duke University Library: owns ELP letters, xxvii
Dunbar, Charles, 60
Dunbar, Mrs. Charles, 60
Dunbar, Miss Grace, 59; letter to, 60

E

East Bay, xxiii
Edwards, Vigerous, 99, 119, 125, 137; letters to, 106–8, 139–41; ELP's memories of, 184
Elizabeth, Princess, 33
Eriskay Island, 71n
Eugene, Prince of Savoy, 65
Evance, Miss, 121
Evance, Mrs. R., 96, 97, 109, 110, 112, 126, 129, 145, 150, 157, 159, 160, 161, 165, 167, 168, 170, 171, 172, 173, 177; letters to, xxiii–xxiv, 99–100, 104–6, 121–22, 146–49, 151–52, 152–54, 166–67
Evance, Master Tommy, 106, 111, 158, 164
Evans, Mr., 44

F

Fairweather. *See* Fayweather
Fandeno, Don Juan de Lean, 55n
Farr, Mr., 157
Fayweather, Miss Fanny, 24, 43, 44, 67; letters to, 12–13, 18, 23, 55, 57, 59; health, 5, 17, 18; goes to Boston, 9, 10

Fayweather, Miss Mary (Molly), 55, 57, 67
Figg, Mrs., 135; Letter to, 81
Fleming, Captain, 15
Folkston, Lord, 77
Fort Cumberland, 84n
Fort Duquesne, 84n
Fort George, 87n
Fort Loudon (Loudoun), 154
Fort Oswego, 87n
Fort Prince George, 125n, 139n
Four Holes swamp, xxiii
Frankland, Captain Thomas, 54, 55; marriage, 62
Franks, Moses, 173
Frederica, Georgia, 54
Frederick the Great, 87n
Freeman, Mr. and Mrs., 109
French and Indian War, 84n, 86n, 87n, 126n, 148n, 165
Friendship, 173, 177
Furer, Mrs., 186

G

Garden, the Reverend Alexander, 42n; ecclesiastical court, 9n; on educating Negroes, 34n; son in London, 78
Garden, John: troubles in London, 78–79
Garden: at Wappoo, xi
Garden Hill, plantation, 10, 13n, 16, 54; description of, xvi; making cotton cloth, 8n
Garrick, David, 74
Garvey, Mr., 54
Geneva, 121n, 181
George II, 71n; birthday celebration, 23n, 57
George III, 174n
Georgia: government, 24
Gerrard, Mr., 98, 99, 108, 109, 110, 112, 123, 139, 142, 143, 145, 147, 148, 156, 169, 170; letters to, 96–97, 134–36
Gibbon (Gibbons), Captain, 157, 161, 164, 168
Gibbs, Colonel, 106
Gibbs, Mr., 106
Gibbs, Mrs. 166, 170
Gilbraltar, 183
Glen, Governor James, xxii, 57n, 58; occupies East Bay house, 98
Glen, Mrs. James, 76; ELP writing to, 77
"Glover, Cousin," 24
Glover, Richard, 82n
Goddard, Mrs., 43
Golightly, Culcheth, 106n, 144

Watson, Mr., 79, 111, 136, 148
Watson, Mrs., 111, 136, 148, 166–67
Webb, Captain, 124
Weldon, composer, 25
West, Captain, 69
West Indies: ELP's birth in, xv
Westminster, 158–59, 160, 163. 167, 172
Weston, Mr. (d. 1759 or 1760): death of, 138, 141
Weston, Mr., 165
Whitaker, Benjamin: goes to Boston, 11n
Whitefield, the Reverend George, 42n; ecclesiastic court, 9; *Journal*, 21n
Wilder, Mrs., 14, 43, 44
Wilkes, John, 182n
William, 25. *See* Deacon, William
Williams, Frances Leigh, xxviii
Williams, John, 18n
Williams, Mary: marries Henry Middleton, 18
Wilton, 77

Wiltshire: ELP travels through, 77
Winchester, Mr. and Mrs., 75
Wood, Thomas, 41
Woodrough, Mrs., 81
Woodward, Colonel Richard, 46n
Woodward, Mrs. Richard, 33, 51, 68
Woolsord, Jacob, 32n
Wormsloe, plantation: publications at, ix
Wragg, Miss, 114
Wragg, Miss Judith, 114
Wragg, Mary Wood (Mrs. William), 80, 114, 172; letter to, 75
Wragg, William, 75n; identified, 114
Wright(s), Master, 81
Wright, Mr., 152, 169
Wright, Mrs., 110, 111, 112, 113, 122, 152
Wrights, Mr., 10
Writ, Miss. *See* Rhett, Sarah

Y

Young, Edward, 130n

Text set in Janson Linotype

Composition, printing by
Heritage Printers, Inc., Charlotte, North Carolina

Illustrations printed by
Meredith-Webb Printing Company, Inc.,
Burlington, North Carolina

Binding by
Kingsport Press, Kingsport, Tennessee

Sixty-pound Olde Style wove paper by
S. D. Warren Company, Boston, Massachusetts

Designed and published by
The University of North Carolina Press,
Chapel Hill, North Carolina